T0128888

SLAVERY AND JIHAD IN THE SUDAN

A Narrative of the Slave Trade, Gordon and Mahdism, and its Legacy Today

Frederic C. Thomas

iUniverse, Inc.
New York   Bloomington

Slavery and Jihad in the Sudan
A Narrative of the Slave Trade, Gordon and Mahdism, and its Legacy Today

Copyright © 2009 Frederic C. Thomas

iUniverse books may be ordered through booksellers or by contacting:

iUniverse
1663 Liberty Drive
Bloomington, IN 47403
www.iuniverse.com
1-800-Authors (1-800-288-4677)

ISBN: 978-1-4401-2259-0 (pbk)
ISBN: 978-1-4401-2260-6 (ebk)

Printed in the United States of America

iUniverse rev. date: 3/31/2009

Contents

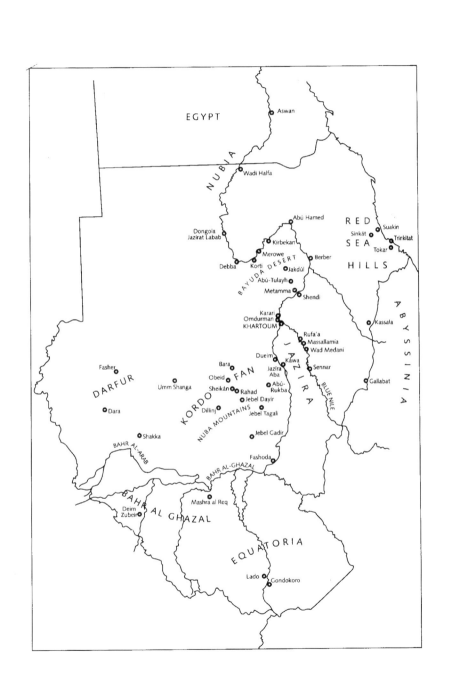

PREFACE

THE UNITY OF THE NILE VALLEY was the rationale for maintaining Egyptian control over the waters of the Nile—Egypt's lifeblood—at the time of Sudan's independence, the subject of my Harvard honors thesis in 1952. A year later, with a Fulbright grant to study Arabic, I went up the Nile to get experience in the spoken language. On arriving in Khartoum, what I remember most vividly was the statue of Lt. Col. Charles G. Gordon in the square next to the Palace. Decked out in his marshal's uniform, sash across his chest, soft Turkish fez on his head, he cut an imposing figure, all the more so because of his austere and somber mien. Astride a stately camel, his back straight, legs crossed over the animal's arched neck, his reins holding its head high, that brooding statue became an inspiration. How I wanted to ride off into the vast deserts of the Sudan!

Gordon was at the center of one of the great sagas that unfolded towards the end of the nineteenth century, a heroic story replete with misadventure. The main protagonists were Gordon, a mystical man of action who sought to eradicate the evils of the slave trade and Muhammad Ahmad—the Mahdi—a holy man who led a rebellion against the Turco-Egyptian regime. Both men became victims of forces greater than themselves, Gordon because there was no great moral gulf in Islam between the slave and the free, the Mahdi because competing tribal interests would not accede to the uncompromising principles he sought to instill.

More loved and pitied than any other figure of the Victorian age, Gordon died a national hero. The English loved him for his indomitable courage and unconventionality. Volumes were written about him. His reputation as a saint-like figure was "crushed under the weight of books." Learning of his death, Queen Victoria, her eyes welling with tears, could only say with abject sadness, "Too late." The army that her government had sent to rescue him had not reached Khartoum in time.

Others thought less of him. Gordon was no hero, they said, but a mercenary who was sent to the Sudan to evacuate the Egyptian garrisons and disobeyed his orders. He was no saint but a weak man who relied heavily on drink and brought young boys into his bed.

Whatever the judgment, his death provoked Britain's implacable hostility against the Mahdi. Smarting from the humiliation of Gordon's death at the hands of the Mahdi, the English wrapped themselves in the flag and, in an outpouring of jingoism, were bent on vengeance. The Mahdi's successor, Abdullahi al-Khalifa, became the archenemy, and history was rewritten. The backlash from Gordon's zeal in suppressing the slave trade, which had been a mainstay of the economy and was not considered immoral, was easily overlooked. His campaign had taken on the fervor of a crusade that mobilized powerful slave trading interests behind the Mahdi. The keeping of slaves, however, was no offense against the religion of traders and slaveholders. A large part of the population was slaves. Without them, Sudanese could not get their work done. The custom of slavery touched the pockets of everyone. In going after the slave trade, Gordon left the people bewildered and resentful.

Amid this confusion and bitterness, the Mahdi filled a need for guidance and purpose. He was one of the great leaders of Islam, combining enormous religious intensity, exceptional charisma, popular support, and shrewd military leadership. He rid Sudan of corrupt rule and exploitation, and told the people of Egypt he would do the same for them. The Sudan was then governed as an extension of Egypt, a vassal state of the Ottoman Empire. In 1821, the khedive Muhammad Ali, the Ottoman viceroy in Cairo, sent armies up the Nile. Two years later, Khartoum became the center of a flourishing trade in ivory and slaves, the land plundered and the people mercilessly taxed. The Mahdi's rebellion stemmed largely from this Turco-Egyptian corruption and incompetence.

The Mahdi promised a way out of a world of tribalism and sectarian rivalry. He sought to unite a tribally divided population behind an overarching religious purpose. He urged the people to arise from their lethargy and regain their God-ordained heritage and identity. Before he appeared, only merchants and holy men frequented the mosques. Afterward, Islam became anchored in the everyday life of the Sudanese. Slaves and slave dealers fought under one banner, and the humblest slave could aspire to the highest office. To many modern Sudanese, the Mahdi was Abul-Istiqlal, the father of independence.

When Sudan achieved independence in 1956, the brooding statue of the Englishman on his camel was removed from the Palace in Khartoum and installed on the Embankment in London. (It now stands at the Gordon Boys School in Surrey.) In 1956, I was living in western Sudan at the time; the pride and jubilation of the Sudanese when they took over from the British colonial authorities was palpable. Being in the Sudan at that historic occasion deepened my attachment to the country and its people.

But exhilarating times never last long. Soon after independence the Sudan became host to one of Africa's longest civil wars, a war between Arabs and blacks that has continued—except for a period of peace between 1982 and 1993—to the present day. A series of Khartoum-based, Arabic-speaking, Muslim-led civilian and military governments became embroiled in a civil war against largely Christian and African peoples in the south, costing two million African lives and forcing over four million to flee their homes. Now on the threshold of a durable settlement, another conflict, also with racist overtones, festers in Darfur, making refugees of an additional 2.5 million black African villagers and costing some 300,000 lives. These internal conflicts have their roots in the nineteenth century during the time of the Mahdi. They arose chiefly from ethnic differences and long-standing competition for scarce resources.

The events described in this book cover a lot more than the struggle and martyrdom of Charles Gordon. It is as much an account of the conditions during a period filled with trauma and turbulence. These conditions have in many ways little changed, particularly outside the larger towns and in the vast expanses of rural Sudan. Ethnic and kinship loyalties, which I studied as an anthropologist in the 1950s, still predominate in the popular culture. Primary allegiance is to the tribe. Herding livestock and tilling the soil remain central to rural livelihoods, and competition for arable land, pasturage, and water resources remains acute.

The story told here is also an account of the interaction of extraordinary personalities who wrote journals at the time. Explorers and adventurers, missionaries and foreign merchants, some of whom served as honorary consuls, and mercenary soldiers in the employ of the Ottoman khedive in Cairo and his governor-general in Khartoum. They all left impressions of what conditions were like. Among them were Copts, Greeks, Syrians, Circassians, Italians, Austrians, and a few Americans. Providing vivid and detailed geographic and ethnographic information, their accounts are of another age, and their observations may sound jarring to modern-day ears. Their voices reflect an imperialist mentality, sometimes overtly racist, and, when quoted here, should not be construed as the author's endorsement—heavens forbid! But these voices provide the flavor and texture that root the narrative within its cultural and historical context.

This is not a definitive history; it is not written to argue a thesis or prove a point. Still, historical fact is never purposely distorted for literary effect. The facts and the characters speak for themselves, letting the story unfold with fragments of conversations and anecdotes, allowing even traces of hyperbole and myth, delusion and conflicting opinions to intrude. It is the narrative that counts. It is never quite clear where the truth exactly lies. So if it is not proper history, is it still true—and if not, does it really matter?

— Chapter 1: Setting —

The Best View of the Town Is from the Blue Nile

Sudan, the largest country in Africa, covers nearly a million square miles. Khartoum, its capital, is two thousand miles from the Mediterranean, at the junction of the Blue Nile, which rises in the highlands of Ethiopia, and the White Nile, with headwaters at Lake Victoria. Hemmed in by the confluence of the two rivers in the middle of unforgiving desert, it gets its name, "Khartoum," meaning the elephant's trunk, from the shape of the land formed by these converging streams.

At the time of this narrative, the low-lying flat land was subject to flooding at high water, which brought on a plague of mosquitoes and malaria. When animals died, they remained where they fell. The sole supply of water was the muddy soup scooped from the river. There were neither drains nor cesspools, and the streets were redolent with noxious odors. Pernicious fevers were rife.

When founded in the 1820s, Khartoum was the last point of civilization on the edge of an immense wilderness of desert and savannah. Beyond the town, the government had little authority. Tribes were left free to administer their own affairs. Tribal chiefs protected their people against raids, regulated transfers of blood money, and settled disputes, which if left unresolved, would erode the cohesion of the tribe and the authority of the sheikh. Acting in consort with clan elders, sheikhs were the interpreters of customary law, collectors of customary dues, and leaders of migrations.

The Gezira, the "island" formed where the Blue and the White Niles came together at Khartoum, was the only important irrigated area. Beyond, as far as the eye could see, was desert. Northward toward Egypt the main body of the Nile occupied a narrow, entrenched valley. Six chains of cataracts prevented it from becoming a highway of migration and civilization. Routes across the desert, which extended nearly as far south as Khartoum, were quicker and more convenient.

In the mid-1800s, the town is best viewed from the Blue Nile. The garden plots of the front row of houses are half hidden behind a green curtain of date palms. The most imposing edifice is the governor-general's palace, surrounded by clumps of trees and large gardens. Built of stately red brick faced with sandstone, its windows are covered by green sunblinds. The men's quarters are on the ground floor, above which are rooms for the harem. On each floor, a corridor runs the entire length of the building. Behind the palace is a lush garden of palms, pomegranates, and grape vines, and down the street that borders the Blue Nile, the extensive grounds of the Austrian mission.

The Palace

The palace looks out on the fishing boats, consular vessels, and trading vessels that throng the riverbank. Flying British and Dutch flags, many of the ships are laden with gum, sorghum, senna, bricks, and firewood. Some are drawn up to the landing stages, discharging slaves.

At dawn one could ride out through the groves along the riverbank and enjoy the cool air and the peaceful murmur of waterwheels. Every hundred yards or so, a bullock or a blindfolded camel is turning one of these "sagiyas," fitted with a chain of earthenware jars. A small boy keeps the animals moving. If the noise stops, his master, sleeping in the shade of a nearby tree, wakes up and beats the boy, who then whips his bullock, and off they go again.

Female slaves with water jars arrive at the banks where Negro boys, sitting under a wild fig tree, tease them. After animated chatter and laughter, the women march back to the town in columns, pitchers balanced on their heads. Muzzles turned out and braying, the donkeys of water-sellers stand in long rows in a swarm of black flies. One of the sellers has only one arm, a crocodile having torn off the other. Despite the danger of crocodiles, people wash their clothes or bathe at the water's edge. A slave works an irrigation scoop called a "shadouf." It's a long pole with a huge knob of dried mud on one end to act as a counterbalance, and a goatskin bag on the other. The man dips the bag into the river and lets the weight of the mud lift it into the air, then swings it round and empties it into an irrigation ditch.

Behind the serene riverfront facade, the daily life of Khartoum throbs in a warren of lanes and flat-roofed one-story houses built of mud brick cemented with cow dung and slime. Here and there, the narrow lanes open into dusty enclaves and bazaars. There is a large mosque with a poor minaret and a Coptic church with a triple dome, a walled enclosure, and a cemetery.

Cavernous warehouses kept by Greeks are filled with musty jams and preserves, moldy macaroni, weevily flour, gritty sugar, sour French and Greek wines, and flat, pale ale. Imported on the backs of camels over miles of desert, or in the rare ships that brave the cataracts of the Nile, this merchandise sells for the highest prices. But, in season, abundant local produce is also available from the long covered markets where much of the life of the town is centered: meats, butter, cheese, milk, sorghum, dates, eggplant, tomatoes, beans, radishes, groundnuts, custard apples, pomegranates, oranges, bananas, and watermelons.

During much of the year the heat is overwhelming—the mean daily temperature more than ninety degrees. Violent storms blow in to add to the human misery. In a perfectly cloudless sky a gloom unexpectedly spreads over the town. The air is suffused with a dull yellow glare. From the southwest, the dust-laden wind appears like a range of immense brown mountains rising high in the air. Engulfing the town in a pitchy darkness, the storm may last for twenty minutes or so before dissipating as quickly as it came, the sun shining as brightly as before.

Before the summer rains begin in earnest the days become more and more airless, the sky, a dull bronze. In the evening rainstorms, accompanied by constant lightning flashes, trail along the horizon. The humid air is full of nasty biting midges, and ants crowd indoors. Water birds cry fitfully. A blinding dust cloud heralds the storm. The rain follows, tearing at the wooden shutters. At times the lightning is almost continuous. But soon the storm is passing away. Thunder dies away into the distance, and the air is refreshed.

In the early 1860s, Khartoum has some thirty thousand inhabitants. A garrison of six thousand, mainly Egyptians and Blacks from Kordofan, provide protection. Coptic Christians, all originally from Egypt, serve as accountants, schoolteachers, and scribes in the local administration. They put up with the local people and the conditions, which they look upon with undisguised scorn. Writes a disgruntled schoolteacher:

"The Sudan is not a residence for a person like me who does not have a Salma or Suad to comfort him. It has a hot wind from which one can smell the breath of a dragon, which the Nile cannot extinguish. Morning and evening storms arrive in tumults and turbulence. Half the people are wild beasts and hating them becomes a jihad. Don't be astonished if they cook a mixture of bone marrow with ashes and smear their bodies and hair with grease like the bodies of camels covered against ticks. They beat their wives with whips...Except for some Arabs among them they would be black, black, black...Three years in Sudan passed without schools of one's liking. How can one hope for schools given the obstacles?"

At some distance from the riverfront are respectable houses belonging to wealthy traders, mainly Greeks but also a few Italians, French, Germans, and Maltese. A sprinkling of Syrians, Copts, Armenians, Turks, Levantines, and an occasional Indian make up the foreign community. The residences of wealthy traders have verandahs, under which the Europeans gather in the evenings to smoke pipes and sip their arrack.

Visitors from abroad are accorded all hospitalities to compensate for the physical discomforts they have to endure. In 1862 one of the first American visitors to visit the town is C.M. Brownell, a doctor and explorer. He takes breakfast with John Petherick, the British consul, and "his lady," Katherine, before going to the house of the American consular agent, a Copt named Setum Chenudi. His luggage is brought from the river landing on the backs of donkeys. A large room, nicely fitted up with cushions and carpets, is provided for him and an evening supper of eight courses sent up with four servants in attendance. The next morning, mounted on a donkey, Brownell explores the environs. Following the White Nile for about a mile, he crosses through the little village of Omdurman and the juncture of the Niles before returning to Khartoum through gardens and groves of date and orange trees, fig trees, and grapevines. He passes by the dockyard where steam engines, hammers, lathes, and punches fit out and repair the vessels upon which much of the river commerce depends. He notes that the gardens of the Catholic Austrian mission have gone to seed, its occupants carried off by disease and pestilence.

Fifteen years later, in 1876, Dr. Wilhelm Junker, a German-Russian explorer, makes his way through the same narrow lanes and dusty courtyards, arriving at a large residence in the middle of a date grove. A double-headed eagle on a golden shield tops the entrance. After rapping on the gate, he is invited in by Martin Hansel, the Austrian consul. He is pleased to note that Hansel still retains a good German accent even though he has lived in the country for more than twenty years. Hansel introduces him to another European, a tall man with a red beard who would be taken for an Englishman but for his hearty *"Guten morgen."* He is Carl Christian Giegler, civil engineer and director of telegraphs, who will become one of Gordon's intimates.

On almost any day, Herr Hansel rides into town on a donkey, wearing a red swallowtail coat and a cocked hat with feathers. No one finds this outfit bizarre, though for day-to-day purposes most foreign residents adopt Turkish clothes with their many buttons and cool freedom. They find European clothes especially awkward for the oriental way of sitting, legs crossed, on cushions or bedsteads. Only later do they seem ashamed to dress in this way and make their own fashions instead. The sartorial preference of Frank Power, the twenty-five-year-old *Times of London* correspondent, is a blue vest against the sun and cummerbund against dysentery. Obsessive fear of sunstroke produces pith and cork helmets, although government officials continue to wear the Turkish fez. Each day the Angelus chimes from the chapel-bell of the Austrian mission above the clatter of Arabs and Negro slaves and the cries of tropical birds. Local gossip has it that the holy fathers and chaste nuns eat and drink lavishly and live in considerable intimacy. Of the forty or so Europeans residing in the town, only three or four are legally married. The rest make do with one or more slaves and have children with them who lead a tolerable life as long as their parents are alive.

Frank Power

On the Prophet's birthday and other holidays, marquees are set up in the central square where tumblers of sugared water and coffee flavored with cardamom, cinnamon, red pepper, and musk are offered to everyone. Almost every other day there is a feast at the home of a rich merchant or high-level official where spacious courts hidden behind nondescript mud walls are decked out with colored lanterns. A large reception room inside is lined with squat, sagging bedsteads known as "angarebs," covered with colorful embroidered cloths and cushions and occupied by guests according to rank. Beginning in late afternoon, the party may last until midnight. When the first guests have eaten, others show up until everyone, down to the donkey driver, has been fed. On special occasions, a military band, stationed just outside, will strike up Italian and French operatic airs, a Straus waltz, or sections from Verdi's "Aida," recently commissioned for the opening of the Suez Canal.

Frank Power, the *Times of London* correspondent, describes one such occasion. Through a rickety gate in a high mud wall, he enters a courtyard paved with colored tiles where tame deer browse. From there, he is escorted to the house of a prominent merchant. His host, a strict

Muslim, does not drink, but his foreign guests are served Bass's Pale Ale and Giesaler's Extra Superior. Not accustomed to eating with their fingers, they are provided with silver knives, spoons, and forks. On the occasion of the departure from the country of the French consul, a wealthy merchant, dinner is served by ten servants in livery, with candles, silverware, cut glass, and flowers. They enjoy champagne, hock and claret, green peas, mushrooms, asparagus, and many fruits from the host's garden. Hansel, the Austrian consul—invariably present at all these functions—is marvelously attired in his consular uniform: red coat, with enormous epaulets, long white waistcoat, and blue trousers. Government officials wear the standard Turkish formal dress, the black stambouli jacket with its stand-up collar. But for a truly special reception the heavy, gold-embroidered pasha's uniform is considered appropriate.

Sometimes the host arranges a pleasurable day's outing at a place known as Mahi Bey's Tree—later renamed Gordon's Tree. This site on the White Nile is the starting point for those traveling deeper into Africa. From there, travelers make their last farewells to their dear ones before entering on a long and perilous voyage. A military band plays Arab and European tunes under a pergola while guests "temper the sun's ardor with frequent libations." After a sumptuous lunch, dancers make their appearance: dark-skinned young ladies with beautiful eyes and flashing teeth, hair loosely plaited in strands greased with mutton fat—an intoxicating spectacle for guests already stuffed with feasting and copious drink. An Italian trader named Santoni says that in his whole five months in the country the first pleasant day he spent was attending a picnic at Gordon's Tree.

The impression that Khartoum makes on other visitors is different. The British explorer Samuel Baker and his wife loathe the town when they are there in the early 1870s. "A more miserable, filthy, and unhealthy place can hardly be imagined," he writes. Johann Maria Schuver, an independent Dutch adventurer, visiting ten years later is more favorably impressed: "If any person should wish to slander a town in this part of Africa, he need only say: 'It is a fevers-hole like Khartoum.'" The bad reputation stems from the fact that Europeans already established there "to their own great profit, endeavor to intimidate other persons," he writes. Schuver finds it strange that this remarkable spot where the two great rivers converge never attained its "natural destiny."

The White Nile and Fearful Sudd

Travel on the Nile calls for a large sailing vessel known as a "dhahabiya," which has a deck, cabin, and, usually, two masts, lateen rigged, and a crew consisting of a helmsman, sailors, caulkers, and carpenters. Later, a decked paddle steamer is added for government service. It has comfortable cabins and can tow lateen-rigged sailing barges called "nuggars" upwind. They carry an armed escort of mercenaries and one or two interpreters as well as sailors, stokers, firemen, and servants, plus whatever donkeys, camels, and horses are needed for transport when the party stops along the way. Soldiers with antiquated muskets pass the time perched on the gunwales or squatting around small fires smoking cigarettes. At prayer times, they wash themselves, slip off their sandals, and perform their devotions to the accompaniment of the steady beat of the paddle wheel aft and the clang of the door of the boiler fire when fresh logs are heaved into the furnace.

Dhahabiya

To travel by steamer is a formidable undertaking. Before setting out, mountains of baggage must be hefted aboard. Teak boxes and well-oiled, canvas-covered baskets, hermetically sealed with soldered tin linings to protect against insects and weather, contain all the traveler needs. People do not travel light in these days. They will be away for two years or more, and need medicines, guns, ammunition, spare cloth, compressed soups, tea, tobacco, matches, brandy, timepieces, prismatic compasses, and writing materials, as well as gifts for the local people met on the voyage: handkerchiefs of gaudy colors, music boxes, magic lanterns, an assortment of toys, glass beads, and silvered balls, which, when suspended from the branches of trees, delight the natives. When all this is stowed away and the steamer is ready to depart, the river landing in front of the government palace in Khartoum is packed with people, many of them wanting to come along and provide services. Others, hoping for baksheesh—a gratuity—besiege the leader of the expedition. As Baker writes:

"One of them, a tall, debauched-looking fellow, excessively drunk and noisy, insists on addressing a little boy named Osman, declaring that he should not accompany me unless I give him a dollar to get some drink. Osman was a sharp Arab boy of twelve whom I had engaged as one of the tent servants, and the drunken Arab was his father, who wished to extort some cash from his son before he parted. The boy showed his filial affection in the most touching way, by running into the cabin and fetching a powerful hippopotamus whip, with which he requested me to have his father thrashed. Osman proves to be a 'capital boy,' a perfect gamin, his ringing laugh and constant impertinence to the crew and soldiers keep the boat alive."

At last, the vessel pulls away from the shore amidst shouted farewells, trilling ululations of women, and a rattle of musketry. When casting off, serious mishaps can occur. Ropes can part, leaving the heavily loaded nuggars to float helplessly downstream, swinging in the current and ramming each other. The Dutchman, Schuver, traveling in the Sudan in the 1880s, describes the ensuing chaos: "The steamer whistled, the crew screamed, the soldiers wailed, the forty-six murderers we had on board clanked their chains until, with a final "hamdu li'llah,"—praise to God—the vessels were sucked into the mud of a sandbank and saved." Once order is restored, the boats are again underway. Arriving where the two Niles converge, they slowly turn and head up the White Nile.

Khartoum at the convergence of the Niles

The river, when full, is two miles wide but still quite shallow. The shelving banks complicate the frequent landings needed to collect wood for the boilers. On the islands and foreshore watermelons and beans are grown during the winter months as the river falls. These crops are watered by means of slowly bobbing shadoufs. Elsewhere the shores are covered with thick brush and dense groves of mimosa. Crocodiles bask on the banks, and a sharp lookout must be kept for hippos, which can smash a rudder and disable the vessel.

Passing Duaim, one hundred and twenty miles south of Khartoum, the main overland route into Kordofan and the western Sudan begins. Farther on lies Aba Island, twenty-eight miles long and thickly wooded.

Shadouf

Progressing still southward, the boat from time to time pulls to shore to collect wood and to buy provisions needed for the voyage: sheep, goats, fowls, even a bullock to be slaughtered and cut up to make sauce for the staple fare of sorghum porridge, as well as maize, millet, sesame, milk, butter, eggs—and, for trading, cotton thread and cloth.

The landscape would be unremittingly monotonous were it not for the wildlife: antelope and herds of hardy, black, long-haired goats, green monkeys, parakeets, cormorants perched with outstretched wings on the lower branches, geese rising out of the tops of trees; and flocks of teal, herons, cranes, and kingfishers. A sandpiper perches on the head of a hippo. When the hippo sinks below the surface the bird hovers near the spot where it will reappear before gently settling down again. On the banks the bush becomes thicker as the steamer chugs southward. Herds of antelopes are seen. In the morning a lion is seen slinking off. After a while thorny acacias give place to leafier vegetation and the predominantly Arab population to the first of the Nilotic tribes. Shilluk appear on the bank—tall, naked figures with lances used in walking stick fashion. Men and boys are spearing fish in the shallows. On the opposite bank, parties of Arab horsemen with broad-bladed spears, sally forth against a Dinka settlement. The river now is more matted. Masses of sedge floating downstream warn of worse obstacles ahead. The boat enters a swamp of stagnant waters and fallen trees, islands of water plants, and plagues of mosquitoes. On board rats and black-beetles are increasingly troublesome. Occasionally, a huge elephant, trunk up, its tusks fully five feet long, will charge toward the boat, then retreat.

Where the Bahr al-Ghazal and the Bahr al-Arab join the White Nile, clusters of thatched huts appear on the banks, their entrances so low that people must enter on hands and knees. Further on, near the Sobat, the waters are covered with papyrus and a weed known to the Arabs as "umm souf"—mother of wool. In the rainy season, these plants are torn loose by the high winds and driven along the narrow, meandering channels until their progress is barred by a bend in the river. The river rises and floats out the masses until they are stopped at a curve. Although the water still flows underneath, passage is again blocked. Huge chunks of the impacted vegetation must be cut away, and what remains is swept down carrying hippos screaming and snorting, and crocodiles whirling round and round. The river then becomes blocked again. This often-impenetrable barrier is the notorious Sudd.

For two dreadful months, Baker's expedition hacks its way through this sea of papyrus ferns and rotting plant life in the suffocating heat where insects choke the air and water birds keep watch along the banks. There is constant menace of crocodiles and buffalo, and at night, the myriad mosquitoes make life hell. Only by going ashore—if they are able to reach firm land in this billowing maze of vegetation—can the passengers build a fire, enshroud themselves in the smoke and, to the snorting of hippos, get some sleep.

Traveling on the Upper Nile is a hazardous existence, especially for the solitary trader with his precious stores of beads and trinkets. He survives among natives who are not always hospitable and whose promises of ivory are not always fulfilled. He relies on local chiefs for landing rights, guides, interpreters, and food. When his stock of trading goods is exhausted, he exists only on what his gun can provide. His precarious livelihood often ends in sickness and death.

In Khartoum, a man with little means can borrow money at a hundred percent interest to form a trading expedition, agreeing to repay in ivory at one and one-half its market value. He is then able to purchase guns, ammunition, a stock of trading goods, and hire a vessel along with some men to whom he pays five months' wages in advance, partly in cash and partly in cloth. Then he is in business. An Italian trader of the early 1850s writes:

"Take my word for it, for a young man it's a marvelous investment. If you make three or four voyages you will become a man of substance, a little gentleman. I have sold glass beads at three times what they cost. I want to winter on the White Nile for it is there that people can procure much ivory against beads. But without beads and firearms for hunting elephants one can do little business."

John Petherick, a Welsh mining engineer, lives in Kordofan in the 1840s and trades in gum arabic until native competition, oversupply, and government constraints paralyze the trade. He accuses the local governor, one Musa Bey, of excluding Europeans from the gum trade and writes to Her Majesty's consul general in Egypt about Musa's notorious cruelty—which includes "depriving eighteen captives of their generative parts." Petherick, a jolly bear of a man, then turns his attention to trading for ivory on the White Nile, which, he says, requires only "a commodious boat and some tons of glass beads, cowry shells, and a variety of trifles." Sometime later, however, the tables are turned. Musa Bey returns to the Sudan—now as Musa Pasha, the governor general—and exacts his revenge. Accusing Petherick, who is always mixed up in one sort of shady enterprise or another, of engaging in the commerce of slaves, not ivory, he deprives him of his Nile trading privileges.

Franz Binder, an Austrian pharmacist turned merchant, tries a different approach and probably profits the most. Instead of mounting his own expeditions—and the risks involved—he invests in other expeditions, holding claims on the ivory they collect, which he can then trade on the Khartoum market. As creditor to merchants going up the White Nile, he acquires valuable assets that are forfeited against loans in default, including trading rights and fully functioning stations stocked with ivory and staffed with native troops, which have become his property at rock-bottom prices. On several occasions Binder also serves as acting Austrian consul and provides armed men for raids against local villages and cattle camps to capture people and animals, which he can then barter against ivory.

BAKER'S IMPOSSIBLE MISSION

For his second journey up the Nile in 1870, Samuel Baker is made a pasha and given a salary by the khedive to annex the upper Nile and, incidentally, to suppress the slave trade. Since his first journey seven years before, slave hunting and trading have increased significantly. The adventures of Baker and his intrepid wife, Florence, enthrall readers back in England. Florence is beautiful, and "Sam," as she calls him, is devoted to her. She goes everywhere with him and supports him in every way she can. She makes for him giraffe-hide

Baker

moccasins and a shirt from gazelle skin, which she dyes a rich brown using mimosa fruit.

Two regiments of soldiers, one made up of Sudanese and the other of Egyptians released from the Cairo jail, accompany Sam and Florence. From among them Baker selects a personal bodyguard of sharpshooters. He puts them into fezzes and scarlet uniforms and calls them his "Forty

Thieves." For transport, he relies on steamers that were constructed in England, completely dismantled in Egypt, and dragged or carried by camels across the desert to the Sudan. Once above the cataracts, the vessels are reassembled and launched on the Upper Nile. The largest is a hundred-foot paddleboat of two hundred and fifty tons with a twenty-horsepower engine.

Baker finds the slave trade ten times worse than when he was in Sudan a decade earlier. Khartoum is so despoiled by officials that a population of thirty thousand is reduced by half. Even though slave trading is no longer legal, slaves confiscated from traders are being enlisted for military service and conscripts are being recruited by methods that have little changed from before. Baker feels it his moral duty to throw out the slavers. Villages along the Nile have become sorry husks, empty of people and animals. "There was not a dog to howl for a lost master," Baker writes in his journal. Foreign traders have ravaged the land wherever they set foot. Their crops repeatedly seized, people have given up tilling altogether. Their waterwheels idle, fields have reverted to desert and scrub.

A massive man with a luxuriant beard, Baker is an unabashed colonialist. He says, "The Negro does not appreciate the blessings of freedom, nor does he show the slightest feeling of gratitude to the hand that broke the rivets of his fetters."

Now, as governor in Equatoria, he must teach the Blacks to live in peace. But to them, Baker is just a different kind of invader, and they fight him. So he must pacify them for their own good. When tribesmen attack with poisoned arrows, he drives them off with guns. When they refuse to sell him grain and cattle, he seizes what he needs. He is uncompromising and sometimes brutal.

Ismailia, Baker's account of his explorations, is subtitled *A Narrative of the Expedition to Central Africa for the Suppression of Slave Trade Organized by Ismail, Khedive of Egypt*. Actually, this was only part of his instructions, which deal also with the exploration of the Upper Nile and improving the lives of the inhabitants. In view of his mission, "the rumor that Baker himself had bought his Hungarian wife" at a Turkish slave auction is especially ironic. Soon he is claiming that he has "crushed" the slave trade, much exaggerating the difficulties. The long-term solution to slavery, he says, lies in economic development, and he endeavors to create "a taste for agriculture." His men cultivate gardens near the camp and are promised prizes for the finest cabbages and carrots.

From Baker's un-nuanced perspective, to be effective in his mission requires absolute firmness in all situations. The keys to success are being a good rifle shot to impress the natives, playing the bagpipes and possessing a magic lantern to delight them, knowing surgery and being well supplied with drugs, and having a never-ending stock of beads, copper rods, brass rings, and gaudy cotton handkerchiefs to entrance them. He is blind to his delicate role as an Englishman and a Christian in the employ of a Muslim ruler. Fifty thousand slaves are being brought down every year, and fifteen thousand Arabs are engaged in the sordid commerce in one way or another. Influential persons in Khartoum possess trading rights over thousands of square miles. Baker's mission is odious to these entrenched interests. They look upon him as an implacable enemy. The fact that his authority relates only to the Upper Nile makes not a whit of difference. He is a threat to their livelihoods. So he quarrels with the slave traders and battles the tribes whose interests he is supposedly there to serve.

Nor can resident missionaries play a part in alleviating conditions. At the Austrian mission station at Gondokoro, Baker meets three demoralized priests who say they haven't made a single convert. They blame their superior in Khartoum, who doesn't listen to them. But in his reports to officials in Europe, Baker maintains that their work is a thriving success. So the hapless clerics are left to suffer in dispirited isolation among a hostile population against whom any resistance on their part would violate their sacred calling.

Stopping at Fashoda on the Upper Nile, Baker invites the provincial governor to join him on the poop deck of his steamer. Over pipes and coffee, he asks, "How many troops have you here?"

"Five companies, in addition to the cavalry and mounted Baggara Arabs who are now out collecting the taxes."

"What is your system of taxation?"

"The people here are very adverse to taxation and therefore I make a tour each year throughout the country to decide what I perceive to be just."

Baker asks if the governor seizes women and children as he does cattle in lieu of tax. Not satisfied with the answer, Baker tells his aide-de-camp to visit the large vessel that happens to be lying close astern.

Shortly, he hears the voice of his aide angrily expostulating with the crew, who are denying that slaves are in the hold. Minutes later a group of captives, mostly girls, women, and children, are dragged up from below. They emerge on deck, disoriented, abjectly sluggish, much to the governor's chagrin. For ten cows one of the children is sold back to her father right on the spot. "This is the Sudan method of collecting taxes," Baker ruefully remarks.

He is struck by the ironies in his predicament. A trader enjoys a monopoly in ivory over a vast area. An arch-slaver with a band of ruffians pays a modest annual tribute of several pounds sterling for the privilege of plundering villages with impunity. Meanwhile he, Baker, is being called upon to suppress the slave trade and improve local conditions. In carrying out these responsibilities, his over-zealousness alienates the natives and provokes hostility against the government. The trade in ivory and ostrich feathers on which Egypt depends has fallen off sharply. The khedive is displeased. Baker's situation is hopeless. His contract is not renewed.

The decline in ivory exports is also due to the methods employed in the trade itself. Elephants that were previously speared for their flesh and fat are now being captured in pitfalls. Their tusks are being brought to the local chief who sells them in the zeribas. Herds are being slaughtered to provide European, Indian, and American markets with billiard balls, umbrella handles, and piano keys. Supplies of Sudan ivory are rapidly declining.

"From white ivory to 'black ivory' was but a short step." Porters are needed to transport the tusks that have been sorted according to size. Four to six men will carry the largest, which may be as long as ten feet, to the river port. At the end of the journey, the porter finds himself a stranger in a strange land, far from kith and kin, from help of any sort. What is simpler than that he himself is sold to bring in yet further profit?

AMERICANS IN THE SERVICE OF THE KHEDIVE

Ismail Pasha becomes khedive in 1863. He has far-reaching ambitions, dreaming of transforming Egypt from an appendage of the backward Ottoman Empire into a modern state. He needs soldiers to organize his army and engineers to carry out surveys and prepare maps.

So he turns to the United States for its technical skills and particularly to American officers with recent Civil War experience.

Some of the young Americans he recruited were destined to play a major role in the Sudan. Among them are Charles Chaillé-Long from Maryland, a border state, Erastus Purdy of California, Henry Prout of Massachusetts, and Lebbens Mitchell of New York. From the Confederate side comes Raleigh Colston of Virginia, Samuel Lockette of Alabama, and Alexander Mason of Virginia. A spirit of adventure motivates some of them; others, particularly Southerners whose fortunes have been wrecked by the Civil War, look to service in Egypt as affording an honorable career and three meals a day for their families. They all serve at one rank below the one they held at home.

Chaillé-Long

Chaillé-Long had been with the Eleventh Maryland Volunteers in the Civil War. Although he had no battle experience, he thinks of himself as a fighting man and longs for action and adventure. He also has experience as a journalist. A slim, fine-boned man with a heavy-lidded, languid look, Chaillé-Long is a favorite with the young women in the small towns and gentrified farms of Maryland's Eastern Shore. Replacing his Civil War chin whiskers with a long, drooping mustache adds to his charms, and the change much pleases him. Chaillé-Long loves a good story and knows how to tell it, making him always welcome in local society. But still, at heart, he is restless and ambitious and would prefer a more adventurous life.

At a Washington reception to which several young veterans are invited, Chaillé-Long is introduced to Thaddeus P. Mott, who also served with the Union Army. Chaillé-Long learns that Mott has an aunt married to a former Turkish minister in Washington, and that, with his military connections, this former minister has been retained by the khedive to engage American officers for service in Egypt. Eager for any opportunity to advance his stalled career, Chaillé-Long presents his case and is told to obtain testimonials from Union military commanders that can be forwarded to the Egyptian minister of war and thence to the khedive.

By Cunard liner Chaillé-Long goes to Europe and then by steamer from Marseilles to Alexandria, and by train to Cairo. He travels with a former chaplain and Confederate officer named Cameron, whom he finds "a queer character." On a hot, dusty day in April 1870, they arrive in Cairo. Facing the onslaught of beggars and urchins, it seems to them a land out of *The Arabian Nights*: a chaos of colors, street jugglers and other entertainers, a babble of tongues and keening ululations, exotic aromas of attar of roses and incense, pounding of drums and ringing of bells, bleating of goats, and grunting of camels, and, floating above all the hurly-burly, the plangent calls to prayer from myriad minarets.

Once Chaillé-Long and Cameron are installed in the Hotel des Ambassadeurs, Cairo's best hostelry, their first order of business is to have tailors fit them out with the official *stambouli*—a single-breasted black frock buttoned to the throat, worn with a black vest and trousers and the obligatory red felt tarbush. Attired otherwise, they will not be recognized as proper gentlemen. Chaillé-Long likens the overall effect to "a bottle of Bordeaux wine with a red seal on top."

Ismail's Cairo is a grand city, a new opera house the khedive's latest extravagance; also an *opéra-bouffe* company, a French comedy troupe, a hippodrome, and a circus. The Suez Canal was inaugurated the year before, and the accompanying festivities still sputter on. American officers are given complimentary passes to the Italian opera and the French ballet. Attending these performances is an unaccustomed luxury for these handsome young men whose full-dress uniforms make them doubly attractive to the ladies of the ballet.

A broad stairway leads to a vast audience chamber of Abdin Palace where the khedive will receive them. Zulficar Pasha, the grand master of ceremonies, ushers them in. Halting within a dozen paces of His Highness, he bends low with his open right hand, palm upward, almost touching the floor, then brings it quickly to his breast, lips, and forehead to show that his heart loves, his lips praise, and his mind reveres his master. Backing toward the door, he salutes and leaves the hall.

The khedive greets Chaillé-Long and Cameron. Aged about forty, Ismail Pasha is less than medium height and compactly built, with dark brown hair, a close-cropped beard and mustache, swarthy skin and black eyes under half-closed lids. His eyes, Chaillé-Long notes, convey

a "sphinx-like expression" of intelligence and sagacity. He is a man of strong convictions and acute observation. Always smiling, he speaks French slowly and deliberately, which Chaillé-Long easily understands, being born of French parents. When the khedive listens, his left eyelid seems to close while his right eye wanders over his visitors. Once he begins to speak, his head jerks aside, his right eye half-closes and his left eye turns full on his listener. People say that he hears with one eye and speaks with the other. "Yes," he admits, "and I think with them both."

Ismail Pasha

The Americans' experience in the American Civil War and their lack of any selfish interest in Egypt has convinced the khedive to recruit them for service in his army. As foreigners and Christians they will undoubtedly encounter some jealousy on the part of Egyptian officers. "Bear it with patience and indulgence, but if this is not possible, do not hesitate to come directly to me for redress," he tells them. "I count upon your discretion, devotion, and zeal to aid me in the establishment of the independence of Egypt."

Pipe bearers enter the audience chamber carrying long-stemmed pipes, called "chibouks," their amber mouthpieces studded with diamonds and sapphires. Next come coffee bearers, bowing low and mumbling apologies, serving Abyssinian coffee in tiny gold cups, also studded with precious stones. Then the khedive stands up and bows his guests out. The master of ceremonies silently reappears and leads them out of the palace to their carriage.

With "Chinese" Gordon to the Sudan

Finding his initial assignment—teaching French in the military school—less than demanding, Chaillé-Long fills his spare time hanging around the Cairo coffeehouses, studying Arabic, and waiting for a more challenging situation. This comes with the arrival in Cairo of Lt. Col. Charles George Gordon of the Royal Engineers. For his

service in China's Opium Wars as commander of the "Ever-Victorious Army," he is referred to as "Chinese Gordon." The khedive, who has hired him to succeed Baker as governor-general of the Equatorial provinces in the extreme south of the country, decides that Chaillé-Long would be the ideal person to accompany him.

Some American officers are chatting in Chaillé-Long's quarters when a messenger from the palace arrives with a note that reads: "My dear Chaillé-Long, will you come

Charles Gordon

with me to Central Africa? Come and see me at once. Very truly, C. G. Gordon." Though taken aback by the abruptness and the peremptory tone of the request, Long smiles and rolls his eyes in feigned bewilderment. But he is never one to let an opportunity pass and accepts without a second thought. In Gordon's office he is greeted warmly by a short, unmilitary-looking man with sympathetic blue eyes. True to character, Gordon again comes immediately to the point: "How are you, old fellow? Come take a b and s. It will help us talk about Central Africa. H.H. has given me a firman as governor-general of the Equatorial Provinces. You are to go with me as chief of the staff. H.H. bade me say that he would receive you tomorrow morning at eight o'clock at the Palace."

Chaillé-Long might be excused for not knowing Gordon's short-hands: "b and s" is brandy and soda, a "firman" is a royal decree, and "H.H." is his invariable term for His Highness the Khedive.

"When do you propose to leave?" he asks.

"Tomorrow night."

"But that's impossible. I have no outfit, no clothing, no shoes. Besides, I must close my house, get rid of servants, horses, and attend to other things."

"Abandon them all. I have clothes and everything necessary."

Gordon thereupon opens a box in which there are boots that fit perfectly. Stores and other necessities are to follow in the care of Romolo Gessi, Gordon's factotum and confidential valet, who has served him well since the war in the Crimea and will play a significant role in the battles to come. So everything is quickly arranged. There is no room for argument. They can now settle down to talk, drink, and smoke through the rest of the night. H.H. will meet with them in the morning, now fast approaching.

Not everyone is pleased with Chaillé-Long's appointment. The British consul-general firmly believes that no one but a British officer should occupy the position. But Gordon will hear none of it. He says, "I do not want a British officer and will not have one. He would be writing home and making trouble for me in London. Besides, I like Americans. I served with them in Crimea." A timid-looking man who speaks in a low, soft voice, there is something in his expression—in his eyes, especially—that exercises a magical power over everyone he meets. "He could charm the birds out of the trees with those bright blue eyes in the sunburned face, with his boyishness and absolute sincerity." Others portray him as a nineteenth-century mystic, but also a practical person who keeps in intimate touch with the real world. He is both an idealist and a realist.

They travel up from Suez by steamer to the Red Sea port of Suakin and then three days by camel—with Chaillé-Long on a pony—across the desert to Berber and then by boat up the Nile, arriving in Khartoum on March 12, 1874. To stick to the Nile all the way, a more direct and more comfortable route, would take too much time because of the cataracts. Upon their arrival, Ayyub Pasha, the governor-general, receives Gordon and impresses him favorably. Ayyub has just finished opening up the Sudd, the tangled barrier of aquatic plants that blocks the Upper Nile, thus putting Gondokoro, Gordon's future capital of the Equatorial provinces, within eighteen days of Khartoum. A

Circassian, Ayyub speaks French fluently, which surprises Europeans unprepared for such sophistication in Ottoman officials.

In these days, the governor-generals of Sudan are invariably Turkish-speaking Ottomans in the service of the ruler of Egypt. None are native-born Egyptians. Most are from Caucasia and Georgia, some Armenian, Kurdish, or Abyssinian. The Sudanese regard anyone with a white face who speaks Arabic with a foreign accent as a "Turk." Under the governor-general are provincial governors and district officers, who are, for the most part, Egyptians with Balkan or Turkish roots. Sudanese are appointed to staff the mosques and the law courts as judges and as muftis who interpret religious law.

Following his audience with Ayyub, Gordon is invited to a banquet in his honor, after which there will be the customary prolonged dance entertainment. Soldiers clap rhythmically with the music while young maidens dance. Their only covering is a thong girdle of thin leather strips decorated with cowry shells. Their hair is done up in small

braids bound with gold and agate balls strung together, or a string of little plates of thin embossed gold. Around their necks, decorations of silver or gold, pearls, or coral; in the right nostril, a pearl; in the ear lobe, a ring of gold or silver wire with suspended corals. They dance in a circle, undulating and beating time with heavily bangled feet, faster and faster with greater abandon, their seductive gestures accompanied with clucking sounds. After gazing intently at them, the enraptured Austrian consul, Martin Hansel, is captivated by the exhilaration of the scene. Prone to play the buffoon, he flings himself in frenzy among the bare-breasted dancers. The governor-general, shouting with delight, seems about to follow suit. Gordon, in disgust, abruptly leaves the room, and the party breaks up in confusion.

—— CHAPTER 2: SLAVES ——

EVERY HOUSEHOLD HAS ITS SLAVES

SLAVERY, IN ONE FORM OR ANOTHER, has prevailed along the Nile for as long as recorded history. In the 1870s, everyone has slaves. Even the Nuba people, who themselves raid for slaves, keep slaves, and the government's slave troops have slaves of their own. No matter how poor, every Nubian peasant possesses at least two. On the upper Nile, deep into Africa, the poorest among the Shilluk have slaves since their woman do not perform household duties.

Master and Slave

Men and women spend time stretched out on lion skins, while slaves rub them with oil.

Slaves are generally well treated and happy. The work is light, and slaves who have adopted Islam are regarded as members of the family. Ignatius Pallme, an Austrian businessman who sojourned in Kordofan in the late 1830s, writes, "I never saw one of these beings ill-treated by his master for doing too little work." "Except for their infernal tom-tomming at night, they annoy no one and go contentedly about their duties," writes Frank Power, the *Times* correspondent. The slave is not to be pitied when he's with a foreign family; his condition is a lot better than with his own tribe. Attempting to run away, however, brings a beating and his legs may be shackled with rings around the ankles. It costs Power four Austrian dollars to purchase a little Dinka boy. The boy asked to let him be a slave in order to be sure of his next meal. When he first approaches Power he is stark naked. His only adornments are two verses of the Koran rolled in a rawhide amulet and tied to his ankles—to protect against falling into a pit or well in the dark or some other mishap. He will need to be baptized before too long. He will shave his master every morning and help the cook, who persists in calling him the "father of all dogs." Power finds the intelligence of such "poor savages" remarkable, although they have no future beyond being slaves, eating four pounds of elephant or hippopotamus flesh at a sitting and some day "entering the crocodile's stomach," as they call dying.

Samuel Baker and his wife Florence establish a similar relationship on their first voyage up the Nile. While they take tea in the courtyard of the British consulate in Khartoum, a Negro boy of about twelve comes uninvited to Florence's side and kneels at her feet. Her first impulse is to give him something from the table, but he declines. His name is Saat. The next day he reappears, kneels in the dust, and implores to be allowed to follow them wherever they may go on their journeys. His story is typical. He relates that when he was about six years old, minding his father's goats, he was seized by "Arabs"—as all nomads are called. He says they thrust him into a large gunnysack slung over the back of a camel and threatened him with a knife should he make any noise. He was carried hundreds of miles across the western Sudan and eventually to the Nile. He was sold to slave dealers, who took him to Cairo where he was sold again. He escaped to the Austrian mission, which sent him to Khartoum. The mission there was already swarming with little black boys who, according to Baker, "repaid the kindness of the missionaries by stealing everything they can lay their hands upon."

Saat is the exception, scrupulously honest and totally devoted to the Bakers. Washed and dressed in trousers, blouse, and a belt, he considers himself as belonging absolutely to Florence. She teaches him to sew, wait on table, and wash plates, and in the evenings allows him to sit by her side. Baker gives him a light double-barreled gun and teaches him to shoot. By the time they reach Equatoria, Saat is more trusted even than Baker's deputy. Nothing could occur among the explorer's escort without his knowledge, and without him, Baker would be unaware of the numerous plots being hatched against him. Whenever a complaint is made, Saat is called as a witness, and the boy bravely challenges the accused, regardless of the consequences. Baker can then charge the conspirator with mutiny and discharge him from his service.

On their return to Khartoum, Saat comes to Baker with all the symptoms of plague. He complains of severe pain in the back and limbs and leans over the ship's side, his nose bleeding profusely. At night he is delirious and the next morning, is raving and consumed by fever. When their steamer stops to collect firewood, he throws himself into the river to cool off. His eyes are suffused with blood, his skin "the color of egg yolk." Florence gives him a cup of cold water mixed with a few lumps of sugar obtained from traders at Gondokoro and buys lentils, rice, and dates to make into soup. But nothing can relieve his condition. Muttering in delirium, Saat sometimes howls like a wild animal. Three days before reaching Khartoum, the fever leaves him but raised blotches have broken out upon his chest and other parts of his body. His only medicine is a teaspoonful of arak every ten minutes on a lump of sugar, which he crunches with his teeth. His pulse is weak and his skin cold as clay. At last, he falls asleep. Karka, a good-natured slave woman, gently stretches his legs out and covers his face with a cloth. The tears pour down her cheeks when in the morning she tells Baker that he has died. On the sandy shore above the high water mark, under a clump of mimosa, a shallow grave is dug for his body.

IT'S THE SLAVE TRADE THAT KEEPS THE PLACE ALIVE

Gum arabic, senna (a popular purgative), hides, and ivory are Sudan's key articles of commerce. But the main reason the Sudan is occupied by Egypt was that it supplies slaves. By 1836, between ten and twelve thousand slaves are being imported into Egypt each year, males, mainly for military service, and females, for domestic work.

Slave Convoy

In November and December, the slave trader and some two hundred armed men sail south with the northerly winds. At a certain point they disembark and proceed to the interior and make contact with the local chief. Impressed by their weapons, the chief sees their arrival as an opportunity to attack a hostile neighbor. This alliance may last for years. Together, they fall upon an unsuspecting village. The firing on the huts takes place before daybreak. The occupants rush out. The men are "shot down like pheasants," the women and children kidnapped, and the cattle driven off. The floors of the huts are dug up to reveal concealed iron hoes. Hands may be hacked off to remove copper and iron bracelets.

Tree trunks, four or five feet long with one end forked and known as "shebas," are then placed on the shoulders of the captives. The fork is wedged against the man's throat and raised to shoulder height. The captives' arms are bound by thongs of fresh antelope hide, which, on drying, shrink and cut painfully into their wrists. Thus constrained, they can walk forward only when the man in front carries on his shoulder the end of the yoke of the man behind. Children are bound to their mothers by a chain passed round their necks, and the whole cavalcade, along with cattle, ivory, and grain looted from the village, marches back to the Nile for shipment to Khartoum.

With the stolen cattle, the trader buys ivory, and for payments of ivory, he ransoms slaves. Relatives redeem their women and children for a few tusks. The trader's native ally on the raid settles for some thirty cattle and a present of a pretty little captive girl. The slaves are auctioned off to the men of the expedition and reckoned against their wages. The rest are landed at various points within a few days of Khartoum and sold to agents. Because the trade is officially illegal, slaves aren't sold openly in the town but in the desert outside. From there they are led off to the Red Sea for shipment to Arabia or Persia or down the Nile to Cairo.

The government leases whole districts bordering the White Nile and Bahr al-Ghazal rivers to Khartoum companies—ostensibly for trading in ivory. These companies raise private armies of ruffians and establish chains of trading stations. A station might be little more than a "zeriba"—a thorn-enclosed compound—where soldiers can be stationed and ivory and captured slaves can be stored. The principal proprietors of these zeribas reside in Khartoum, where they are better placed to bribe the authorities not to interfere in their nefarious business. Treating all of them as likely swindlers, the government extorts whatever it can, and many traders find it more profitable to steal slaves and cattle than to trade for ivory.

In the 1850s, when government duties and taxes force European merchants to leave, the Nile trade is taken over by northern Sudanese—known as the "Khartoumers." Allied with indigenous chiefs, they carve out personal fiefdoms for raiding and trading. A network of their stations flourishes across much of southern Sudan. In the Bahr al-Ghazal the most permanent stations, known as "daims," have subsidiary zeribas under them. At the head of each is a "wakil," who receives a share of the profits. Because the owners are away much of the time, wakils have a great deal of autonomy. They command a workforce of hunters and interpreters and a small army of Blacks, recruited locally and known as "bazingers." Local people living in the vicinity produce food for the zeriba and serve as porters.

Not all Blacks in the zeribas are the product of raids. In times of drought or famine local people bring their children along with ivory to the markets of the Arabs, and many of the children end up in the zeribas as slaves. One may ask, "Where does this black man come from?" The Arab answers, "There is a black race which sells themselves. Each man comes and says, 'Father, I want you to put me up for auction.'"

A story is told of a little boy who sees his father and mother die of starvation. At night, alone and afraid, he climbs into the tree to shelter from wild animals, but soon, weak and hungry, he falls from his perch and injures himself. Some passing Arabs pick him up and take him to the nearest zeriba that becomes his new home.

Rooted in the society, slavery has been absorbed in the Arab social system for generations. By Islamic teaching and Ottoman law slaves have rights, and slave origin is not an absolute barrier to advancement. A slave soldier or civil servant of the Ottoman sultan can rise to become a general or governor, and a few do. In the slave market, the customer first asks if the slave is willing to serve him; an element of reciprocity is respected. In the Sudan, every household—Turkish, Egyptian, Syrian, Greek, Armenian, and Sudanese—has domestic slaves. They work alongside free peasants in the fields, herd cattle, and do household work. They are not necessarily considered social inferiors and are often treated with considerable kindness. There is hardly a family in northern Sudan whose ancestral blood isn't mixed, so color loses importance as a racial distinction. Slaves are allowed a rich social life, participating in festivals and ceremonies, music and dancing. They may be brought up as sons, circumcised, given Muslim names—or peculiar names, such as Sabah al-Khair (good morning) and Jurab (leather bag), for males, and Sabr (patience) and Bahr al-Sahwa (sea of lust), for females. They are taught to call their master "my father," and, when of age, they are freed and given freed women as wives. The well-to-do owner may set up the faithful servant in a household of his own, and the family tie remains as before. A slave concubine who bears a child to her master can be elevated to the status of mother of the child, and the offspring considered equal to freeborn children and share in the father's estate. By the early 1880s, an estimated two-thirds of Khartoum's population are slaves.

Intimate relationships serve the needs of men far from home and family, as excerpts from the diary of a traveler in Sennar on the Blue Nile in 1836 describes:

"A young Galla girl named 'Azamiya, whom I bought the other day for 1200 piastres, came with me. I seem to be entering a dazzling, ethereal world when I contemplate the ingenuous figure of this adolescent walking by my side; the same feeling of joy and well-being of a mother looking upon the fruit of her first love was born in me...

My little 'Azamiya has been ill these last five days during which time she has taken only a little water ... She asked if she could lie in my bed, and I carried her there. Nearly all night she held me close to her. We were both naked...[A month later] I was in bed but, as I could not hear my poor 'Azimiya breathing, I got up and by the light of the lamp I saw that she was dead. I sent for Sa'id Efendi, the Arab doctor, to certify her death when my tears nearly choked me. I called Fatima, the black freed slave, to wash the body and wrap it in a shroud."

The real barbarities lie in the traffic in slaves. For every ten slaves who reach Egypt, an estimated fifty die along the way. But in private relationships, also, unspeakable cruelties are described, nearly always at the hands of foreigners: a Turk hangs his slave girl to satisfy a jealous wife, a Frenchman castrates his slave for befriending the slave girl who is his master's mistress. In the early 1860s the government forbids "Franks"—as foreigners are called—to strike their slaves and compels them to send their slaves to the Islamic judge for justice. It is incongruous, one traveler comments, "how people, who, when in Europe, bristle at the very mention of slavery, can find it so agreeable to possess slaves themselves when they are here."

Plundering the country from all sides, many administrators sent to the Sudan in Ottoman times become immersed in the slave trade. They are of Kurdish, Armenian, Syrian, or other Turkish nationality rather than Egyptians who have been in the country for centuries and have intermarried with the local population. According to a local proverb, "The grass never grows in the footprint of a Turk."

In response to pressure from anti-slavery groups in Europe, the khedive Ismail visits the Sudan in 1858 and proclaims the abolition of the slave trade. A brief cleanup of the bureaucracy occurs when a new governor-general, Musa Pasha—John Petherick's nemesis—arrives in 1862. But before long conditions revert to their former state, and "the nose again recalls the savory old times."

Khedive Ismail appoints Samuel Baker to bring the regions of the Upper Nile and Bahr al-Ghazal—where traders in ivory and slaves are ravaging the local communities—under Egyptian control. His appointment offended many Egyptians and Sudanese as a living symbol of the ascendancy of Christian Europe in the dominions of the khedive and his putative sovereign, the Ottoman sultan. Arriving in Kodok in the Upper Nile in 1869, Baker estimates that fifteen thousand men are engaged in slave trafficking. He even finds the governor himself away on a slaving expedition. This, he notes, is how taxes are collected. The U.S. consular agent in Khartoum, an Egyptian Copt named Azar Abdul Malik, reports in 1871 on the involvement of top Egyptian officials in the slave trade. He urges his government to join with Great Britain to put an end to the abomination, but the State Department ignores his recommendation.

The underlying conditions are not propitious, in any event. Government influence and resources are limited. Ordinary Sudanese consider payment of taxes to a distant authority in Khartoum an unwelcome intrusion from which they get no benefit. The Egyptian garrisons in outlying areas live off the land as an army of occupation, extorting taxes in kind through armed raids on cattle herds and village grain stores. Paid irregularly and addicted to foraging and plunder, the soldiers are the curse of the country. Under the command of Turkish-speaking officers, they include Nubians, themselves former slaves, and an irregular cavalry of "Bashibazuks," a hodgepodge of half-caste Turks, Albanians, and other denizens of the Ottoman Empire for whom nobody has a good word. The name comes from the Turkish for crackpots—crazy in the sense of brave—and is associated in many minds with atrocities in Bulgaria and the depredations of ruthless Arab auxiliaries.

"I am not ashamed to say that I feel the greatest sympathy for every race that fights against the rule of pashas, baksheesh, bribery, robbery, and corruption," Frank Power writes. No sooner does an enterprising farmer erect a waterwheel but he is taxed, not only for his wheel but also for the produce of his garden. If he stops using it, he can end up in prison and have his hut burned. If someone has a trading boat, he will be fined for failing to fly the Egyptian flag. That such laws are arbitrary and the penalties excessive overshadow any reforms made by the government. Not all the government authorities are heartless tyrants of course, but there is plenty of reason for their serious image problem.

THE GREATEST SLAVE TRADER OF THEM ALL

Al-Zubair, son of Rahma, is a Jaali Arab from the Nile valley north of Khartoum. A tall man of powerful physique and swarthy hue, with mustache and small beard, his stern features and arresting eyes suggest a combination of intelligence, strength, and serenity. He wears European clothes and a tarbush in public. Quick witted and sagacious, he is strong-willed and generous, fond of learning and conversation with pious people, and unprejudiced with regard to other religions.

How did Zubair become the most powerful slave trader in the western Sudan? Here is what he says:

Zubair

"I was born on the island of Wawissi in 1831 of the Christian era. On my seventh birthday my father sent me to the Khartoum school where I learned to read and write and was instructed in the Koran and also taught metaphysics. When I was twenty-five years old, I took my uncle's daughter as my wife and became a merchant.

When I learned that my cousin was going to travel with Ali Amuri, one of the most important traders in the Bahr al-Ghazal, I decided to join him. At first, Ali Amuri treated me as a man would treat a dog. He gave me neither cakes of fine bread, nor coffee nor sweetmeats. In this unworthy state, I continued on my way, until the woods that fringe the waters of the White Nile gave way to the limitless marshes of the Bahr al-Ghazal. Ali Amuri gave me an old, worn-out rifle. Savages attacked us with hordes as numerous as the flies on a dead bullock. I brought one of them, the size of an elephant, to the ground with a blow between the eyes and, seizing his loaded rifle, fought for an hour. Afterwards, Amuri brought me cakes and exquisite meats and dainties and kissed my knees and my head, saying that I had been the cause of their deliverance from the lips of death. At Meshra al-Rikk, beyond which vessels cannot proceed, we disembarked with our merchandise. We arrived where Ali Amuri had a station.

At this time, there were many merchants scattered throughout the Bahr al-Ghazal, each with a zeriba to which he could fly for shelter and into which he could put his goods. Most in demand were beads of all sorts and colors, cowries, and tin. These they exchanged for ivory, rhinoceros horns, ostrich feathers, rubber, iron, copper, and other products of the country.

In 1857, the natives attacked the zeriba of Ali Amuri, but I led his men and opened fire on the savages, routing them and killing large numbers. When the merchants heard of my success, they flocked to me. Ali Amuri loved me exceedingly and gave me a share of his profits, but I determined to commence trading on my own.

I returned to Khartoum and bought a boat and much merchandise. I hired some Blacks as porters and started to explore new country that had never been previously visited by merchants. I traded until I had accumulated a lot of ivory, ostrich feathers, and other valuable products, which I sent to Khartoum with my cousin who sold them and returned with more merchandise. I made my capital at a place that was afterwards known as Daim Zubair. I decided to open up a trade route from there to Kordofan because the journey by way of the Nile was long and dangerous. I sent messages and presents to the sheikhs of the Rizaigat Arabs, who were settled along the route that merchants would have to follow. Each one took the oath on the Koran, and we agreed on the dues they could extract from the merchants who used that route.

Later, they broke faith with me and intercepted the merchants and destroyed their caravans. I invaded their country but progress was slow because they had many horses and could encircle us. But in the end we prevailed because in their country there was no water, and they were compelled to come down to the rivers of the Bahr al-Ghazal where we could defeat them."

Thus, in his own words, Zubair tells how Daim Zubair became the most important trading station in the western Sudan, dealing in slaves, ivory, guns, ostrich feathers, gold dust, and precious stones. In 1870, Georg Schweinfurth, the Baltic explorer and naturalist, visits the place. Surrounded by tall palisades, the entrance is secured by chains where unwashed and ragged slave merchants—"hawkers of living human flesh and blood"—squat, keeping a wary eye on their property. Visitors are conducted into carpeted rooms and served coffee, sherbet, and pipes. In the innermost hut, Zubair, who has a bullet wound in his ankle, lies on a couch behind a curtain. Attendants are close at hand and fekis—holy men—sit outside, murmuring endless prayers. A chair is pulled up to the side of the invalid's bed for Schweinfurth. A draft on his bank account in Khartoum is honored so he can purchase soap, coffee, boots, pipe-bowls, Lucifer matches, and other needs.

Zubair is an amiable and very open man and the best shot in shooting competitions on steamer trips. He doesn't raid for slaves himself. Instead, he has created a personal fiefdom in an area as large as France within which ordinary traders in slaves and ivory, Arab and Egyptian alike, can operate. His revenues come mainly from the duties he levies on them. His reputation for humaneness is such that slaves belonging to others seek to join him. He finds a place for them in his private army where they are trained to shoot with a tripod, which they carry with them.

After defeating the paramount chief—the nazir—of Bahr al-Ghazal, Zubair proposes a two-pronged attack on the independent sultanate of Darfur to the north. The government in Khartoum is unable to rule these remote parts, but the khedive in Cairo accepts his proposal. Zubair, however, takes action on his own, killing the sultan and marching into El Fasher, the capital, before government forces can arrive. Rumor has it that the fekis of Darfur, who are held in great reverence, make amulets that can vaporize the lead bullets of the enemy, and that Zubair has twenty-five thousand silver dollars melted down into bullets that the amulets cannot affect—an apocryphal tale, but such is the reputation of Zubair.

Under the sultan, the settled non-Arabs have been able to keep the nomads out of Darfur. By subduing the sultanate, however, Zubair opens its pastures and cultivations to the Arab nomads on the frontiers, thus unleashing intermittent conflict that has reverberated to the present day.

Darfur is added to the Egyptian Sudan, and Zubair is made a pasha and invited to Cairo. Hoping to obtain a firman from the khedive making him the legal governor, he accepts the invitation and leaves his son Suleiman in charge of his vast trading enterprise. He takes with him a battalion of his Black troops armed with rifles, one hundred horses of the best Arab stock, one hundred and sixty-five *kantars*—about ten tons—of ivory, four lions, four leopards, and sixteen parrots. Accepting these presents, the khedive gives him a comfortable residence and tells him that he is "to consider himself a permanent guest"—a gracious way of placing him under house arrest.

Zubair claims that he has done as much as Gordon to end the slave trade. "I never sent a single slave to Cairo or a single eunuch. When I captured slaves, instead of selling them I formed them into an army of my own, giving them good pay and a life of adventure, which they liked. Many of these southern Sudanese are great fighters, and many of them joined me of their own free will. They would not have done this if I had not treated them well."

— Chapter 3: Cultures —

Khartoumers and Jellaba

Year after year, small bands of itinerant Arab merchants and a few Copts and Greeks arrive in southwest Sudan with guns, glass beads, and brass wire to trade. They come in the winter months, do their business and return home before the summer rains set in. Large-scale traders follow in their footsteps. But before long they find that the ivory they collect isn't sufficient to maintain their armies, and they turn to slaving instead. Zubair can acquire no more than one hundred and twenty hundredweight—maybe three hundred loads—of ivory, surely not enough to maintain his fighting force of over a thousand men.

On the White Nile it becomes increasingly difficult to evade the authorities. Slave vessels are being seized and human cargoes are dying in large numbers. New routes inland must be opened. It is more profitable to trek slaves across the desert to Nubia on the Main Nile, instead of via the White Nile as before. Zubair and other Khartoumers turn away from Meshra al-Rikk, the main river port in Bahr al-Ghazal, in favor of an overland route through Kordofan. The darb al-arbaeen, the forty-day desert track direct to Assuit, becomes the major link with Egypt for the export of slaves, ivory, rhinoceros horns, ostrich feathers, gum arabic, tamarind, and natron. To make this journey from Darfur necessitates five thousand camels.

Shilluk and Dinka, situated on the east bank of the White Nile and the Nuer River near its junction with the Bahr al-Ghazal, furnish the bulk of the slaves. When the Nile route is closed down, Khartoumers turn their attention to the Nuba tribes in the hills of eastern Kordofan and to the Dinka, who have moved westward into Bahr al-Ghazal, as sources of slaves. The wakils of the Khartoumers are not numerous but their troops are well armed. In the thrall of their zeribas, the Dinka lose cattle by the thousands, and many give up stock raising altogether. Others are hired as porters or for compulsory labor far from home. Their culture is plundered as well. There is a market for their pottery and woodcarvings in Khartoum. Irregular troops of slave traders gather up whatever they can lay their hands on and sell it when a merchant returns to the capital.

Driven off the Nile, traders swarm into Kordofan. In a single year in the early 1880s no fewer than twenty-seven hundred traders make their way into Kordofan, Bahr al-Ghazal, even to Dar Fertit in the extreme southwest. They range from the small itinerant Jellaba traveling about with a couple of donkeys and buying up two or three slaves at a time to great merchant princes like Zubair who deal in the thousands.

When a government official visits a zeriba in Bahr al-Ghazal, the wakil's troops put on white parade jackets and form rank and file to welcome the distinguished guest. They fire their muskets to the accompaniment of piercing shrieks of joy from their women. The wakil, controlling his mount with the bridle and the pressure of his thighs, displays feats of horsemanship. He gallops towards the esteemed guest and, almost upon him, turns sharply aside. When the official is Ibrahim Fawzi, Gordon's adjutant, the wakil presents him with a dozen boys bound with a cord from neck to neck. As Wilhelm Junker, a German-Russian explorer there at the time, remarks, "Fawzi was by no means a stickler to find presents of slaves incompatible with his principles and position; on the contrary the more he got the better he liked it." Fawzi gives him two parrots in return.

Zeriba owners complain that the good times ended when the government monopolized the commerce in ivory. As long as it was free, traders could make a tidy profit, selling contraband arms and ammunition on the side. But now they have to give baksheesh to every government official or else face one hindrance on top of another. One wakil complains to Junker that, on his last journey to Khartoum he had to distribute thirty-five slaves among sub-governors and clerks. So the traders make less profit than before, Junker says, while the Blacks remain "the luckless fowl, plucked of every feather."

Itinerant traders were known as "jellaba"—"packmen"—because of the satchels slung across the backs of their animals. The Jellab is thin and sinewy, with deep-set eyes, mustache and beard little more than a tuft of hair under his mouth, and three parallel slashes on his cheeks. He entrusts his land to kinsmen and loads his donkey with trade goods. Farewells done, he shoulders his lance and sets off at a steady pace. A short stick, one end gently curved and the other with a short nail, serves as both bridle and spur. Jellaba are ubiquitous along the meandering tracks of the Sudan, passing from village to village and arriving in twos and threes on market days, their trade goods in woolen saddlebags covered with a bullock's hide on which they are spread out in the market.

They are Nubians—their ancestral home in the valley of the Nile north of Khartoum, once the ancient kingdom of Nubia. Many are Jaaliyin of Arab admixture whose ancestry is traced through a certain Ibrahim al-Jaali to the uncle of the Prophet. Born traders, they hear from earliest childhood tales of kinsmen living far away. "Foreign parts ease the hearts," is their saying. Zubair is a Jaali, and like him, they travel abroad to fulfill their destiny. "The north gives birth; the south gives manhood." A girl waits until the day a cousin from the Diaspora returns to marry her. Onerous taxes on waterwheels and the fragmentation of land under Islamic laws of inheritance contribute to their dispersal. With less land, they borrow grain that must be repaid at harvest when the price is low and end up repaying more than they have borrowed. Trapped in this cycle of indebtedness, the only recourse for many is to search out opportunities on the frontier.

Another Nile Valley people, the Shaigiya, are centered on Shendi, the first major town north of Khartoum. They aren't traders at heart, like Jaaliyin, but warriors feared for their cavalry. With broadswords and coats of mail they are known for staunchly resisting the Egyptians coming up the Nile in the early 1820s, though their swords were no match against the musketry and artillery of the invaders, and they eventually capitulated. Because of their experience in soldiering, they have been enlisted in the irregular formations where they serve as tax collectors—and are exempt from taxation. Their ruthlessness earns them an unenviable notoriety. Each province maintains its own force of these irregulars, who are widely loathed.

There are Nubians who speak Arabic in addition to their own language, the most important being the Danagla, or Dongolawis, their forebears having come from the vicinity of Dongola at the bend of the Nile. Traditionally, they have been farmers and boat builders. Many also have served as auxiliaries and tax collectors in the Egyptian administration or as irregulars in the slave-raiding forces of the zeribas, and some had important administrative positions. Jaaliyin with their noble pedigrees look on the Danagla with disdain, claiming they are descended from a slave named Dangal.

Jellaba are reputed to shun all activity apart from trading, beer drinking, and endless talk. They are liars and thieves, many say, knowing no gratitude and understanding only how to flatter. Gordon has nothing good to say about them, particularly the Danagla under his authority. However, European traders depend on Jellaba for services and entrust their merchandise to them when other business takes them away, so these slurs seem to have little veracity.

Jellaba get their trade goods on credit in the town market—the "suq"—where blacksmiths and locksmiths, tanners and leather workers, weavers and dyers, potters and makers of palm leaf mats and baskets, and other artisans gather. The suq usually takes place twice a week. Peasants from surrounding areas arrive with grain, cotton, liquid butter, and cotton piece goods to sell. Foreign merchants act as middlemen and creditors.

A Greek merchant might spend his entire working life in the sleepiest Nile village and return home only to spend his declining years and die. Perched in his booth with wares spread out before him, he is always open for business. His boldness and enterprise are legendary. When British and Egyptian forces advance up the Nile in the 1890s, Greek merchants are already ensconced in their stalls to fill the soldiers' needs—tinned biscuits, bully beef, jam, milk, tobacco, razors, soap, enamel bowls, oil of geraniums, and patchouli.

Before leaving for a spell in the interior, the Jellab visits the sheikh of his village, a duty not easily neglected. He is greeted with the customary courtesies and provided an angareb on which to recline while chatting over tobacco and coffee. Then he leaves his village—maybe for a period of months or even years.

Once away from the Nile, he attaches himself to nomads who know the country and offer protection. Arriving at a distant village, a bowl of "merisa"—millet beer—as well as sweet and sour milk and some hens are offered, all of it free; they never go hungry. Traveling with Arabs, Jellaba remain somewhat aloof since their culture and language are different. They touch food only with the tips of fingers and find the bedouin habit of drinking milk directly from udders repugnant.

Many Jellaba settle as traders in El Obeid and other large towns. They obtain calico from Sennar and cotton sack cloth from Egypt, double-barreled guns of Belgian manufacture, Turkish pipes, slippers, and fezzes as well as beads, cotton, and salt to barter for slaves and ivory. A brisk commerce opens to Egypt with trade in ostrich feathers and gum arabic. Some find land to cultivate along the Blue and White Niles or in the oases of Kordofan. Others become moneylenders or fekis with their rosaries and their long, white robes, the oracles of the village, the doctors, letter readers, and writers of verses for amulets. Traveling in Kordofan in the late 1830's, Ignatius Pallme finds most fekis among the Danagla—"the most rigid observers of Mohammedan religion, with one single exception, that they are very fond of brandy."

Some of these traders penetrate deeper to the southwest, by which time the term jellaba becomes synonymous with slave dealer. Zubair is the best known. They may arrive with their donkeys and trade goods in January and leave by March or April. A few settle for longer period in the zeribas of bigger merchants and serve as holy men and teachers. Shakka in southern Kordofan, which is beyond the reach of government officials and their exactions of baksheesh on each slave, becomes an important trading center. It is larger than El Obeid and full of slaves. There, the Jellab can obtain oxen for carrying his burdens into the forests and swamps of Bahr al-Ghazal. He can lay in a stock of butter to barter in the zeribas he will visit. He may hire a few Baggara to manage his oxen and trade his donkey—if it survives the journey—for a slave. Being also of Nubian origin, the soldiers, clerks, and storekeepers in the zeribas welcome him, so the cost of his travel is next to nothing. When he later returns home, needy young Blacks attach themselves to his caravan, each surrendering to virtual slavery in order to get a cotton shirt and a gun of his own.

There is a thriving market for this human merchandise when Jellaba return. Even the humblest peasant needs a slave girl to wait upon his wife and another to help on his land. A slave girl is needed to grind corn since grinding enough for a family is tedious and entails a full day's work. Only with slaves can the Persian waterwheel—the sagiya—be used for irrigation. It is taxed at a fixed rate, so labor is indispensable to make it profitable. Likewise in the savannah, the availability of slaves determines how much land can be cultivated.

Slaves are also needed to fill the ranks of the Jihadiya—the Black battalions of the army. They are better able than Egyptians to deal with the climate, which causes the mortality rate among Egyptians to be high. Besides, Arabs are averse by nature to serving in the regular army, so Blacks have to be conscripted instead, forcibly if need be. Anyone who complains of mistreatment will probably end up in the army. Female slaves will be turned over to the military depot and married off to the troops—usually from the same district as themselves.

Slaves: what would the Sudan do without them?

WILD SONS OF THE STEPPE

The cattle nomads—or Baggara—range across the borderlands between Arabs and Blacks. Of darker complexion after generations of intermarriage with the indigenous population, they live in the forested savannah where camels cannot survive because of the tsetse fly. With their lean, fly-bitten cows, the Baggara are allies of the slave traders, an alliance that has had important consequences ever since.

Georg Schweifurth, the naturalist and traveler, visits Daim Zubair in 1870. He describes Baggara gathering around him as he draws pictures of their cows, but always at enough distance to avoid the evil eye of the "Frank." They are a hawk-eyed, lithe people with handsome features and sparse beards tilted forward, mustaches carefully combed to bristle, head shaved or hair rolled back from the forehead in tresses. They never wash, and once they put on a frock it will remain, torn and ragged from thorns and smelling of milk and animals, until it falls off in rags.

Baggara are devoted to the well being of their cows. Riding bareback ahead of the herd on a young ox with a cord passed through its nose, the herdsman calls each cow by name when it lags behind. Hearing its master's voice, each understands and obeys.

Baggara Family

Baggara women are also on oxen, along with their cooking utensils, stores, and wood frames for their huts. In camp, wearing ear and nose rings, lumps of amber around their necks, and bosses of silver across their foreheads, they move about freely with faces uncovered, indeed with no more covering than a skirt. They never walk in front of men nor eat or drink in front of them. Shaking hands takes place only between equals, so proffering the shoulder or forearm suffices as salutation. But the woman's tongues are greatly feared. If they sing against a man's courage, they can drive him from the camp.

In camp, the men while away the hours lounging on angareb bedsteads. Old men sew garments, repair sandals, and shave their friends' heads. Young men take the cows out for grazing, milk them when they come back, and fetch wood for the smoky fires that will ward off flies and mosquitoes. Women churn milk to make butter, cultivate small plots of sorghum, and fix the evening meal. The brief twilight allows time to milk the cows and eat supper. Afterward, men and women in separate groups sit around wood fires and chat until it's time for bed. During the night a few young men, armed with light javelins and shields and a drum to warn of danger, patrol the perimeter of the zeriba. Only the scream of a night bird or the distant roar of a lion or the howl of a hyena interrupts the stillness. Fearing lions and leopards, no one ventures outside unarmed.

The Baggara hunt gazelles, geese, and ducks, and tame and pluck the feathers of ostriches. They cultivate sorghum and water their herds from the pools that collect during the rains. When the water holes dry up, they migrate along well-established routes to dry season pastures and water. Oxen carry their belongings and hut frames.

Baggara Camp

A few family members remain behind with some milch cows, which get liquid from the small melons that grow in the sandy soil. With the rain come tsetse flies, driving Baggara and their cattle back to the drier regions to the north. The fly's bite spreads trypanosomiasis, bringing on lethargy, hallucinations, and painful sensitivity to the slightest touch. Near the end, the patient loses the ability to feed himself, slips into a coma, and dies.

Baggara donkeys can go a couple of days without water, and their ponies—ugly beasts, all head and tail—are used to recover stray cattle and hunt down ostriches. Baggara sheikhs may own Dongola horses, which are more elegant and much prized. The care they devote to them is proverbial. An hour before sunset they are fed as much grain as they can eat. Watered only once a day even in the height of summer, they are given fresh milk mornings and evenings.

Jellaba used to depend on Baggara as guides on their slave-hunting forays. Raids, known as "ghazwa," are mounted regularly in the dry season to capture men for the army and women as concubines, and Jellaba follow to the raiding frontier. A force of regulars, Arab auxiliaries and Bashibazuks, is assembled and camels requisitioned to carry riders, baggage, water, and tents. Before the expedition can set forth, some of the camels must be trained to accept loads and allow riders to mount and dismount.

Ignatius Pallme provides a harrowing account of a raid in 1839 in the Nuba Mountains. The raiders halt near a hill they intend to storm and order the local chief to furnish a number of slaves. If not, camel-riding Arab auxiliaries commence their charge with a great hue and cry, spears held high, oblong shields covering their naked bodies, shaggy locks whipping in the wind. The thunder of cannon causes more alarm than effect. In the midst of this pandemonium sanctuary for the Nuba lies in their steep hills. The Egyptian infantry laboriously scale these, clambering over rocks up narrow defiles where the Nuba, rallied by the shouts of their women, roll down boulders on them and launch poison-tipped spears and arrows. Thus, they hold off the invaders, who are ascending on hands and knees with their heavy, useless muskets slung across their backs. Ultimately, however, the Nuba are overrun when they run out of water—since their hills have no springs.

Jellaba traders generally treat their captives humanely; they represent capital to them. Not so the Egyptians whose captives are saddled with the six- to eight-foot sheba yokes. Stopping for the night, their necks are so compressed that sleep becomes impossible. The boiled millet given them is so hard to be virtually unchewable. Children swallow it like pills and their bodies swell. Pallme describes how, on one occasion when an old woman can't go a step further, an Egyptian soldier strikes her with his musket butt. Incensed by this blatant cruelty, her son knocks the soldier to the ground with his yoke, and other captives throw themselves on the troops before they are able to take to their arms. During the ensuing melee, some fifty captives take flight and make their escape.

On returning to El Obeid, most of the captives are sent to Egypt, and the rest are drafted into the local garrisons. The cattle are set aside as food for the garrison and as part payment of arrears in the soldiers' pay. A captain might get four adults and three children, and every two enlisted men one adult to sell. Jellaba buy any remaining slaves unfit for military service at rock-bottom prices to barter for ivory or sell at public auction. Afterward, an ant-like caravan of captives plods wearily across burning sands to the Nile markets. Without enough water and grain along the way, half of them may die before reaching the river.

In the 1840s, cattle collected as tax are sold to the Jellaba, who sell them back to the Baggara in exchange for slaves—for which there is always a market. So Jellaba wind up as taxpayers on behalf of Baggara. In the event of default, government troops will be dispatched to the Baggara camp where they will be entertained with beer and food and given large nose rings of gold and slaves for each officer. Subsequently, the Baggara are given the right to pay taxes in slaves, which ensures that their livestock will not be placed in jeopardy.

The Nuba Mountains, where the Baggara have been coming for years as friends, became their primary source and now they come with hostile intentions. Lying in wait near wells frequented by villagers, they rush in, seize women and children, and gallop off. Back in their encampment, the thorn bushes surrounding their matted huts serve as a zeriba in which the captured Nuba are chained and kept under guard.

By the 1860s, the government is making regular troops available to Baggara, who themselves lead slave raids. From defending their livestock, they are inured to war and always ready to plunder. In a horse, cow, and slave culture, their ability to attract and lead men on raids brings them power and influence. Mounted, they are formidable, armed with a broad-bladed, flat sword resting against the side of the saddle under the thigh, a large stabbing spear carried in the hand, and small needle-bladed throwing spears, capable of piercing chain mail, clustered in a quiver.

Arguably the most warlike people in the Sudan, Baggara live in a continual state of hostilities, even among themselves. It seems that all they care for is warring and adding to their stock of cattle. When asked to show their authority to collect taxes, they reply, "The beard orders...Isn't this beard enough authority?" So it is not just the Jellaba slave dealers with which the government has to reckon, but also the Baggara tribes that give them support. Bilad al-Sudan—the land of the Blacks—is where Baggara are thoroughly adapted. Their mode of thinking and way of life is akin to that of the Blacks, in the midst of whom they had long lived. "This is our land—we know no Effendina (khedive) here," they say.

BELOW THE BAHR AL-ARAB

To the south of the Baggara, and below the Bahr al-Arab, a main tributary of the upper Nile, are the Dinka. Protected by the malarious nature of their country, sixty thousand square miles covered with their immense herds of cattle, they live in small family homesteads strung out in clusters over miles. Each homestead has a hut for sleeping, another for cooking, and a cattle byre, and is surrounded by small clearings where sorghum, corn, peanuts, sesame, okra, yams, and other vegetables are cultivated. But it is cattle that preoccupy Dinka lives.

Smudge fires are kept up at night to drive away mosquitoes and flies, and tall, spectral figures shift the cattle about.

Dinka Cattle Camp

At first light the cows become restless. Young Dinka take them to graze in pastures where flies are less prevalent. Carrying a small gourd of drinking water, younger children free the goats and sheep from their byres and take them into the bush. It is a wonder that lions don't devour them more often.

In the late afternoon, the cattle drift back to the settlement where milking is accompanied by much grooming and cleaning. The milk is put straight on the fire, warmed, and poured into gourd churns to make butter. This is the Dinka's proudest hour, since they are the loyal servants of their cattle and will risk their lives for them. They drink their milk and, through small incisions, their blood, and slaughter a cow only as a sacrifice to spirits and ancestors—never because of a craving for meat.

If not tending cattle, they work the gardens around the village. Men dig holes for planting, using long sticks with sharpened tips. Women and their children follow, dropping the seeds into the holes and covering them with their feet. They sing to the rhythm of the hoe.

To escape the mosquitoes, villages are situated away from the river, so fetching water is a time-consuming task. Women sweep out the houses, collect firewood, pound sorghum, prepare home-brewed beer and, at dusk, light the fires in readiness for the return of the cows. Avid hunters, Dinka drive their prey among trees where the hunter can dismount and stab it with a long spear. In larger parties they remain out for days, hunting elephants.

In the late 1860s, driven from their ancestral lands along the White Nile, the Dinka moved into the forests and marshes of Bahr al-Ghazal, but again they are thwarted as the slave and ivory trade shifts westward. Tall and well built, none less than six feet, Dinka are much in demand for the black regiments, and Arabs keep Dinka to tend cultivations and as concubines. So Dinka live in fear that the slavers will come and carry them off, bundled in large skins hung on the flanks of camels. Children, frightened into silence with the warning, "There come the camels," flee into the bush whenever they see a camel and rider entering the village, whoever it may be.

"The owl is a wise bird that sees things in the darkness," the Dinka say. Its cry alerts the village of an impending attack. Startled awake they hear in the distance the roar of the hungry lion that will protect them by attacking the horsemen coming to seize their cows, women, and children. Scouts are sent out to trail the horses, but the crisscrossing of hoof prints makes it difficult to see where they have gone. Later, Dinka raid an Arab zeriba and recover some cows.

Living in such proximity with Arabs, fragile alliances may be formed. Ngok Dinka reached understandings with the Rizaigat, a major Baggara tribe, who are allowed onto Bahr al-Ghazal if they come in peace. Other Dinka established tenuous links with Humr Baggara, providing protection when they bring down their herds during the dry season. Similarly, Hawazma Baggara have links with particular Nuba hill communities. Nuba herd cattle and cultivate land for the Baggara and entrust their cattle to them in exchange for grain.

The only schools are those of Christian missionaries, who disparage the Dinka as primitive and degenerate. The missionaries teach that Islam is a violent religion that preaches that non-believers be brought to the faith by the sword. While only by accepting Islam and Muslim names can they enter the mainstream of Sudanese society, the more they adopt Arab ways, the more their pride in being Dinka. They are proud of the black color of their skin, while the Arabs and those who call themselves "Arab"—and whose color might be as dark as theirs—demean them and call them slaves, free as they are. Indeed, there are some Arabs who are as black and Negroid-looking as any African can be. But in the Sudanese context they are nonetheless "Arabs."

Contact with the outside world brings only misery. Dinka hardly distinguish among the waves of invaders except by the use of such varied terms as Arabs, Turks, Egyptians, and Dongolawis. Dinka chiefs are slain, people killed, cattle seized, crops burned, and houses destroyed. Tormented by these confusions and contradictions, Dinka cherish their independence, and cattle are the prime symbols of their identity. Moving the animals to cattle camp in the rainy season is a joyous occasion. Young men sing to their cows, extol their beauty, and decorate the huge lyre-shaped horns of their bulls with tassels. In their special breed of cattle is the ideal wealth.

Their elders tell them that Arabs are morally depraved as shown by their trading in slaves, hunting human beings like animals and subjecting them to the indignity of slavery. When one asks whether they also haven't themselves captured Arabs in war, they admit that they have, but only in retaliation. They also say that the people they capture are always adopted and assimilated into their families as relatives. To them, slavery is totally alien and inherently Arab. That's the way they think God created the Arab. The Dinka was created differently. The Dinka scholar, Francis Deng, writes:

"All the cattle of the Dinka, the Arab took. He took even the sheep and goats and grain at home. People used holes in the trees to hide seeds in the hope that in the right season they would try to cultivate them again. A man's son would be seen and, if liked, it would be said, 'This child is beautiful; I'll take him.' He would take a child and put him in his big bag on a horse and take him away. At three o'clock at night or at four o'clock while people were sleeping, without any word or any warning, they would burn down the villages.

The Dinka would beat the drums of war and say, 'We have to go and attack the Arabs.' They would kill them just as they had killed the Dinka, and the people who had been captured by the Arabs would be released. Only the cattle would remain with us. But a human created by God was never made a slave by a black man. Slavery is not known to us. If there are slaves among us, it is people your great-grandfather took from Khartoum to save them from slavery."

The Land between the Niles

In the early 1880s, Johann Maria Schuver traveled through the Gezira, the land between the two Niles before they converge at Khartoum. Robust, bombastic, and noisy, with a wry sense of humor and an ear for languages, Schuver is much liked. Unlike other Europeans, he stays off the beaten path and lives close to the people. Many thought he was a Turkish spy. They call him "Abu Kalb"—father of a dog—because of his two dogs (one of which is eaten by a crocodile). His guide is often a slave trader, who tells him about his business. Schuver likes the people he meets and settles down with them for a time. Although not trained as a scholar, his detailed accounts are later found to be highly accurate.

In the spring when the sun bleaches the grass to straw, the cows are driven every third day to the Blue Nile. If this is not possible, water must be lifted in goatskins from deep wells. The Arabs tell Schuver that they can live for several months without a drop of water, provided they have a dish of fresh milk every morning and some curdled camel milk in the evening.

Schuver finds the lack of shade more intolerable than the blistering heat. Having few leaves, the thorn trees offer about as much relief from the sun "as a stretched fishing net." He passes through scattered hamlets where living conditions are austere, but the people are unceasingly hospitable, providing shells filled with sweet or curdled milk, chickens stewed in butter, sorghum mush, over which they pour "mullah"—a thick sauce made of Jew's mallow and described by Schuver as "almost like elephant's spittle." They never ask for money. Such hospitality is unheard of on more frequented routes, where the people have been repeatedly provoked, he says, "by the chicanery of soldiers passing through."

The main town on the Blue Nile is Sennar, once the proud capital of the Funj kingdom. In Schuver's day, it features a jumble of mud brick dwellings with flat roofs and windowless walls, a white stumpy mosque, and not a green spot anywhere. Sennar's only importance is a garrison for three hundred badly dressed and neglected Jihadiya. Its exports are modest: small amounts of wax, senna, tamarind, henna, gum, and ostrich feathers. The Jellaba in Sennar kill ostriches with a musket ball or lance or pluck the feathers from captured birds. From the outlying villages and hamlets they buy salt and cotton cloth, which they exchange in Abyssinia for slaves.

The suq opens late in the morning so people from the countryside can attend, and activity peaks during the hottest hours. Women, their eyes embellished with antimony, and their fingertips with henna, shepherd flocks of crooked-nosed, long-tailed sheep and goats into the square. The big traders and moneychangers are Greeks, known as "Rumi," although a few might be Syrians or Armenians. "Merisa" made from millet is the universal beverage. "Without merisa, no Sudan, and without Sudan, no merisa," writes Schuver. "I can compare the best bilbil—its other name—only to horse's piss…I know Negroes, who for periods of several weeks, take no other food."

As elsewhere, the central government exerts a feeble presence and earns only feeble allegiance from the local population. With Jellaba providing support, it conducts raids against villages that are delinquent in paying tribute and abducts slaves as punishment. Hearing disputes is the responsibility of the "mamur," the principal local official, who ranks at the bottom of the government hierarchy. He is not from Sennar but from Mosul on the Euphrates.

According to Schuver, when one Arab accuses another of stealing a camel half a dozen witnesses carrying spears attend the hearing, "swearing on the Koran, the Prophet, the beards of fathers and on the sins of mothers and wives." They refer to a party in the dispute as "a son of a dog, a son of a thief, a son of a whore, a perjurer and a kafir." Afterward, the mamur, who carries the government's archives in his pocket, makes his decision. This, Schuver says, is how Turco-Egyptian justice is done.

THE WESTERN FRONTIER

Along the Nile and its tributaries, the date palm is the main cash crop. Digging sticks are used to turn the soil and waterwheels to irrigate the land. This is in sharp contrast to the terrain in Kordofan to the west, which is rolling steppe with scattered thickets and isolated peaks and, to the southwest, flat, fertile soil, and thickly wooded plains.

Kordofan Village

Hamlets of conical straw huts shimmer in the glaring light, roofs finished off by a stick run through an ostrich egg and a bottle at the top for the ultimate in architectural decoration. Around each cluster of huts are fields of millet, fenced with dry bushes thrown carelessly together. Farther out are gum gardens and grasslands. Along winding footpaths, languid groups of men shouldering lances, women with water jars, flocks of goats and sheep, and herds of cattle pass from village to village. In the dry season, the plants are withered, and no birds sing. Only the gum acacia and tamarind offset the burnished landscape and provide a modicum of shade. The leaden air is impregnated with fine sand. Barely discernible in the sepia haze, a merciless sun scorches the land and, at twilight, turns into a blood-red disk.

With the first summer showers, this barren land is miraculously transformed, the tawny earth renewed and carpeted in green, the bushes cloaked in flowers and myriad butterflies, the grass in places high enough to cover a horse and its rider. Wild geese and whistling teal preen themselves in the morning sun, flapping and calling to each other as they root on the grassy edge of the pools that have collected, frogs croaking everywhere joyously. The soil is alive with scarlet beetles. In the fields, men make holes in the soil with a twisting motion of their wooden tools as a rainstorm and its thunder fade in the distance. Women follow, sowing the seeds and treading down the soil. They sow the high ground and ridges and later, when the water soaks in, the depressions and hollows. After the sowing, they beat drums. "Of a truth," they say, "Allah is generous and merciful."

Several weeks later, people are standing amid the stalks, as small birds in countless hundreds, scarcely larger than insects, explode upward and circle above and then settle back again on the field. Should the locusts come, there will be no harvest—that is the will of God. They can fill the sky with their whirring bodies and, when they have landed, devour every sprig of new growth. But the locusts can be harvested and roasted, providing welcome nourishment in times of hunger.

Wadis, bone dry for months, are recharged. Women washing clothes pour water into shallow basins dug in the sand. Boys, with long sticks and cries of "ai-ee, ai-ee, get-get," drive the groaning camels in circles, keeping them back to await their turns at the basins. She-camels are big with young or have their young frisking at their heels. Away from the wadi and standing water, sheep and goats and herds of camels and cattle collect near a well in the pitiless glare, and black flies swarm like a pestilence. Arabs sit their horses and herdsmen stand, stork-like, leaning on their spears, the sole of one foot pressed against the shin of the other leg, and wait their turn.

Two men, facing each other at the wellhead, chant a monotonous lament as they raise a leather bucket with a palm-fiber cord, hand over hand.

At the well

Poured into gourds and troughs, the water is opaque. Women and children drive back the sheep and goats to wait their turn. There is no confusion; the scene is orderly and respectful.

Bulrush millet—"dukhn"—is the principal crop, uniquely adapted to Kordofan's sandy soil. This staple food is much preferred to the sorghum—"durra"—that grows in richer, clayey soils. A man, his wife, and a slave can cultivate fifty acres. The earth is cleared of grass, and they dig lines of holes in which the seeds are placed before the rains that come in May or June. The crop appears and is harvested at the end of October. Threshed and ground between two stones and mixed with water, the flour is heated in an earthen dish, greased with butter, and baked into flat wafers called "kisra." These wafers and the thick, glutinous polenta called "asida" are the food of the people. The flour is boiled, and a ragout of dried okra and strips of meat, served up with onions and hot red peppers, is poured on top. Millet is also made into beer. To a visitor, it may look as if a handful of ashes has been thrown into a bowl of water, but it has a refreshing taste. Sorghum grown in low-lying clay soil doesn't make as strong a merisa, but that doesn't seem to matter, as it is consumed with every meal. Used as forage for horses and camels, sorghum is less heating than millet but also less digestible if not thoroughly chewed.

In the nineteenth century, El Obeid and Shakka are the main towns. At mid-century, El Obeid—described by the Austrian Ignatius Pallme—comprises several villages, mostly huts of straw or clay with a coating of cow dung. The government house is the only imposing structure: an audience chamber and the scriptoria for the Coptic secretaries, and opposite, an open space for executions. Without even a single minaret, the town overall is not particularly pleasing except during the short rainy season when the soil is covered with luxuriant vegetation, beautiful flowers, and high stands of millet.

The slave market takes place every day. It is "easier in this country to find a slave than a dollar of ready money," writes John Petherick, who later becomes an ivory trader on the White Nile and British consul in Khartoum. He describes market-days in El Obeid in the early 1850s: Jellaba arriving in small groups and spreading their goods out for sale; Baggara women in single file astride oxen, laden with bundles of wood and bags of sorghum, butter, fowls, eggs, and cotton; Kababish nomads down from the north with camels to sell; women squatting on low stools with fruit, vegetables, sour milk, merisa, and balls of grease—the native pomatum used cosmetically by both sexes—laid out before them. Between the lines of vendors spear-bearing Arabs stroll proudly back and forth. A donkey with cocked ears and raised tail, ridden by a half-naked lad perched on its rump, trots quickly by.

A butcher makes his first purchases and, as soon as a price is agreed, the beast is slaughtered on the spot and its meat laid out on angarebs for sale. Bargaining is an integral part of every purchase, casual onlookers intervening in the process, even suggesting a compromise. When agreement is reached, payment may be in Egyptian piastres, Spanish dollars, British sovereigns, or in ells or cubits of common cottons— measured from the elbow to the tip of the fingers. The best exchange rate is for Maria Theresa dollars.

Townsmen wear a loose white cotton shirt tight at the neck and reaching to the ankles, and, on their shaven heads, a small white calico skullcap. Government employees wear the tarbush. Village chiefs cover themselves with a single voluminous piece of coarse white cotton, wrapped about the body and over the shoulders, and on their heads a large turban. Nomads, their hair grown long and plaited in thick braids running back from the brow, wear only a cloth wrapped around the waist. Maidens wear nothing more than a leather-stripped skirt or, if freeborn, a thin transparent scarf covering their heads, and older women, a single piece of cotton cloth, one end draped around the lower part of the body and the other thrown over the left shoulder, leaving the right shoulder, breast, and arm exposed. They spend half their time adjusting these robes, taking care to cover head and shoulders for the sake of modesty. Their hair, plaited in tight little braids, is saturated with mutton grease and sometimes sprinkled with the powder of aromatic bark and decorated with bits of colored cloth, cowry shells, and beads.

The town makes a good impression on the missionary, Fr. Stanislao Carcenari, who in 1862 finds El Obeid the most delightful and the cleanest town, its shade trees well cared for. Of a population of one million, two thirds are Blacks. It is the seat of the governor who is responsible directly to the khedive in Cairo. The greatest part of the trading of the Sudan is located here, and the principal merchants of Khartoum are coming here to live.

A two-day journey to the north is the town of Bara, the country abode of rich Dongolawi merchants who are adept at irrigation. Their homes are of mud brick and flat-roofed amid gardens of wheat, tobacco, pepper, and onions. The richest gum gardens are just beyond, in the sandy hills. After the rainy season when the thorny acacia trees lose their foliage, children and the poor collect the amber nodules of gum that have exuded through fissures in the bark. Relative size determines quality since, when stored, the larger nodules are better able to withstand the dampness that destroys the crystals.

To the south and west of El Obeid, through dense and thorny woods rich in ebony and into undulating sand country, there are places where water can't be obtained from wells. Instead, small melons are cultivated to provide liquid. They are virtually tasteless and full of black seeds, and their husks are fed to camels.

For liquid the people depend on mammoth baobabs, known as tabeldi, which have small crowns, thick trunks, and bizarre shapes. They dig a ditch around the trunk to collect water during the rains. The trunk is filled through a hole at the top, its branches serving as gutters. A single tree can hold as much as a ton of cool and fresh water, enough to provide for many camels. After filling the tree, the ditch is leveled so no one can tell if the tree is full or not. By selling the water to travelers, the owner of fifty or more tabeldis can become a rich man. To save themselves the trouble of drawing water, Bashibazuks who are out collecting taxes fire their muskets into the trunk and drink from the holes.

Tabeldi Tree

In 1821, the viceroy of Egypt sends his son-in-law, the Defterdar, into Kordofan with forty-five hundred infantry and cavalry. Tribal irregulars rally against the invaders and hurl spears at their cannons. Wearing only a cloth wound lightly around the waist and armed with but shield and spear, they are no match against the musketry of the Turco-Egyptian troops. Struck by bullets, they put their fingers in their wounds and wonder how they were made. Women pick up the spears of the fallen and joined in the fight. When the battle is over, their shrieks are heartrending as they tear out their hair in frenzy and despair.

Stationed in Kordofan the Egyptian troops are not accustomed to the climate and, toward the end of every rainy season, suffer from fatal fevers. In time they are replaced by Bazinger slave troops better attuned to the climate. Having been in the private armies of traders, they have experience with muzzle-loading muskets and rifles and prove to be better soldiers than the Egyptians.

Supreme authority resides with the governor, who reports directly to the khedive in Cairo. A ferocious mustache curling up from the corners of his mouth epitomizes his absolute power. He can remove sub-governors and chiefs at will and give their posts to others, who annually pay him an agreed sum plus cattle, sheep, and grain. Onerous levies on waterwheels and other irrigation devices discourage cultivation. Property becomes virtually his own and tax collection a military operation. Danagla and Bashibazuks go from house to house and keep part of what they collect.

A village that doesn't meet its tax obligations has to furnish the equivalent in slaves, which are publicly sold for the provincial account. Not surprisingly, the government is heartily disliked because of the rapacity of Bashibazuks, although some of the fekis and spiritual leaders—who, by the way, are exempted from taxes—can be equally unscrupulous.

Cattle nomads are turned into slave-raiders on behalf of Jellaba, who hunt slaves for the government on a half-share basis. Camel nomads are fleeced unmercifully. Compelled to transport gum arabic and grain to Nile river landings, their herds are pillaged when the hot weather drives them to watering places vulnerable to attack. Their double-barrel rifles and cartridges made of paper are no match for the government's breech-loading Remington rifles and brass cartridges.

Any apparent injustice on the part of the "pasha," as the governor is called, gives evil repute to the word "Turk." The term is indiscriminately applied to anyone with a light skin who wears a fez, whether a genuine Turk, Syrian, Albanian, European or, as most often the case, an Egyptian. By the time of the Mahdist rebellion "Turk" has become synonymous with infidel.

Audiences with the provincial governor are spent smoking pipes and drinking endless cups of Abyssinian coffee. An assembly of notables and tribal elders, complaining of taxes or some other matter, can be found in the pasha's divan or reception salon, all talking and gesticulating at once. The matter settled, there is a lapse in the heated exchange until someone raises a fresh point, and the hubbub starts all over again, more lustily than ever.

A foreign visitor, Sidney Ensor, traveling in the western Sudan in the early 1870s, is put up in comfortable government quarters where he spends afternoons at backgammon—of which Turkish officials are passionately fond—and evenings at sumptuous meals or listening to opera music and watching dancers. He accompanies the governor and his personal physician, a Greek, on official visits to outlying villages where village elders come forward, eager to kiss the pasha's hand. Fresh chibouks and coffee are followed by more backgammon—at which Ensor loses three sheep to the pasha and half a flock to the doctor. On their return to Government House the military band strikes up the khedivial anthem.

Outsiders obliged to stay overnight in a village are sheltered in a rectangular-shaped "rakuba" made of straw, closed on three sides, and furnished with mats. An angareb is brought out and a carpet spread over it. A pipe is prepared, and a large bowl of camel's milk or merisa is placed on the ground by a slave girl. An august group of village elders then enters. Out front, others sit in the open, the women apart. Shy youths, overcome with curiosity, hesitate before also settling down nearby. Womenfolk and girls edge forward to get a glimpse of the dignitaries. A sick person may be presented to the governor's physician, since the foreign hakim ranks above all others when local doctoring normally involves dubious potions or a passage from the Koran on scraps of paper to be chewed and swallowed by the patient. Ensor found that the patients brought before the Greek doctor are mainly women, "all of the semi- or full Negro type, since the Arabs keep their thoroughbred Arab wives at home in seclusion...The fee per visit was half a sheep, half a goat, or nine fowls...The women would club their halves together... and the doctor was rapidly accumulating a large farm."

A long-legged sheep, with its prominent hooked nose, is brought forward and its throat severed to the spine. While being roasted its stomach and liver are cut into small pieces in a wooden bowl, over which the gall bladder is squeezed and red pepper added, and the whole concoction is served up still warm. People tuck up their right sleeves over the elbow and are invited to eat with the word "bismillah"—in the name of God—by the sheikh of the village. Hands plunge into the dish. During the meal not a word is spoken, and when it is over, merisa is served. What's more, no thanks are expressed nor any expected.

After the meal an entertainment is often presented, as Petherick describes in his account. By the light of a sputtering kerosene lantern and the dying embers of the fire, dancing girls form a semicircle in front of the angareb where the honored guest is reclining. Young men stand behind, clapping their hands and singing. As the tempo quickens, a dancer, wearing a scarf over her shoulders, throws it open, exposing her breasts, and then springs to the center, accompanying the change in measure with her right foot. Throwing her head well back and her chest forward, raising her hands, she slowly advances, moving head and chest backwards and forwards. The onlookers ecstatically shout "Allah, Allah" as the tempo quickens. One bound forward brings her up to Petherick. Bending her head right and left, she salutes him with her tresses of greasy plaited hair. He writes, "By moistening a small gold coin, a rubyeh, in my mouth and sticking it to her forehead, she retired apparently as much pleased as myself."

The "false dawn" comes an hour before sunrise, a wave of cool air passing over the village, which Arab poets call the "breath of dawn." The braying of donkeys and barking of dogs mingle with the high-pitched cadences of children chanting the Koran. A feki has awakened his pupils before sunrise to start memorizing the phrases inscribed the day before on their wooden slates. When there is enough light there are ablutions and prayer, the collection of firewood for the feki to sell, or work to do on the feki's land, or grinding his corn. The student who shows insufficient diligence may suffer strokes of the "kurbaj," the heavy hippopotamus-hide whip, leaving him unable to move. His wounds will be treated with hot butter until healed.

Feki and Pupils

The traveler's party now prepares to get underway. The camels, grunting and spitting, are brought to their knees for loading. Guttering embers of the evening are stirred to life and tea is brewed. Villagers come out to watch the departure. If it takes place in winter, the party can't strike camp until mid-morning, as the camels are stiff from the cold and can barely move when loaded. When everything is loaded and cinched tight, the sheikh rides ahead on his donkey to lead his guests out of the village.

When Darfur to the west of Kordofan becomes an Egyptian province in 1874, the khedive sends out two expeditions, both under American Civil War veterans, to report on the country. Erastus Sparrow Purdy, who has fought on the Federal side, enters Darfur. Raleigh Edward Colston, who has fought for the Confederacy, goes into Kordofan and then links up with Purdy. Their instructions are to set out together up the Nile until they reach Wadi Halfa, where Colston is with five hundred camels and drivers. Purdy continues along the Nile until he strikes the route to Darfur, thence southwest to El Fasher and the copper mines at Hufrat el-Nahas.

During this reconnaissance through unknown regions, Purdy's servant becomes mortally sick and asks his master to look after his son, who lives in a distant village. Purdy gives his promise, locates the boy, cares for his needs during infancy, and sends him to a school in Egypt run by American Presbyterians. Learning later that the boy has "galloping tuberculosis" and that his days are numbered, he writes to the school: "His father served me faithfully. See that he wants nothing. Draw on me for all necessary expenses, and when the inevitable happens, give him a Christian burial and place a cross on his remains."

For more than a year. Purdy explores the vague frontiers of the khedive's newest province. On his return to Egypt, his fortunes deteriorate sharply. A wrongful suit is brought against him by an Italian hotelkeeper in Cairo for non-payment of grossly inflated bills, and he is discharged from the Egyptian army. An ill man and deeply in debt, he dies in Cairo in 1881.

Soon after leaving the bend of the Nile, Colston realizes that his camels are in no condition to undertake the journey. They straggle into camp well after dark, and the next morning many of them are too weak to be loaded. Colston sends frantic messages to the governor of Dongola for more camels. He himself has suffered earlier from lumbago and other ailments and was already sick when he entered Kordofan. Overexposed to the sun, he begins to lose control of his legs and falls from his mount. In his last report, he describes his plight: "My left leg showed symptoms of paralysis. But I preferred to die in the desert rather than abandon the command, which His Highness had done me the honor to give me." Despite suffering day and night, he valiantly keeps going by horseback, taking barometric readings and making his surveys. With a soldier's pride, he refuses to quit. When no longer able to ride, he is transported on a stretcher by soldiers who are relieved every half-hour. His suffering is intense. "Oh, Night of Hell!" he cries.

In June 1875, the chief of staff in Cairo sends a telegram to Henry Gosalee Prout, a Federal veteran, who is undertaking surveys along the Red Sea coast: "His Highness, expressing great sympathy for Col. Colston and great satisfaction with the high sense of duty displayed by him in continuing, as he had done, to advance with his command under such adverse conditions of health, was pleased to direct me to send orders by telegraph confirming you in command of the expedition. Choose the most healthy of the unexplored portions of Kordofan, and work there with the expedition. Communicate frequently with me and send reports and maps as soon as practicable. Do your best for comfortable return of Col. Colston to Khartoum."

After six months' rest in El Obeid, the swelling in Colston's legs has subsided, and he is able to return to Cairo and eventually to the

United States. There he loses all his savings on unwise investments and spends his last years in the Confederate soldiers' home in Richmond, Virginia.

Prout carries on where Colston left off. He orders fresh quinine from Cairo and fresh camels and men from the governor of Kordofan. For nine months he probes into every corner of the province. His reports earn him unqualified praise. He is promoted to the rank of major and, succeeding Gordon, made governor of Equatoria, the province furthest south on the upper Nile. On the strength of his investigations, he determines that the country west of the Nile, having so few resources, will be wholly unable to repay Egypt the cost of occupation. But there are thousands of square miles of fertile soil along the Nile that, with irrigation, might be made highly productive and provide considerable benefit to Egypt.

— CHAPTER 4: GORDON —

GORDON IN EQUATORIA

In 1874, Charles Gordon replaces Baker as governor of the Equatorial provinces. Charged with establishing a series of military stations on the upper Nile and, almost as an afterthought, abolishing the commerce in slaves, it is up to him to win back the confidence of the local people lost under Baker's inflexible regime. With a few hundred Egyptian and Sudanese soldiers, he is expected to suppress insurrections, build roads, establish fortified posts, enforce a government monopoly of ivory, and send enough money to Cairo to pay for the expenses of his multifaceted assignment. "What I shall have done will be what I have done" is his reaction to these formidable responsibilities. He is forty-one years old.

As governor-general of Equatoria, Gordon is given an annual salary of £2,000 sterling. It is all he asked for, whereas Baker had received five times as much. Money and material things mean nothing to him. A man of great piety and simplicity, he is completely selfless, putting aside the normal comforts of life. When he accepts the governorship, he writes to his sister Augusta, "Events will go as God likes."

His journey up the White Nile is done in one of the government steamers that Baker brought into the country in 1870. To get to his new headquarters at Gondokoro, a thousand miles to the south, takes almost a month. En route, Gordon gives everyone something to do to keep busy. When he decides to stop to take on wood, everyone troops out to hunt for food or undertake some other task.

Gondokoro is a decrepit river port of about a thousand conical straw huts enclosed by a palisade beyond which no one could venture without an armed escort. Rats eat the food and then scurry to the river where they are snapped up by crocodiles. All that remains of the Austrian missionary station, which has been vacant since the last pastor died of dysentery a few years earlier, are tumbled walls and blackened pots.

Foreigners approach Gordon, upon his arrival, wanting employment. Many of them prove useless. They have come to shoot crocodiles and hippos, to write about their experiences, and make names for themselves. They are given good salaries and responsible posts, leaving subordinate posts to be filled by Nubians, principally Danagla from villages north of Khartoum.

The narrow strip of Danagla cultivations is unable to meet the needs of their families, so they spend much of their lives elsewhere as boatmen, merchants, ivory hunters, and slave traders. Literate in Arabic, they take positions in the Egyptian administration as clerks and tax-gatherers. Being handy with rifles and better able than Egyptians to cope with the climate, they also serve as irregular troops. They feel little loyalty toward the government and little sympathy with its campaign against the slave trade. Subordinate positions as watchmen, porters, and messengers are filled by natives, often bazingers, the freed slaves who had previously worked in the zeribas.

In Gondokoro, Gordon's staff includes Americans, Englishmen, Frenchmen, native Turks, Egyptians, and Sudanese. A senior post is given to Abul-Suoud, a notorious slave trader himself, and, therefore, in Gordon's opinion, qualified to deal with the slavers, although in Khartoum "everyone's jaw dropped," as he wrote to his sister. Previously imprisoned by Baker, Abul-Suoud is grist to Gordon's mill, like everyone else.

Gordon's office is a large divan—office tent—where he sits, perspiration pouring off him. Tropical rains and long marches through swamps have played havoc with fine linen uniforms, so he and his officers dress in coarse homespun cotton cloth that immediately becomes soaked with sweat. At sunset, the daytime heat gives way to chilly dampness and an onslaught of mosquitoes. Burning Keating's insect powder works for a while, but the carbolic acid Gordon brought with him turns out to be useless. To escape the mosquitoes, he goes to bed early after reading from his Bible. The next morning at first light he again opens the Bible and then, inspired and uplifted, emerges from his tent to grapple with the problems of the day. His food is usually dry biscuits, bits of broiled meat, and boiled macaroni and sugar—no vegetables. But eating isn't important to his life. His servants are an Arab cook and two skinny little Shilluk boys he picked up in exchange for some sorghum when coming down from Khartoum. "As I do not talk Arabic, and they do not talk English, conversation is nil. It is the same with the authorities; they come, and instinct tells me what they want, and then they go."

Unable to count on his staff, his solitude is unrelieved and would have been intolerable if he hadn't plenty to do. He creates tasks only to keep himself busy. "Inaction is to me terrible, and I do not know what on earth to do from morn till night, and this is indeed the more trying…I feel sure that the tedium of this life does as much to make people ill as the malaria. It is a country of delays." Sheer activity in itself, whether of importance or not, fends off stagnation and boredom and keeps Gordon going. In his journal, he says, "Writing orders to be obeyed by others, thinking of the various trifles, even knocking off the white ants from the stores; that is one's life; and speaking materially, for what gain? The gain is to be called 'His Excellency.' Yet His Excellency has to slave more than any individual: to pull ropes, to mend this, make a cover for that—just finished a capital cover to the duck gun." Reading is confined almost entirely to his Bible, which he reads and rereads assiduously. Each day he prays, having placed a hatchet and a flag at the door of his tent to indicate that he is not to be disturbed. An outpouring of memoranda to officials, even to the khedive in Cairo, and a stream of letters to his beloved sister spew forth. His only recreation is smoking his pipe or a cigarette, which he does endlessly, admitting, "If you sit in all day and smoke, you can't be surprised at your liver getting congested. Difficult as it is to do it, it is only by forcing yourself out, by cutting down a decayed tree, or some such exercise, that you can keep your health out here."

The troops Baker left behind were paid in liquor or slave girls sent from Khartoum. So Gordon must return to Khartoum, confront Ayyub, and obtain a supply of Austrian dollars to pay his soldiers. He wastes no time getting rid of anyone who has been dealing in slaves. Meanwhile, his senior staff is beginning to sicken and die, and Abul-Suoud goes back to slave trading, the only life he knows.

Money from a government that is chronically in debt finds its way at irregular intervals to Gordon's Equatorial provinces where it is distributed among his officials. Meanwhile, fleecing the local tribes and taking bribes meet their immediate needs. When the tribute from tribes is not enough, plundering is the only option. How else can officials feed their innumerable servants?

The fluctuation of arrears, advances, and settlements in different currencies and dispersed locations creates an accounting nightmare, which keeps a host of Copts busy. The bashkatib—chief clerk—consequently has exceptional authority, second only to that of the local governor himself, and often serves as his deputy. Many of the governors can't read, so they rely on bashkatibs with their Arabic to keep tax records, house rates paid by townspeople, dues from women who make sorghum beer, bribes to hide taxable property, etc. Opportunities for graft, fraud, and deception are ubiquitous. Clerks can read into the orders and records whatever they like, and the governor usually seals the envelope and makes it official without bothering to look at it.

As with Baker before him, slavery and slave trading become a thorn in Gordon's flesh. His adjutant, one Ibrahim Fawzi, is also secretly involved. At Fashoda—a critical choke point at the mouth of the Sobat, a major tributary—Gordon appoints a well-connected Shilluk as governor. Instead of suppressing the slave trade, however, he allows himself to be bribed by Egyptian officials and becomes a trader himself, exchanging ivory, ostrich feathers, and hippopotamus hides for cotton cloth, glass beads, brass wire, and slaves. Gordon can do little to stem the illicit traffic. Governors downstream complain that they can't seize steamers with slaves and ivory coming from Equatoria because they have no jurisdiction over arrivals from Gordon's provinces. Often, natives bring their children to Gordon's station in order to exchange them for some grain. "Lads and women came to do certain work for the soldiers…the station was much more amusing than their homes," Gordon writes. Slaves freed from traffickers often choose to remain at Gondokoro rather than take the long and dangerous road back to their homes. When two vessels sail into Gondokoro with cargoes of ivory and ebony, Gordon finds ninety-six slaves concealed underneath the deck boards. They are set free and settled in the little agricultural colony he has established. He calls them "volunteer slaves" and says they are quite content.

That slavery is so deeply entrenched poses a dilemma. No civil servant, Egyptian, Turk, or Sudanese, condemns it in principle or holds that slave trafficking is a crime. Slaves are being imported into Khartoum not as trade items but as personal property, and the clerk at the river landing can easily certify that those listed on the manifest are, indeed, domestic servants.

Even Gordon himself employs many ex-slavers, the most notorious being Abul-Suoud. He recruits soldiers by buying slaves or enlisting captured slaves and making soldiers of them, sometimes against their will. He argues that he needs soldiers to put down the slave dealers, creating a vicious circle. Anyhow, he writes, "The slaves I buy are already torn from their homes; and whether I buy them or not, they will remain slaves." And, since everyone depends on slaves, to liberate them without compensating their owners would be robbery. Or so he claims.

One after another of his staff falls victim to marsh fever. Before sulfate of quinine replaces absinthe as a preventive, there is little that can be done. Stricken by fever, the patient raves and suffers horrendous headaches. After drinking great volumes of tamarind water, a few hours' sleep, and profuse sweating, the worst is usually over. First to expire is a young Englishman, then the German botanist, Witt. A fortnight later, only a month after reaching Gondokoro, Gordon's French secretary and interpreter, Auguste Linant, dies and is sorely missed. Anson, another of his staff, just twenty-five years old, never reaches Gondokoro, "but lies in an ant-hill, the only dry ground there is on the banks of the Nile." The American, Major Campbell, becomes so ill that he has to be sent downriver to Khartoum where he succumbs. Writing to his sister, Gordon calls the place "a complete hospital…it is only my iron constitution which has pulled me through as yet. Do not let me perish up here."

Chaillé-Long, who served as Gordon's chief of staff, is a survivor. He attributes his immunity to the bilious fever he suffered each year when he was a boy on Maryland's Eastern Shore. He and Gordon are in many respects alike—ambitious, stubborn, and jealous of fame—and soon come to detest each other. Unknown to Gordon, Chaillé-Long has been given a secret mission by the khedive. Striking off on his own, he heads south into Uganda to convince M'Tesa, the king, to become a vassal of Egypt. In lectures and newspaper articles about his explorations, he later presents a most unflattering portrait of Gordon: how his anger is ungovernable, how he will cuff the face of his Arab aide-de-camp or kick his Alsatian servant until he screams. He describes Gordon's fits of melancholy during which he shuts himself up in his tent for days at a time, a bottle of brandy at his elbow and the hatchet and flag at the door; how he lashes out when Chaillé-Long chances to enter his tent during one of these bouts; and how, the next morning, Gordon reappears brisk and cheerful. "Old fellow, now don't be angry with me. I was very low last night. Let's have a good breakfast—a little b. and s. Do you feel up to it?"

Chaillé-Long's accounts are filled with contradictions and inconsistencies. Aside from his daily half-hour of prayer, for Gordon to shut himself off for days is not in keeping with his character. That he is a curious fellow, there is little doubt. He is most certainly overbearing and not easy to get along with. Chaillé-Long says, "Gessi paid dearly for the privilege of being Gordon's intimate by being kicked whenever his master's ill-humour required it." Certainly, Gordon is impulsive and relies heavily on intuition, which, for him, contains almost divine sanctity. He is contemptuous of bureaucrats—"arrant humbugs" he calls them. He is, as the Arabs say, "foq al-qanun"—above all ordinary rules. He has extraordinary faith in himself, which allows him to vacillate in his moods and decisions without the slightest qualms. At first supportive of Abul-Suoud, who, in Gordon's opinion, has "exerted such zeal and energy that the inhabitants are living in peace," he later calls him "a despicable creature."

That he is completely honest and exceptionally generous there is no question. Gessi speaks of the pleasure Gordon finds in giving to others and the reluctance with which he accepts anything in return. Junker tells fondly of how Gordon instructed all his heads of stations to provide him with porters and other assistance and how he gave him some bottles of Warburg fever tincture upon which Gordon himself depended for his own health.

Gordon admires the local people and doesn't try to reform them. In this respect, he is unlike Baker and many other expatriates. He allows his Black soldiers to fish for Nile perch and tilapia, brew native beer, choose wives among the tribes, dance at the full moon, and turn toward Mecca for their daily prayers. But he has nothing good to say about his senior staff members, who are for the most part Danagla.

"You have but little idea of what work I have up here with one limp, wretched interpreter, who is always sick, and an officer in command of troops utterly incompetent, thinking of his comfort and safety only. How trying these Arabs are. The fact is that the Arabs are as much foreign to these lands as Europeans are. You have little idea how frightened these Arabs are of the Blacks…."

He also says, "No one can conceive the utter misery of these lands—heat and mosquitoes day and night all the year round. But I like the work for I believe I can do a great deal to ameliorate the lot of the people." However sincere his intention, Gordon alienates the established interests—the slave traders, tribal chiefs, government officials, and witch doctors. When he leaves Equatoria toward the end of 1876, little has been accomplished other than a few miserable forts, several thousand bewildered, homeless, freed slaves, and a slave trade as robust as it was when he arrived. Here he is—a Christian confronting an institution condoned by Islam and working virtually alone, sustained only by the remote authority of the khedive in Egypt. When the khedive asks him to continue his good work, Gordon points out the futility of making great efforts to open up Equatoria to civilization while the rest of the country is the scene of a corrupt administration and the brutalities of the slave trade.

HE GAVE ME THE SUDAN

When he leaves Equatoria toward the end of 1876, Gordon never plans to return to the Sudan—but within a year he is back. The khedive believes that Gordon, more than any other man, can clean up the corruption of officials and channel taxes back into the Egyptian treasury. He appoints him governor-general with the rank of marshal and gives him a splendid uniform with a coat covered with gold lace worth £150. For an Englishman and a Christian to be made ruler over a predominantly Muslim territory was indeed remarkable. Gordon could proudly write to his sister, "He gave me the Sudan."

He arrives in Khartoum just after his predecessor, Ismail Ayyub, has been dismissed. In a fit of pique, Ismail has smashed the windows in the palace and slashed the offices to pieces.

On May 5, 1877, amid great enthusiasm, beflagged boats, and six stately elephants in the charge of their Indian attendants, Gordon is formally installed. He decrees that the inhumane rhinocerous hide whip, the kurbaj, should be abolished as an instrument of punishment and wastes no time in sacking Turks and Egyptians and replacing them by Sudanese. He often chooses obscure civil servants for important posts—some of whom lose their positions within a fortnight. Every day new decrees are published, officials appointed, and others dismissed. Unconcerned by what others think of him, Gordon makes a lot of enemies. In the eyes of British officials, he is a loose cannon.

At all hours, he is sitting at the large mahogany desk, wearing his red fez and white linen uniform, a trim, alert figure "with eyes like blue diamonds," his secretaries at his side, and tobacco jar close at hand. When Carl Giegler, the former director of telegraphs, who had been acting governor-general, comes to call on him, Gordon's first words are: "My dear fellow, whoever you are, I have no time to see anyone now." Where are the customary civilities, the pipes and the coffee? What a bizarre chap. Surely a more cordial reception might be expected. On another occasion, Giegler is announced and led into the divan where Gordon is dictating orders to his secretary. "He greeted me coldly, motioning me to a chair and handing me the latest *Times* while he continued dictating."

Although Gordon speaks little Arabic, he tries with the aid of the several dictionaries at his elbow to convey to his secretary what he wants to say. Brow furrowed in thought, he will say aloud what he wishes to mean while his secretary, Busati, who speaks neither French nor English, somehow manages follow the chain of thoughts and set down the commands as Gordon wanted. His dictating finished, Gordon says to Giegler in his usual low, soft voice, "You came rather too soon. Go home now. I have a lot to do." It so happens that he is at the time preparing a recommendation for Giegler's appointment as his deputy. That evening he comes up to him, a mischievous, narrow smile on his lips, and blithely remarks with a wink, "You never dreamed of that, did you?"

Gordon wears a white officer's uniform with the insignia of a general. For special occasions, he wears the heavy, gold-embroidered pasha's uniform. Every high official travels with two or three orderlies to deal with crowds seeking an audience. Gordon has several, two of whom he nicknames "Cow" (the more faithful) and "Gazelle" (the swifter). They accept the petitions that are addressed to Gordon and tell petitioners to come back the next day. The antechambers of the palace are constantly humming with people who have been summoned or have come on their own to discuss some matter or other. Gordon is never free of this inundation. Even when he is on camelback, they run along beside him, yelling their complaints up at him and throwing dust on their heads.

Egyptian administrators control only a few square kilometers, but Gordon intends to master the entire country of a million square miles. Arrayed in his white linen uniform with sleeves rolled up, he sets out on vast tours of inspection. "I expect to ride five thousand miles this year, if I am spared. I am quite alone, and I like it. I trust God will pull me through every difficulty. The solitary grandeur of the desert makes one feel how vain is the effort of man."

His journeys are truly prodigious, riding on and on for weeks at a time, nothing but emptiness around him, to reach a place where there is a crisis and there impose his will. His sudden arrival at some distant headquarters leaves officials dumbfounded. "I came flying into this station like a madman in a marshal's uniform and only one man with me. The escort did not come in for an hour-and-a-half afterward." Being the governor-general, his arrival is an occasion of celebration, drums beating, music playing, and the shrill cries of women. The local governor and lesser officials, the small foreign community, and the principal merchants come out to meet him. "The old trod on the young because of their happiness," is how one eyewitness describes the frenzy of emotion. Gordon, they are sure, will bring relief from the injustices inflicted on them. Nomad Arabs arrive at the provincial headquarters from afar to present their petitions, which Coptic scribes write up on payment of some piastres.

Then off again at a slashing pace, his dromedary stepping out in gallant style, guided by a cord attached to its left nostril, nose up in the air, head practically in Gordon's lap. Only in the gathering dusk does he slacken his hold to enable his mount to better follow the darkening track. There is also need for caution since, without warning, the camel might accelerate its pace and risk breaking into a gallop, throwing Gordon onto its neck.

Gordon has an underlying fondness and respect for camels. When he sees a dromedary he likes, he will ask if he can buy it. "The camels and I are of the same race—let them take an idea into the heads, and nothing will take it out. If my camel feels inclined to go in any particular direction, there he will go, pull as much as you like ... Only gentlemen camels travel, the ladies stay at home looking after their families; the boy camels travel with their families for a year or so, but carrying nothing so as to accustom them to their work."

Dashing back and forth across the arid wastes in often blistering heat fills him with discomfort:

"Every fortnight I have a new skin to my face. Thanks to some glycerin, it is not painful; but the sun is fearfully hot. About seven miles from Dara I got into a swarm of flies, and they annoyed me and my camel so much, that we jolted along as fast as we could. Well ahead of my escort, I came upon my garrison like a thunderbolt. Imagine to yourself a single, dirty, red-faced man on a camel, ornamented with flies, arriving all of a sudden…Such a road through the forest! You are nearly torn to ribbons through which your camel will drag you if you do not look out ... We can't go a yard at night; so all our traveling is by day, which is very hot work."

An important Baggara sheikh named Ali Julla accompanies him on some of these hectic journeys and describes:

"Gordon summoned me to guide him. He had with him a company of camel troops and with him was Busati Bey who translated for him, for in those days he knew little Arabic, and he trusted Busati. Gordon used to dress in white; sometimes he wore a tarbush and sometimes a hat. When riding a camel, he had his sleeves rolled up above his elbows. He had five riding camels, which he called by the names of the sheikhs who had given them to him. I had a horse and a donkey, but when he saw that I could not keep up with the camels, he bade me ride one of his, which afterward he gave me…When I guided him to El Obeid, he was very pleased with me, and gave me a sum of money and a robe, and forty-five slaves. He was very generous. He was a great man, Gordon."

Only in the solitude of these arduous journeys does Gordon find real peace of mind: "I would infinitely rather travel alone in these countries than with a companion. One goes gliding along. The camel's cushioned foot makes no noise, and you learn yourself. During my long, long, hot, weary rides, I think my thoughts better and clearer than I should with a companion. The quiet of the desert is something wonderful and the air is perfectly pure. I have a splendid camel; it flies along and quite astonishes the Arabs."

Gordon keeps going at this frantic pace with little sleep and food. "I have no pleasure in eating or drinking and do both to keep myself alive. Imagine journeying some thirty miles a day, starting at half-past three in the morning and halting at nine or ten; and then starting again at three in the afternoon and going on till seven, day after day, through the sandy plain covered with dried-up yellow grass and scrub-trees; the heat terrible during the day, the nights bitterly cold."

Lytton Strachey says Gordon is a "pious toper" who liked a brandy and soda for breakfast and then more again when he retired. On the other hand, he is admired by the Sudanese who "despise the Englishman who gives way to drink." That he was a heavy drinker seems preposterous. The way Gordon carried through his camel rides is evidence enough. Who can live through what he does if he is not temperate and abstemious? How can he cover a hundred miles in two days, on sandy soil, where the camel's pace is usually not more than three-and-a-half miles an hour, and withstand the discomforts and the heat? In addition, he suffers throughout from a kind of eczema, an intolerable itching, which feels as if he is being bitten by mosquitoes at night.

"To die quickly would be to me nothing, but the long crucifixion that a residence in these horrid countries entails appalls me. I do not think I can face the cross of staying here, simply on physical grounds. I am a perfect Job. I have almost entirely given up smoking. If I had gone on with it much longer, I believe my heart would have stopped altogether. When I get to Obeid I shall have ridden on camel twenty-three hundred miles this year...."

In a man with angina pectoris and prickly heat rash that has turned into boils, and a horror of meals besides, his physical endurance is a miracle. "In camel riding you ought to wear a sash round the waist and another close up under the arm-pits; otherwise all the internal machinery gets disturbed." But these are minor afflictions compared to his constantly nagging self-doubts.

"I own nothing and am nothing. I am a pauper and seem to have ceased to exist. A sack of rice jolting along on a camel would do as much as I think I do. In the fearful heat, I wish I were in the other world. This is such a country, so worthless, and I see nothing to be gained by its occupation."

When he returns to Khartoum, he lives simply and austerely. The easy luxuries of his class and station are unknown to him. His clothes at times verge on the shabby; his meals are frugal. At heart a man of action and restless energy, he dislikes dealing with reports and accounts, fawning officials, and endless petitions. "A lover of danger and the audacities that defeat danger," he rides into the camp of insurgent slave raiders with an interpreter and small escort, and passes coolly along the ranks of scowling brigands who can only stare at him in silence—as if he is wearing invisible armor and can't be harmed by bullet or spear. But he is unable to achieve inner peace. His constant self-questioning is only put to rest when he is facing difficulties and hardships.

In Khartoum, he is occupied from dawn till late at night with mundane responsibilities, which he finds tedious and uninspiring. He is inexperienced in the routines of administration and gets no joy from them. He is impatient with niceties and illiterate in Arabic. "My huge palace is a dreary place. I can't go out of it without having people howling after me with petitions that I will let their sons out of prison, or such-like things; and they follow me wherever I go." Having to see personally that his orders are carried out quickly and exactly dismays and frustrates him. A clerk who enjoys his confidence is found to have "eaten"—that is, embezzled—fifty thousand Austrian dollars in less than six months. When a Nubian is arrested and charged with killing a slave, Gordon orders that he be tried immediately. Knowing the delays this will entail, he stipulates further that the trial be completed within two hours; if not, he will have the culprit brought to the palace and shot. He is obsessively impatient with bureaucratic dithering and procrastination.

"I sent out an expedition, which stayed out nineteen days and did nothing. The officer in command took a heavy bribe—£200 in money,

£50 worth of feathers, and ten camel-loads of durra—from the chief of the tribe he was to attack, not to attack him. If this proves to be true, I will have him shot and not wait for the khedive's sanction. But it will not be proved, for the witnesses, guilty of the same sort of actions, will try to screen him."

Gordon's love of animals and their idiosyncrasies interjects a modicum of levity in what is otherwise dreary routine. He finds humor in the antics of the animals around him.

"The steamer has just brought four little hippopotamuses, which are in my yard and which are very tame. They are like huge pigs…so plump and soft and cool-skinned. They have only little teeth. The little elephant smelt them but did not like them at all (a nasty fishy smell, no doubt). The hippopotamuses, however, would have been friendly with the elephant, but after a few overtures on their part, he butted at them, and when in the pond with them he flicked water at them with his trunk.

This morning, without any apparent reason, the two ostriches rushed at a black slave in the garden, and striking at him with their toes nearly killed him. One stroke from their toes tore off the poor man's nose. The culprits I have ordered to be sold into slavery and annually plucked. The proceeds of their sale are to be devoted to purchasing the freedom of the wounded slave, and to giving him a good baksheesh. It will be a just retribution."

When he is working, Gordon dislikes interruptions but welcomes company in his palace, where his hospitality and generosity are unbounded. He finds a house nearby for Rudolf Carl Slatin, the young Austrian officer who joins his staff, and asks him to share his meals with him. He invites Wilhelm Junker, the German explorer, to eat at the palace and sends him off with a supply of his precious "fever tincture" when he leaves for the malarial districts in the south. When Junker comes back years later, Gordon tells him that he had received a collection of ethnographic specimens, which are still unpacked, and asks if he'd like to choose from them what he wanted. When Junker finds it hard to decide what to take, Gordon tells him to take them all.

Wilhelm Junker

Another guest at the palace is the journalist, Frank Power, who describes Gordon as "a most lovable character—quiet, mild, gentle and strong; the way he pats you on the shoulder when he says, 'Look here, dear fellow, now what do you advise?'"

En route to Uganda, Bishop Comboni of the Austrian Roman Catholic Mission tells Gordon about a young English sailor, Frank Lupton, who wants to come to Sudan. Without a word to Comboni, Gordon telegraphs Lupton and hires him. He gives Comboni and the other missionaries seventy pounds in gold when they leave, since they weren't able to obtain money beforehand, and he sends his orderlies with two bags of macaroni to deliver to their steamer. When they are later caught in the Sudd, that gift of macaroni may be what saves their lives.

Gordon appears never to have been in love or to have indulged in thoughts of earthly pleasure and domestic joy. "Marriage spoils human beings," he says. He is less at ease in talking to women than to men. The presence of ladies, fashionable ladies especially, makes him uneasy. Women belong to some foreign culture, of which he doesn't know the language.

He is at his best among young children. A close friend in England describes how "he would run halfway up the stairs to the nursery, calling out 'Naughty, naughty' to the children's great delight. He calls them angels, touching their shoulders and saying, 'Where are your wings?'" Under siege in Khartoum, Gordon takes pleasure in the native children and their response to him, especially the boys, both browns and blacks—the former are a perfect bronze color.

Before coming to the Sudan, when supervising the erection of forts at the mouth of the Thames, he reaches out to the poor and unfortunate, taking provisions to hungry families or visiting a bedridden old woman to light her fire. When they die, they send for "the Colonel" rather than for the clergy. He houses street urchins in his official residence, where he feeds, bathes, clothes, and teaches them, eventually finding them jobs, and he corresponds with them after they have gone away.

He is particularly fond of boys, ragged street urchins and rough sailor-lads. Although he never married, it is not that evident that he was homosexual. Or is homosexuality simply too deeply buried? Or can it be that his life involves a perpetual struggle against the evils of the flesh?

Files of men, women, and children linked to each other by iron chains from rings around their necks pass along the desert tracks of the Sudan. Some carry the yoke, making it difficult for them to walk, as armed Bazingers on the flanks spur them on. In front on donkeys, a loutish bunch of Jellaba rides, impassive, without a flicker of guilt. A dead Negro pierced with a spear lies by the road, the fate of a slave too weak to walk.

Coup de grace of an exhausted slave

75

By the late 1870s these long strings of captives are encountered less frequently, but evidence of Jellaba passing small numbers of them down is everywhere. Human skulls by the side of the road dismay Gordon. "Why should I, at every mile, be stared at by the grinning skulls of those at rest?" He orders that the skulls be piled in a heap "as a memento of what the slave dealers have done to their people."

He intercepts a party of seven slave dealers and twenty-three slaves, some of them children not more than three years old. The slavers are chained and put in prison. The men and boys they captured are conscripted into the ranks, and the women become the wives of the soldiers.

Another time he meets on the trail three Bashibazuks who look clearly guilty. Seeing some figures sink into the high grass a short distance away, he says to his secretary, Berzati Bey, "I smell slaves; look under those trees." Fourteen slaves are flushed out and set free. The Bashibazuks are beaten, and their camel and two donkeys as well as their clothes and the £15 they have in cash confiscated.

Another man claims that the seven women with him are his wives. "I can't disprove it," Gordon writes. "There are numbers of children— the men say they are all their offspring...One day I noticed a very small black boy in the path, who would not get out of it. Put up on the croup of the camel, he denies belonging to a slave party we passed. He says, 'Give my master a piece of cloth for me. I should like to stay with you.' Poor little soul! He values himself at a dollar, which is the price of the piece of cloth he named."

Gordon raids the camps of slavers and interrupts the slave traffic whenever the opportunity arises. Sixty-three caravans are intercepted between June 1878 and March 1879. His doggedness and ubiquity flabbergast officials and earn him the implacable hatred of the slave-trading aristocracy—some of whom, though of Egyptian ancestry, hold foreign passports and do not pay taxes, even though they cultivate land and keep slaves.

For all his missionary zeal, Gordon is ever the realist. He makes no attempt to interfere with domestic slavery. But he orders the Catholic missionaries to cease giving asylum to runaway slaves, and when they refuse, writes a letter to the Pope, asking him to keep his priests from defying government policy.

He draws a sharp distinction between domestic slavery—the custom of the country—and the hunting of natives to sell into servitude, which is reprehensible in any culture. So he sees no discrepancy in acting vigorously against slave raiding while letting domestic slavery die a natural death. His position is thus at odds with that of the abolitionists, who are aghast at the idea of chattel slavery of any kind. He has sympathy for slaves but no tolerance at all for abolitionists. "It is the slaves who suffer, not Europe. Our professional humanitarians are no more anxious to abolish slavery altogether than masters of foxhounds are anxious to abolish foxes."

For him, the solution is simple: compel runaway slaves to return to their masters as long as they are not being mistreated. Require registration of slaves to prevent any new slaves being treated as property. Have Europeans give each of their slaves a paper of enfranchisement and do not allow them to take free men into slavery. Slaves will then come forward and ask for freedom. If well treated, the freedman will remain a faithful servant, but he will want a paper to carry round his neck to show that "he is free as the bird in the air."

Gordon agonizes over what to do with the emancipated slaves:

"Poor souls, I can't feed or look after them. If I released them, who would care for them? Their homes are too far off to send them to. Don Quixote would have liberated them, and made an attempt to send them back some forty days' march, through hostile tribes, to their homes. I can't liberate them from their owners without compensation, for fear of a general revolt. People will also say, 'By buying slaves you increase the demand, and indirectly encourage raids.' I can't take them back to their own country. I must let them be taken by my auxiliaries, or by my soldiers, or by the merchants. If I let them loose they will be picked up in every direction, for an escaped slave is like an escaped sheep—the property of him who finds him or her. These wretched slaves have their likes and dislikes; some would sooner go with their Jellaba merchants, some with the local Arab tribes, and some with the soldiers; even if they could, they would not go back to their now desolate homes where they would be attacked by more powerful tribes and made slaves by them."

At the very least, Gordon is able to remind his soldiers that if they take Muslims as slaves, they do it against the prescriptions of the Koran. He hopes the slave merchant will take off their chains and consider them as valuable as cows, and take care of them. And he, Gordon, can go after the slave raiders with a vengeance. That much is clear.

Zubair and his confederates have for long been carrying on the odious trade with impunity. Gordon's predecessor had made Zubair a pasha, and he was invited to come to Cairo. But Zubair was now under virtual house arrest, leaving his son, Suleiman, in command of the Jellaba slave-gatherers and their Bazinger auxiliaries in the southern districts of Kordofan and Darfur. With Gordon now governor-general, they are brought under the rule of an Englishman who was known to be Zubair's bitterest foe.

In September 1877, Gordon rides out with a small escort of Bashibazuks to confront Suleiman with an ultimatum.

"I was met by the son of Zubair—a nice-looking lad of twenty-two years who looks a spoilt child that a good shaking would do good to him, lolling about, yawning, fondling his naked feet—and rode through the robber bands. There were about three thousand of them, men and boys. I rode to the tent in the camp; the whole body of chiefs was dumbfounded at my coming among them ... I gave them my ultimatum that they should cease their pillaging or I would disarm them and break them up ... The pantomime of signs, the bad Arabic, etc., were quite absurd. There are some six thousand more slave dealers in the interior, who will obey me now they have heard that Zubair's son has given in."

They listen in silence and then go off to consider what Gordon has said before sending a letter confirming their submission—"and I thank God for it," he writes. Thereupon, he appoints Suleiman, Zubair's son, sub-governor of Darfur with a monthly stipend of £50. But Suleiman doesn't yield for long. Without provocation he massacres the entire Egyptian garrison at the headquarters town of Deim Idris "down to the very babes," seizes a large store of government ammunition, and proclaims the independence of Bahr al-Ghazal.

Gordon learns that El Obeid merchants have been selling arms and powder to Zubair, and afterward to Suleiman with whom they sympathized. The contraband is being secretly dispatched through Jellaba who are being paid in slaves—six to eight slaves for a double-barreled gun, one or two for a box of caps. Believing that Zubair is stirring up trouble, Gordon occupies his Khartoum property and discovers large cases containing richly ornamented saddles. Suspecting that the saddles are destined as gifts to Darfur chiefs in order to induce them to join up with Suleiman, Gordon orders the Jellaba to evacuate districts south of the route from El Obeid to Dara in southern Darfur. Then, when his order is ignored, he tells the Baggara sheikhs to seize the slave merchants, which they do with enthusiasm. By using Arab tribes to attack the Jellaba, Gordon stirs up latent antipathies that find outlet during the Mahdist rebellion and persist to the present day.

Every Arab in Suleiman's force has fifty slaves and every Bazinger five or ten. When one of his captains sets up his standard of revolt, the wind brings it to the ground. To turn away the anger of heaven four oxen are slaughtered and a Negro boy is sacrificed. The flag is dipped in the boy's blood, raised a second time, and a second time it falls. Learning of this inexcusable brutality, Gordon has the captain shot.

Zubair writes to his son: "Free Bahr al-Ghazal from the Egyptian troops; attack and make yourself master of Shakka." At that point Gordon orders Romolo Gessi to march against Suleiman.

GESSI TO THE BAHR AL-GHAZAL

When Gordon is serving in the Crimea, Romolo Gessi is employed as an interpreter. Besides Italian, French and German, he also speaks Greek, Turkish and English. He once ran a *café chantant* with a gambling den in Romania. Later, he set up a sawmill near the mouth of the Danube. While Gordon is the British representative to the International Danube Commission, he resides in the same town as Gessi. They both espouse the cause of the Romanian peasants who are suffering under Turkish rule. When Gordon is offered the position of governor of Equatoria, he invites Gessi to come along with him.

Romolo Gessi

79

Gessi's capacity for decisiveness gains him the title of "The Garibaldi of Africa." Compact and determined, a genius in practical mechanics, "he ought to have been born in the 16th century." He reassembles sections of a large steamer, christened the Ismailia, which have been shipped overland to Khartoum by Baker and are lying in the dockyard storerooms. His responsibility includes the procurement and shipment of supplies that Gordon needs in Equatoria.

He is full of plans, such as how much money can be earned by speculating in corn or in some other get-rich scheme. He knows people in Italy who will finance a commercial expedition to Sudan. He has a gift of being able to elicit backing for any project, investors so taken in by what he says. Gordon once said to Carl Giegler, "Do you know Gessi yet? If I were to order him to kill his own mother, he would certainly do it." Giegler later tells of a time when a hippopotamus surfaced near a boat Gessi was rowing. "It was so near I could have grasped its head. Gessi wanted to shoot it, but we forbade him as the animal would surely have gone wild and sunk the boat in no time." These aggressive instincts, Gordon believes, are needed in dealing with Suleiman.

In July 1878, Gessi leaves Khartoum on a paddle steamer, two nuggars in tow with three hundred regular soldiers, guns, ammunition, and a small, eight-ton cannon. He passes in front of the palace where Gordon appears on the balcony and waves his hand in a final farewell. The shoreline is lined with spectators who gaze on those who they say Gordon is sending to certain death.

A month later, Gessi is setting out for the interior on a splendid Arab horse. His party includes his private secretary and the expedition doctor, Dr. Zycchinetti, both riding donkeys, and a contingent of foot soldiers. They pass through Rumbek, the starting point for expeditions to the interior—"A safe retreat for the scum of the earth…a pigsty…a place of hopeless neglect, disorder and filth," according to Junker, who was there shortly afterward.

It is now the rainy season, the country a vast lake, elephant grass ten feet high and, in places, water chest high. Through this flooded land, past native houses built on scaffolding to protect against white ants as well as lions and leopards, Gessi's party finally reaches the river port of Meshra el-Rikk, the main entrepot in the interior.

Meshra al-Rikk

The captains of vessels in from Khartoum and the wakils of zeribas welcome him with coffee and tamarind-water and a full meal, as well as a quarter of an ox for his soldiers.

In every zeriba in Bahr al-Ghazal are a thousand soldiers or more, armed with guns and lances. For attacking a native village they are given a share of the cattle and slaves, while the ivory they collect becomes the property of the wakil. Much of the cattle are later exchanged for ivory. "What is their use to natives who never eat meat, who can live on roots alone, and they have their durra, which they cultivate." Some of the cows will be slaughtered and the meat dried for provisioning the trade vessels.

When the rainy season ends, Gessi departs Meshra al-Rikk, his last link with Khartoum. In March 1879, he attacks Deim Idris, the zeriba of the former Darfur governor, Idris, now Suleiman's main camp. He fires on its wooden huts and palisades of tree trunks, driving Suleiman out. The news of this humiliation brings a cry of despair from the slave traders, who are also under attack from the north. In Kordofan they are being chased out of their haunts by Gordon, "riding like a scourge of God…even out of Shakka itself, the main depot…and this place is clean of them, I hope, for ever," writes Gessi.

The Jellaba rally behind Suleiman. Their fekis preach crusade against the government. The revolt spreads. Subdued in one place, it breaks out in another.

After taking Deim Idris, Gessi feverishly rebuilds the palisades on ramparts of earth as Suleiman's soldiers set up their standards only thirty yards in front. Gessi's troops fire on the standard bearers, who are replaced immediately by others when they fall. His grapeshot scythes through the enemy, creating havoc. Soon there are a thousand dead piled up around the ramparts. In the confusion many of Suleiman's slaves try to flee, as do some Bazingers, who have little heart for the fighting. Jellaba cut off the heads of those trying to run away, but many make their escape. Corpses poison the air, and vultures and hyenas feed on them. Gessi's camp becomes a hotbed of fever. Still defiant, Suleiman dispatches letters to Baggara chiefs in southern Kordofan and Darfur, urging them to renew their allegiance and add their forces to the struggle.

Conditions are so bad that one can no longer operate in Bahr al-Ghazal. Jellaba must now take their trade elsewhere. "But are you not afraid that the trade will be prevented in other places too?" Gessi asks. "It is possible, but will Gordon remain many years among us! And, after him, will another Gordon come? Has not Muhammad allowed us to possess slaves, and who has the right to suppress the Prophet's laws? Really, can we live without slaves? Who would grind our durra and cultivate our fields under such an ardent sun? Once slavery is destroyed, the Sudan will become a desert."

Like Gordon, Gessi knows where the evil lies: "I have seen master and slave sitting eating from the same dish, sleeping under the same roof, and sharing the same cup of merisa. I remember a Greek ordering his female slave to go away, but she refused and for three days remained sitting on the house steps. 'Why do you not go? You are free.' 'I do not want to leave you, my master. If you absolutely want to get rid of me, you must sell me. At least, he who buys me will take care of me.'"

The real evils lay in the commerce. Slaves obtained from Baggara are being taken north in small numbers to depots in Kordofan and sold. They skirt the big settlements. But their trail is easy to follow: Skeletons along the way, tumbled walls and ruins of huts, abandoned posts where cattle were once attached at night provide signs enough.

Gessi attacks the caravans mercilessly. One day, eight slave dealers are brought into his camp and with them twenty-eight children chained together. He has the dealers shot. A few days later, he hangs another batch. In the course of his campaign, thousands of captives are released and some of them are restored to their homes.

Village chiefs tell Gessi how Suleiman abducts wives and children, burns villages and standing crops, and how they, the people, live like wild beasts in the high grass with nothing to eat except the leaves of trees. They show up at his camp, ready to help him track Suleiman and even the score. They bring armed men and whatever ammunition they have, but never enough, usually only small amounts of powder and shot. A bent and grizzled Dinka, bare-chested and barefoot, emerges from his mean hut. With bloodshot eyes fixed on Gessi, he opens a leather sack and takes out a small pot of honey. "It is all I possess," he says and begins to weep. Tears come to Gessi's eyes.

"Let us destroy their infamous commerce in human flesh. If we lose this opportunity, dear Gessi," Gordon writes, "you must know that all your labor will have been in vain." He realizes that no act will be more popular in anti-slavery circles than the execution of Suleiman. "I shall give Gessi £1,000 if he succeeds in catching Zubair's son. I hope he will hang him."

Gordon meets with Gessi in a village eighty miles north of Shakka, and they spend several hours talking together in Gordon's tent. The meeting gives Gessi fresh impetus. He promises that he will soon rid the land of Suleiman. He keeps up his attacks on the zeribas, setting fire to the palisades, sending rebels, enveloped in smoke, fleeing in all directions, and horses and mules reduced to cinder. He gathers up the spent balls and cuts the amount of powder in cartridges, but there is never enough to attack the huge zeriba at Deim Suleiman. Smallpox breaks out in his ranks. No precautions are taken to isolate the sick. "No one can escape his destiny," the Arabs say. His troops suffer from lack of meat and salt. Only the Blacks, who feed on human flesh, stay healthy. They cut off the feet of the dead, the choicest part, open the skulls, and preserve the brains in pots.

With its ragged train of freed slaves and camp followers, Gessi's weary force passes empty, darkened hamlets, guttered buildings, crumbled walls, blackened pots, and abandoned fields where crops have been destroyed or carried off by the enemy. Emaciated villagers are more anxious to save their single, sorry ox and their wife and hungry children from the rapacity of Suleiman than till their fields. They can't feed Gessi's tired, sullen soldiers.

In one darkened village, a white woman, almost naked, holding a baby to her breast and a look of terror on her face, runs out of her hut. Tears pour down her cheeks as she tries to kiss Gessi's feet. Her husband, a government artillery officer, "was massacred by Jellaba slave dealers, and she had been carried off as their prey."

Rain falls intermittently in torrents, and no one can be found to act as guide. Still, Gessi's forces doggedly track Suleiman, sending out skirmishers on the flanks to protect against a surprise attack. Vultures circling overhead reveal where wounded Bazingers were killed so that they wouldn't fall into Gessi's hands and inform on Suleiman's movements.

Gessi sees women crouching in the long grass. They are carrying little bundles of antelope's flesh in strips. The women belong to Suleiman's soldiers, and they stay behind to smoke and dry the meat. He sees corpses of spindly boys and girls, overcome with hunger and fatigue, their throats cut, and mounds from which the fingers and toes of buried men protrude—doubtlessly Arabs since dead slaves and Bazingers would have been simply left to the vultures. Gessi sees "a poor little girl with a beautiful face, her head resting on her left arm as if she had fallen asleep, but it was the sleep of death." He can scarcely restrain his tears. Some of his Jellaba prisoners gaze vacantly on her, their faces expressionless, and then "offer up their last prayer, invoking the assistance of the Prophet before justice is done according to the rules of war." Only thus can the victims be avenged.

The pursuit of Suleiman pushes Gessi and his troops into southern Darfur, dragging in their train women, children, and slaves. Water is scarce, and if lions don't eat them, they risk dying of thirst. As night descends, the distant braying of an ass guides them to a tiny hamlet where they obtain water. There Gessi learns that Suleiman is up ahead exchanging slaves for cattle and making forced marches to Jebal Marra to join Harun, pretender to the throne of Darfur. He presses on for several more days to within four hours of Suleiman, who is at a village named Gara.

It is now July with thunder and lightning and winds beating wildly in every direction. Gessi orders that no fires be lit and silence maintained. In a shower of rain just before dawn, he moves up and, with only two hundred and ninety troops against Suleiman's much larger force, posts his men in bushes near the village to conceal them and surprise the enemy while still asleep. His message to Suleiman: "I give you five minutes to surrender; that time passed, I shall attack you from all sides."

In minutes, the camp is awake, the Jellaba bleary with sleep, their women and children screaming, and Bazingers fleeing, leaving slaves behind. Suleiman and eight of his leading sheikhs file out from the village, astonished when they see that a much smaller force has forced them to surrender. "What! Have you no other troops? And I had seven hundred men!" exclaims Suleiman exasperated with dismay.

Two years earlier, Gordon had told Suleiman that if he and his allies went on with their slave hunting, they would answer with their lives. Gessi is now in a position to carry out this threat. Finding their horses saddled and loaded with food and arms—a sign that they were planning to escape—he invites Suleiman and his eight sheikhs into his tent for coffee. Gessi's soldiers enter after them, bind their wrists, stand them in a row, and shoot them, one after another. Afterward, they bury them.

A group of the anguished widows of Suleiman's soldiers make their solemn way into Kordofan and eventually to El Obeid. Dressed in white with hair uncovered, they bemoan the loss of their husbands and family members. Since the days of the Prophet, women like them have battled for the banner of Islam. They are prepared to seek vengeance or give their own lives for the cause. After the bravery of their men, they can't accept humiliation and defeat. They can't be treated as residue of battle not worthy of killing, as "remains of the sword." Their leader is al-Aza bint Idris, whose tormented cries stir the hearts of the people of El Obeid: "We left our homes, preferring jihad and migration. We are the people of war. We are the people of the sword…We do not die on our beds like the cowards, humiliated and without dignity. We put ourselves in the place of men to defend our homes and our land."

Aza's eloquence kindles the resentment against the government. "My condition is like that wished only on the enemy, a condition like that of a sheep facing slaughter, like that of a person bit by a snake when the poison starts to enter his blood, like that of the mother who is losing her baby."

When the Imam Muhammad Ahmad—al-Mahdi—hears the lamentations of Aza mourning her husband and provider of her children, tears fill his eyes, and the others around him begin to cry. And when the Arabs of Kordofan learn of the disaster that has befallen Suleiman in Darfur, their hearts become empty. They now anxiously await only a call to fight in defense of their existence and to regain their manhood. In declaring his mission, the Imam Muhammed Ahmad offers the opportunity they have been waiting for. Sooner death "for the cause of God"—fi sabil Allah—to living in humiliation and deprivation. Like an angry river that floods everything in its path, nothing can stand in their way. They adopt jihad to escape a deep sense of deprivation and wretchedness. Their slogan is echoed everywhere: jihad fi sabil Allah... fi sabil Allah.

His pledge fulfilled, Gessi and his exhausted troops toil down the road to Suleiman's capital in Bahr al-Ghazal. The huge zeriba of Daim Suleiman, surrounded by twenty-six-foot high palisades, has inner courts and spacious dwellings with conical roofs.

Daim Suleiman

Gessi takes over Suleiman's residence, which is built in the style of a two-storied house in Khartoum. Gordon says, "Gessi has kept his word. I did not doubt that he would. I knew him to be the only man capable of such acts." He adds that thousands of slaves were freed after the defeat of Suleiman.

Junker, the German, whom Gordon had assisted when he started out on his lonely journey into unknown regions to the southwest, thinks back to his final meeting with Gessi. Mounted on a mule and accompanied by his officials, Gessi has escorted him out of Deim Suleiman, which is as far as he had reached by that time. He knows that Junker intends to spend some years wandering through remote lands unattended by the then-customary bodyguard and harbors dire thoughts regarding Junker's ultimate fate. Junker remembers with nostalgia their final parting, which took place beneath a large tree: "A silent leave-taking, a mere grasp of the hand and the usual Arab farewell greeting for the native officials, a warmer embrace for Gessi as a dear friend, and who I never saw again."

By then, Gordon has left the Sudan. He had spent five years in the country and ridden more than seventy-five hundred miles in the last three. Exhausted and in poor health, he is also deeply discouraged when his friend the khedive Ismail is dismissed by the sultan and replaced by Ismail's young son, Tewfiq, whom Gordon doesn't like. In July 1879, Gordon resigns, harboring bitter thoughts of how his efforts as governor-general will probably be ruined by his successor, Raouf Pasha, whom he has already sacked twice.

Still, on leaving Khartoum, Gordon concludes: "I like the Mussulman; he is not ashamed of his God; his life is a fairly pure one; certainly he gives himself a good margin in the wife-line, but, at any rate, he never poaches on others. Can our Christian people say the same?"

Muslims might look upon him as a militant Christian marabout—a dervish with supernatural powers—but he admires their religious convictions. He cleaned out their mosque at Dara—which Zubair had made into a powder magazine—restoring it for worship and reopening it with due ceremony, and the people blessed him for it. He washed his hands with sand, his eyes riveted on those standing around him. From his annual pay of £5,600, he has covered the expenses of journeys he has made to every corner of the Sudan without burdening the state treasury with even a para—the smallest Ottoman coin. When he departs, he possesses seventy-two camels, purchased with his own money, and gives fifty of them to the government. Also in the end, he concedes that even the slave merchants might not have been as nefarious as purported to be. Can slavery be abolished when it is "a fundamental to the Muslim way of life…when many slaves would not have exchanged their masters for freedom?"

Meanwhile, Gessi has banished the Jellaba from forests that have been furnishing eighty thousand slaves a year. Villages arise again along the paths. Natives hiding in the marshes filter back and begin farming again. Gessi establishes schools and an arsenal for building riverboats. He encourages the production of rubber, cotton, pomegranates, and lemons. As ever, he is full of schemes, ideas, and energy.

But Gessi's achievements come at great cost to his health. His feet are painful and swollen grotesquely from the guinea worm, which can't be avoided when the horse's hooves sink so deep in the mud that he must dismount often and go on foot. He punctures the blister that formes, and blood and water come out, followed by a guinea worm "as thick as a violin string." It retreats again, the wound closes, and the severe pain returns to torment him.

His sheer doggedness makes him enemies; they call him an "arch-schemer and trickster." Khartoum's slave-trading aristocracy denounces his methods. Raouf Pasha, who expects orderly reports, tidy accounts, and scrupulous carrying out of orders, judges him too independent and reduces his rank. A disgruntled Gessi writes to Gordon: "I turned the Bahr al-Ghazal into a garden. The people were all with me. My strength lay, not in brutal force, but in the love of the chieftains and their followers. From all sides, ivory, caouchouc, and other products were brought in, increasing the revenue by tenfold."

Just a year after Gordon has relinquished his post, Gessi, finding his position intolerable, also resigns. He takes passage in September 1880 from Meshra al-Rikk on the steamer Safiya with nuggars in tow. Although it's soon evident that the boat may not get through the Sudd, Gessi, being Gessi, stubbornly refuses to allow the flotilla to turn back. He realizes his folly too late. The floating vegetation hopelessly blocks farther progress. Men spend all day in the water working to clear the way. Gessi blames the captain, who, he says, has failed to take on enough wood to feed the boilers—and, besides, owes his post to his wife being the mistress of the governor-general. Plagued by mosquitoes, no one can sleep. They stumble about in the dark, treading on each other and bringing on howls and curses. Food runs out. Hippos can be heard in the distance but can't be reached. Passengers cut up the skins that wrap their belongings, soak them in water and remove the hair so they can boil them and roast them to eat. Soldiers eat their shoes. The distraught mother of a one-year-old boy, who has eaten nothing in three days, implores Gessi, "As I can't give milk to my son, take him."

Everyone sits listlessly on deck, head bent, numbly awaiting death amid irremediable despair and decay. "Scarcely does someone die than he is devoured during the night by the survivors." Of the five hundred and fifty who initially embarked, hardly a hundred are left at the end of two months. "And now must I die ingloriously in the middle of a river after surviving the deserts of Darfur?" Gessi moans.

Sick and weakened, he eventually arrives at Fashoda, then Khartoum, where he refuses to rest and perhaps recover his strength. Instead, half alive, strapped to an angareb on a camel, he manages to continue on to Suakin on the Red Sea and there, finally, by boat to Egypt.

Taking his wasted hand, the khedive says to him: "Courage, Gessi. Egypt has need of you."

"I should like to serve her, your Highness, but, as you can see, I am nothing more than a corpse. I die because I have done my duty."

Gordon could only write to his sister: "Gessi! Gessi! Gessi! How I warned him to leave with me ... Your life is bound up with mine. He knew me to the depths."

— Chapter 5: The Mahdi —

Holy Men and the Mahdi of Allah

In the religious life of the Sudan the feki fills a vital role. When his study of the Koran, however rudimentary, is finished, he adopts a peripatetic lifestyle. With his donkey, an umbrella, a Koran, and little else, he leaves his village on journeys that may last for months, even years, availing himself of the hospitality of the villages through which he passes.

Feki Preaching

As a spiritual guide and a healer he is respected. A shelter is placed at his disposal and a small plot marked out by stones to serve as his mosque. His services are in demand because Islam offers status and membership in a wider society whereas unbelief is tantamount to enslavement.

He opens a religious school—a "khalwa"—and he is seen, even today, sitting under a tree near the suq, with a group of young boys gathered around him. As he dictates, his pupils inscribe on wooden slates his words, which they intone until fixed in memory. When he dies his grave becomes a shrine—a domed tomb, a ring of stones, or simply a cairn marked with fluttering flags. In the Gezira and other settled parts of the country, the main roads are chains of these Koranic schools. As the population grows, flat-roofed, mud-brick houses replace the thatched, conical roofed huts, and the whitewashed domed tombs of religious sheikhs stud the landscape.

A holy man heals the sick, writes sacred phrases on scraps of paper and inserts them in amulets to ward off the evil eye and exorcize the demons that afflict the deranged. In the backcountry he is the only mediator between man and Allah. When an influential holy man dies, he is regarded as a saint—a "wali." People for whom the sacred, the unseen, and the supernatural are very real ascribe miracles to him. Saints possess baraka—"special virtue"—given by God and transmitted by inheritance or contact.

Sufi orders—known as "tariqas"—originally formed around saints, give Islam a vital meaning closer to traditional beliefs and practices than the sermonizing of orthodox clerics and jurists. The saint's possessions become relics and his domed tomb—a "qubba"—becomes the shrine of a cult dedicated to his memory and a place of pilgrimage. Devotees may take a handful of the holy sand inside back to their homes for good luck. The wali's influence extends beyond tribe and region.

Even after death he guides the believer as he did during his lifetime. The head of the Sufi order is the "khalifa," who has inherited the saint's baraka. Addressed simply as "sidi"—my master—he provides guidance and support to his acolytes. When approaching him, visitors fall on their knees and kiss his right hand and address him without looking at his face. When leaving, they put a few coins under the cushion on which he sits. Members of the order are known as dervishes, literally meaning "the poor" to designate those who devote their lives to self-denial and prayer. They are given a robe, a turban, and a cloak.

Communities of these holy men dot the Nile banks, providing hospitality and protection to travelers. With its own grain reserves, the order reaches out to the poor and persecuted.

The Badrab Islamic center at Umm Dubban, fifty miles southeast of Khartoum, is well endowed and easily reached. Its walls enclose the qubba of Muhammed Wad Badr al-Ubaid, a khalwa and dormitories for students, patients, and visitors, and residences for the khalifa, his assistants, and functionaries. Large crowds gather for the Prophet's birthday and other religious festivals. The baraka of Wad Badr permeates his shrine, and belongings are left there for safekeeping. To visit is to pay homage to the saint and to ask for his help by mediating with Allah.

Wad Badr's forebears are originally from the vicinity of Mecca, but little is known of his genealogy—which is remarkable in a country where genealogies, true or fictitious, are socially indispensable. Little trained in orthodox dogma or any particular Sufi doctrine, he spends much of his youth visiting the tombs of religious sheikhs. In 1847, he decides to settle permanently in Umm Dubban, where the soil retains rainwater, and there build a mosque and a school. His khalwa becomes a center for those seeking material and spiritual assistance and a sanctuary for oppressed slaves and peasants. He dies in 1884 during the Mahdiya.

His successor, the khalifa, inherited his baraka. He begins each day with solitary prayer and meditation. Afterward, he instructs his followers in Sufi principles, listens to the problems of his students and disciples, and resolves conflicts that may arise. In the evening, he cares for the sick, the needy, strangers, and widows. At night, he meditates alone before checking the food and sleeping places prepared for students, followers, and guests. His disciples give free labor, grain, animals, and money, a large part of which is used to support indigent members of the community. Food is provided daily for five hundred people in the community. "If it were not for my food, who would come to me?" Wad Badr asks.

In July 1880, the Safiya, the steamer that Gessi takes, halts off Aba Island, one hundred and twenty-five miles south of Khartoum, where there lives a holy man who studies the Koran every day and fasts in a cave hollowed in the earth. The whistle sounds four times, and the crew prostrates in prayer. A Coptic passenger tells of when he once visited this holy man he and his friends are greeted courteously and given cups of sugared water and sweet milk, and, when they have all drunk freely, their cups remained as full as before. This holy man can turn bullets into water. He has the light brown complexion of a Nubian, a mole on his right cheek, a black beard, and large limpid eyes. Smiling, he shows regular, flawless teeth and, between the two upper middle ones a v-shaped space—a "falja"—a sign that he would be especially lucky.

Ancient tradition has it that toward the end of the world a man of the Prophet's family will come forth at the appointed hour among the people and guide them in the true religion. He will be named "al-Mahdi al-Muntazir"—the Expected Guide. According to some, he will be the forerunner of the Messiah, to others, that he will be Christ himself. When he appears all doubts will be swept aside.

This is a time when the people are governed by force and alarms, paralyzed by tax gatherers, despot pashas, and predatory Bashibazuks who think only of enriching themselves. A new brand of Islam, introduced by the Turks and preached by the official hierarchy of clerics, is alien to their beliefs and resented by their Sufi leaders. There is also bitterness toward the Christians in senior positions and their European lifestyle.

Muhammad Ahmad, who will later be seen as this Mahdi, was born on an island in the Nile near Dongola in November 1845. Upon his father's death, his uncle takes him to Aba Island where Danagla artisans are frequently called upon to build and repair Nile watercraft. After the usual khalwa education, he joins the Sammaniya Order. The sheikh of the order announces that when his son comes of age, a feast will be held to celebrate his circumcision, and all the usual rules against worldly pleasures will be waived. There will be music and dancing and rich food. Muhammad Ahmad protests vehemently against such sacrilege. The sheikh is incensed. He orders that the painful yoke used on newly captured slaves be fastened on his neck and expells him from the order. Later in the day, riding home from the mosque at the head of a procession of friends, disciples, and musicians, the sheikh comes across Muhammad Ahmad stretched out in the dirt and says scornfully, "Miserable Dongolawi, how true is the saying a man from Dongola is a devil in human shape." Even when Muhammad Ahmad later returns in penance, sprinkled with ashes, there is no forgiveness. "Get away, you wretched Dongolawi ... a devil in the skin of a man; I shall never forgive you."

In the face of this harsh rebuff, Muhammad Ahmad retires to Aba Island where he lives in a cave.

The Mahdi

He wears a simple robe of coarse cotton cloth with a belt and a skullcap of palm straw. He has two wives, both named Fatima. They bring him sorghum porridge or fish in his wooden begging bowl and wash and sew patches on his torn robe. His only furniture is an angareb. Pupils gather around him, and his reputation as a holy man soon reaches the ears of the sheikh of a rival order, who invites him to become a member.

With begging bowl and iron-tipped staff in hand, and quills and inkstand tied to his belt, Muhammad Ahmad embarks on the life of a dervish, wandering through the towns of the Gezira and Kordofan. He visits important khalwas and becomes an ascetic. His message is stark and unequivocal: "Put aside everything that has the slightest resemblance to the manners and customs of the Turks and infidels. Avoid the vices of envy, pride, and neglect of the five daily prayers, and practice the virtues of humility, endurance, eating little, drinking little, and making visits to the tombs of holy men...The cursed tax gatherer should be driven into holes and caves, the bribe-taking official from off the field he had usurped, and the Turk should be thrown to jabber his delirium on his own dunghill."

He travels into Kordofan where Gordon's zeal and ruthlessness—in attacking the Jellaba, killing the son of Zubair, and Sultan Harun of Darfur—has stoked groundswells of discontent and calls for vengeance. It is not so much Gordon's prohibition of the trafficking and sale of slaves that most angers everyone, but the confiscation of slaves in the care of their masters, which is making the Sudan "like a cart without wheels or a bird without feathers or a lock without a key...What was the crime of their women and children?...What was the crime of the orphans whose fathers he killed?" Is Gordon's seizing labor and livestock essential to the economy in fact a crusade against Egyptian rule and Islam itself? The prohibition of slave trading and the establishment of a state monopoly in ivory hurt the pocketbooks of slave and ivory dealers and fill them with resentment. Slave trading is legitimate and besides has benefit in converting pagans to Islam. So religious and business leaders welcome him.

Accompanied by his disciples with their shining faces and spotless clothes, Muhammad Ahmad makes a strong impression. In his book, Babikr Badri describes that effect when he visits his village on the Nile: "Often when we were students, we would attend the sunset prayers with him and listen to his reciting the Koran in his reverent, humble voice." In El Obeid, the people become aware that a new dervish from the Nile has arrived when they hear the recitation of a Sufi "dhikr"—remembrance—a formula they had never heard before. The incantations continue throughout the night as Muhammad Ahmad and his followers circle the town until dawn and time for morning prayers. Ordinary people approach this new holy man and ask for his blessing. The time is propitious for reviving the true religion. Under his guidance, all submerged suffering is released in an unbridled outburst of religious fervor.

Back at Aba, one of the first to recognize Muhammad Ahmad
as Mahdi is Abdallahi ibn al-Sayyid, the son of the soothsayer of the
Taaisha Baggara. At one time, Abdallahi hailed Zubair with the title
of Mahdi, but Zubair refused to accept it, saying, "Men who profess
to have inherited the divine spirit come and go like geese in the time
of heat, while God alone remains unaltering and unaltered." On his
deathbed Abdallahi's father, who was noted for his ability to read
omens in the sands, urges his son to seek out Muhammad Ahmad.

Abdallahi's only transport is a donkey, which he can't ride because
of a gall on its back. But it carries his water skin and a bag of sorghum.
His clothes and his dialect mark him at once as an outsider. He is jeered
and taunted by the Nile people he meets on the way as a bumpkin from
the western Sudan. "What do you want? Go back to your country.
There is nothing to steal here. What are you going to the Mahdi for? He
would not soil his lips by even mentioning the name of your race."

When Abdallahi finally reaches the Mahdi, he begs to be allowed
to become a disciple and swears submission. "From the first moment I
saw his face I knew that he was al-Mahdi al-Muntazir." Together, the
two men recite the "fatiha," the opening verse of the Koran, and their
lives become bound henceforth. "He is of the Mahdi…and the Mahdi
is of him." The bond between them is likened to that between the
Prophet and Abu Bakr, the first Caliph, and Abdallahi becomes the
Mahdi's successor—his khalifa.

Muhammad Ahmad invites all the important sheikhs to come
to Aba and proclaims himself the awaited Mahdi. "There is no god
but Allah and Muhammad Ahmad is the Prophet of God, and is the
successor of God's Prophet." The news is carried along the caravan
routes and discussed by the men in the coffee houses and the women
at the wells. In several villages, eggs are found with "mahdi" written
on them. The common people throng to him to obtain the baraka. His
blessing in food satisfies their people, and the watering holes near their
encampments are overflowing.

Among the earliest to join him are Baggara of the White Nile.
Others follow, including the Fallata, who become his most ardent
followers. Coming mainly from northern Nigeria, where they have been
told that the Expected One will arise in the east, they pass through the
Sudan when performing the "hajj"—pilgrimage—and settle there.

The first of Moharram of the year 1300 of the Muslim era is near at hand when, by local legend, the Mahdi is destined to appear. Belief in the Mahdi takes such a hold that in Khartoum the governor-general, Raouf Pasha, fears for his own authority. He sends a mission headed by Abul-Suoud—the same person whom Gordon dismissed for using his position to deal in slaves—to convince this "mahdi" of the error of his ways. Arriving at Aba Island fifteen hours later, Abul-Suoud is courteously received. He is granted permission to speak.

"The Hikumdar—governor-general—heard of the Mahdiya and rejoiced in it. He now requests that you come with me to him so as to support you, and to sustain you, and to follow you. You claim to be the Mahdi, but the "ulama"—the learned—need evidence to be convinced. Come to the town of Khartoum and provide the proof that they need; so they can question you."

Muhammad Ahmad replies: "I am supported by God and his Prophet—prayers and peace be upon him—and have no need for the support of the ulama and the Hikumdar. I am the ruler whom the whole Muhammadan community is in duty bound to obey."

"Muhammad Ahmad must abandon his claim and come at once to Khartoum," Aboul Suoud insists.

To which the Mahdi lashes back: "Must! I am not to be ordered, and if the Hikumdar wants war, I am prepared for it."

Leaping to his feet, the Mahdi so startles Abul-Suoud that he pees on himself in fear. The interview is cut short, and the Egyptian emissary returns ignominiously to Khartoum.

Shortly afterward, the hapless Aboul-Suoud is again sent out, but this time with two companies of Egyptian soldiers, each under the command of an adjutant-major. One of them wants to advance at once, the other claims it would be better to wait until daylight. The force becomes split. It is the rainy season, and the ground is a sea of mud. Abul-Suoud is the only person who knows where the Mahdi's village is, but he stays on the steamer. When some locals met on the way are asked where the Mahdi can be found, they are unsure.

Then, without warning, the Mahdi's followers come down on the Egyptians in a storm. Some have spears and swords. Having been told to equip themselves "with stones and clay and even wood and straw," many are unarmed. Only the Mahdi is mounted. The Khalifa Abdallahi, walking beside him, suggests that he dismount so as not to expose himself to enemy fire. At that moment his horse is shot out from under him, sending the Mahdi to the ground. Dervish spears rain down on the Egyptian soldiers, who fire wildly. Without time to reload they rush back to the steamer, leaving one hundred and twenty dead behind. On board the steamer, Abul-Suoud orders the artillerymen to load their cannon and fire at the advancing mob. "Where is the powder? Where are the bullets?" they shout in confusion. In the ensuing chaos, one cannon shot lands twenty yards from the attackers, who retreat. The Mahdi, hit in the right shoulder by a bullet, is the only casualty. The Khalifa Abdallahi dresses the wound and conceals it so that the Mahdi's followers won't lose heart. His victory with spears and clubs against the firearms of the expedition sent against him is hailed as a miracle—in the hands of God.

Like the Prophet's migration from Mecca to Medina more than a thousand years earlier, the Mahdi now performs his own "hejira" — migration. His Ansar—his "helpers," those who are truly devoted— accompany him. It is the month of Ramadan and the height of the rainy season, an unhealthy time of year. The enemy will be weak from fasting and sickness and their baggage camels and mules will have to drag heavy artillery pieces across muddy terrain, putting them at a disadvantage.

Two hundred and fifty miles to the southwest is Jebel Gedir in the Nuba Mountains where there is a stone on which the Prophet himself is said to have rested. Arriving there at the end of October 1881, the Mahdi establishes his abode among Baggara who are still chafing from Gordon and Gessi's recent campaigns. Furthermore, Kordofan in western Sudan is a crucial base for rallying Jellaba who are poised to join the rebellion. The Mahdi publishes his visions of audiences with the Prophet Mohammed and summons the tribes to unite behind him. Many slaves are attracted to him when he instructs slave owners to treat their charges in accordance with the sharia. Runaway slaves should not be mistreated, and converts should not be enslaved. Those forced to adopt Islam and the disgruntled members of slave-raiding bands that have been broken up by the government, should join in a holy war—a jihad—against the infidel Turks. They are assured that enemy bullets will turn to water and the Mahdi's baraka will protect them in battle.

At Jebel Gedir, one of the most barren and unfriendly places in the borderlands between Arabs and Blacks, the austere life and deprivations are not to the liking of some of the Mahdi's original followers. Coming from a more benign and civilized Nile environment, they return home. The Baggara, however, brave and tough fighters who pasture their herds in every valley and nook of the Nuba Mountains, become Mahdists heart and soul. Their allegiance is reinforced by the Mahdi's marrying the daughters of some of their leaders. A sheikh from Darfur gives him Aisha, who becomes his chief wife and is named "Mother of the Believers," a title given by the Prophet to his first wife.

When Muhammad Ahmad, a follower of Sammaniya Order, asks other orders to abandon their separate paths and join him, the heads of smaller orders respond, but the Khatmiya, the largest order, remains loyal to the government. Sheikh Wad Badr also stands firm against the Mahdi. The Nuba, although nominally Muslim, never waver in their contempt for the Baggara, now Mahdist allies, whose depredations had first driven them into the hills. So loyalties initially remain divided, but as victory follows victory, the Mahdist movement gains momentum and spreads rapidly.

Khartoum makes a fresh attempt to quell the Mahdi. Yusuf al-Shallali is sent out with a force of four thousand from Fashoda on the White Nile. Gessi's former second-in-command in the Crimea and in his campaign against Sulaiman in Bahr al-Ghazal, Shallali is an exception in the regular army in being himself Sudanese. Joined with another two thousand troops dispatched from El Obeid under the command of Abdallah Wad Dafallah, they set out to attack the Dervishes. All of El Obeid comes out to witness Wad Dafallah's resplendent departure amid the booming of the war drum and the blaring of the elephant trunk trumpet, pipes, and horns. Alas, the war drum falls to the ground from the camel bearing it, and elation turns abruptly to dismay and foreboding. A bull is sent for and slaughtered on the spot to avert this dire omen. With heavy hearts, the army marches out to confront the Mahdi.

Shallali orders some captured Mahdist spies put to death, cutting off their limbs in full view of his soldiers. Their calm defiance to the very end has a demoralizing effect on the government troops. If his people show such courage, this Mahdi must have something going for him, they say. Is his mission divinely inspired? Arriving in the vicinity of Jebel Gedir, Shallali's weary and dispirited soldiers don't even bother to build a proper perimeter. They simply gather scrub in the vicinity and slap together a makeshift barrier that can be easily breached. From the hilltops, lookouts spot Shallali's column and light signal fires. Relayed along the ridges, this warning gives the Dervishes time to prepare an ambush. At night, they come down like a storm, annihilating the government troops and killing Shallali—in his nightshirt at the door of his tent.

Like the shift in winds to the north that dispels the suffocating heat of summer, this victory infuses fresh impetus to the Mahdist cause. Word is passed around that supernatural forces are acting with the Mahdi, that fire burned the dead bodies of his enemies, and that his name will be found written on eggs and on leaves of trees. This is no crazed religious fanatic of whom the wastes of Sudan abound. This is no disreputable hothead with a rabble of tribesmen at his back. This is the embodiment of a religious crusade founded on a widespread and profound sense of injustice. The Mahdi leads no ragtag force of angry civilians but a disciplined army that must be faced with all seriousness.

Learning what has transpired, the foreign merchants in El Obeid rush to return to their homelands. Egyptian soldiers and slave troops in outlying garrisons seek refuge at provincial headquarters, bringing in the government's money with them. On the way, Arabs attack them and take the money. Danaqla who worked for the government flee from the outlying towns with only the food and water they can carry on a donkey or on their own shoulders.

Outsiders refer to the followers of the Mahdi as Dervishes—a slur among some Sudanese—but the Mahdi calls them Ansar, like the Companions of the Prophet. They are organized under three khalifas, each with a flag and a war drum. As principal khalifa, Abdallahi is given a large horn—the "ombaya" made from a hollowed-out elephant's tusk. He carries the black flag and commands the Baggara. Ali Wad Hilu, gets the white flag and commands the people of the Gezira and White Nile. A man of unquestionable piety, he is educated in Islamic theology and is a chief among the Dighaim and Kinana. Muhammad Sharif, a young cousin of the Mahdi, is entrusted with the red flag and, under the supervision of Abdul Rahman al-Nujumi, a Jaali merchant, the command of the Danagla. Beneath these khalifas are emirs, sheikhs of tribes, and tribesmen with their many camp followers and animals. Some of the best emirs are former soldiers of Zubair. Everyone, irrespective of rank, wears a simple, shirt-like garment as a mark of virtuous poverty—the "jibba" of homespun cloth, wide sleeves, and colored patches.

With the Mahdi

In August 1882, the Mahdi and his army of thirty thousand set out. With a population of one hundred thousand, El Obeid is the most important commercial and government center of Kordofan. The time is right. The rains have just set in, and water is plentiful. The Mahdi's horsemen approach the town on four sides, at rifle-shot distance, and call out: "If you yield, you will be safe, otherwise the Mahdi is coming with his many troops to defeat you with the sword of might. He gives you one day. Whoever comes to him will be safe and his property as well, but whoever does not come will be considered ungodly and will be killed."

Two messengers are sent ahead to tell the governor to yield and avoid bloodshed. The merchants are told to come out with their families, leaving their property behind where it will be safe. The messengers, each with a spear and a sword, are escorted into the governor's office and give him the Mahdi's letters. He summons officers, omdas, and the principal merchants. "Now, what will you do, humbly submit or stand firmly and defend your honor like men?"

"We will fight until God has shown what He wants." The Koran is brought out. The officers swear that they will never yield to a false prophet. But the merchants, who have been secretly in touch with the Mahdi, say that they must take the matter under consideration before giving an answer. Each of them has a few hundred men under arms, so they have a lot of local influence.

Leaving his office, the governor overhears the messengers telling some soldiers how the angels and devils obey the Mahdi and fight with him. The governor is infuriated when he hears this threat. He allows the messengers to perform their ablutions and pray. Then, in full view of the Mahdi's horsemen who have been waiting outside, he has them shot.

The people of El Obeid now know that attack is imminent. All night, they feverishly dig a trench around the town as they grumble that they are digging their own graves. At daybreak, a muffled rumble of voices in the distance fills the silence. Clouds of dust on the horizon hide the approaching hordes. When gusts of wind blow away the dust, horsemen can be seen galloping wildly about, then disappearing back behind the dust. The noise swells to a crescendo like the rumble of advancing thunder. Above the pall of dust, Dervish flags and banners become visible.

The Egyptian regulars and Jihadiya who man the garrison are armed with Remington breech-loading rifles, which have shown their deadly power on the battlefields of the American Civil War. They shoot farther and more accurately. Instead of loose gunpowder, which is useless in the rain, they use brass cartridges, which are quick to load. The enemy has only swords and spears.

The attacking horsemen collect durra stalks to fill in the trench that lies ahead. Flags flying and amid cries of "Allah dayim Allah baqi"— God is eternal—they encircle the town. In open terrain their advantage lies in not giving defending soldiers a chance to use their firearms, and their swords and spears can win the day. But here at El Obeid, they are facing an enemy that is dug in and has time to prepare. They are met with a withering fusillade of cannon and rifle fire, which pours into the seething mass of men and animals. Defending the town against the onslaught, "master and slave behave like brothers and the soldiers and local people behave like twins." So hot are their rifles that the soldiers need to cool their hands with water. The air is filled with angry shouts, the wails of women who fear becoming the captives of merciless Arabs, the panicky whinnying of horses going down, and the pitiful cries of dying men falling in the dirt. At length, the Mahdi has no choice, ten thousand Dervishes have fallen; he gives the order to retreat.

It is an ignominious defeat, the first for the Mahdi. Abdallahi tells him to return to Gedir. Elias Pasha—having been dismissed by Gordon and now with the Mahdi—urges him to remain close to El Obeid and await modern arms and ammunition. If the enemy chooses to follow up its initial victory by coming out in the open, they can employ their own familiar guerilla tactics. If not, they should lay siege to the town until the defenders starve or surrender. A magnificent comet appears in the eastern skies just before dawn at the close of the month. It is the Great Comet of 1882, and the Dervishes see it as a portent of their ultimate victory.

Meanwhile, Abdul Rahman al-Nijumi, one of the principal emirs, is besieging the government town of Bara, two days to the north. A feki named al-Minna Ismail, chief of the Jawamaa, joins in the final assault. The feki's reputation for piety is enhanced when, as a prisoner of the Turks and confined in irons at night, he is found one morning outside his cell, free of chains and waiting to be let back in. Why is he now showing no sign of interrupting his prayers and not attacking Bara with the others? While he is praying, however, fires break out inside the town, destroying the food stores. The townspeople go out to collect watermelons and come under fire. When all hope of relief is lost, Bara surrenders.

Still, myths infuse and cloud actual events. The prayers of Minna don't set the fires, but the betrayal of Nur Angara, who had once been with Zubair and is now second-in-command of the Bara garrison. In secret collaboration with the Mahdi, he conspires to set the fires that lead to the collapse of government resistance. He then sheds his Turkish military dress, puts on a jibba, and becomes one of the Mahdi's favorite emirs. But in the telling of the story, Minna is credited with driving out the defenders so that Bara could be taken without firing a shot. The splendid victory is said to be an act of God in response to the devout feki's intervention.

On account of his esteem for Minna, the Mahdi marries his daughter when she is ten years old and, taught by her father, already well versed in the Koran. Later, however, Khalifa Abdallahi accuses Minna of illegally appropriating booty, and relieves him of command. He is shot, and his body is buried near the withered stump of a mimosa tree. It grows into a big tree, and other trees spring up, and his grave rests in complete shade.

At the Mahdi's camp outside of El Obeid, Father Joseph Ohrwalder also sees the Great Comet as an auspicious omen. A tall, handsome young man, the Austrian priest is a missionary in the Nuba Mountains when the Dervishes overrun his station. "We rang the Angelus bell for, heaven knows, how many years." Taken to El Obeid, he does not accept to become a Muslim though warned that otherwise he would die the next day. The appearance of the comet just prior to his martyrdom does much to console him. He spends the remaining hours of darkness in prayer. At dawn, brought before an assemblage of Dervishes, the priest is bending his head for the deathblow when the Mahdi rides up on a white camel and says, "May Allah lead you into the way of truth." Believing it wrong to kill captives who have surrendered peaceably, he spares the priest's life.

Ohrwalder describes in his journal the Mahdi's huge camp where forty thousand Dervishes have assembled and thousands of cooking fires created a sea of flickering lights stretching to the horizon: "During the night they gathered in groups and, seated on the sand, sang the Mahdi's praises, the two principal singers keeping time by beating the ground with their sticks while the rest joined in the chorus at the end of each verse. Every emir's dwelling was identified by two flags planted near its entrance, and beside them lay the war drums that were beaten day and night, almost without intermission. Besides all this, the neighing of thousands of horses rendered the din still more unbearable. The whole air was infected with the most sickening stench."

While most of the El Obeid merchants have already defected, the besieged garrison and remaining townspeople fear they can expect only death from the Dervishes if they surrender. When camels and cattle have been eaten, they turn to donkeys, dogs, mice, crickets, and cockroaches. Digging into the ground, they search for termites to eat. Hundreds die of starvation, scurvy, and dysentery, and many are left unburied. Too gorged with carrion to fly, birds are killed and eaten. Afterward, there is only gum arabic and leather to eat. The gum brings on diarrhea and causes bodies to swell, and more die.

Finally, on January 17, 1883—largely because of emir Nujumi's lenient treatment of the garrison at Bara—the governor and his officers surrender. They are granted their lives. But when the Mahdi learns that they have been trying to get in touch with Khartoum, he changes his mind and hands them over to tribal chiefs —to do whatever they wish with them. Black soldiers from the zeribas, who have been serving in the government forces but have no particular loyalty to Egypt, are enrolled as Jihadiya irregulars, where they are issued captured rifles and become the backbone of the Mahdi's army.

After the fall of El Obeid, the Mahdi is venerated almost as much as the Prophet himself. The water in which he washes is distributed to his followers, who, drinking it, hope to cure their ills. He regularly leads prayers in the mosque, a huge open-air rectangle surrounded by a mud wall with no protection from the merciless sun. A sheepskin is spread on the ground for the Khalifa. The Mahdi then appears, his eyes painted with antimony. He wears a short, quilted jibba, spotlessly clean and perfumed with sandalwood, musk, and attar of roses—the "Scent of the Mahdi." During the Mahdi's prolonged sermons, Ohrwalder and the other captives remain kneeling, their legs becoming so cramped they can hardly walk.

He issues proclamations from his new residence in El Obeid: "Let all show penitence before God, and abandon all bad habits—the degrading acts of the flesh, the use of wine and tobacco, lying, bearing false witness, the clapping of hands, dancing, improper signs with the eyes, tears, and lamentations at the bed of the dead, slanderous language, calumny, and the company of strange women. Clothe your women in a decent way, and let them be careful neither to speak to unknown persons nor graze cattle in the company of men. Wear the jibba, which the enemy fears, and the turban. Go barefoot and keep the head shaved; the wearing of the fez is especially prohibited. Pray at the prescribed hours. Adore God, and hate not each other, but assist each other to do well. The only honorable way to die is in battle in service of the Mahdi. The blasphemer is to be hanged, the adulterer scourged with whips of rhinoceros hide, the thief to have his right hand and left foot hacked off. Give a tenth part of your goods to the treasury of Islam—

the 'bait al-mal'—to be used for public and charitable purposes. Do not succumb to your customary instincts, namely, to seize booty in arms, slaves, beasts, goods, and money for personal benefit."

Before long, however, the Mahdi's emirs are leading lives not unlike that of the despised Turks, and he is furious. One emir is forced to give up twenty of his wives. Smoking is punished with a hundred lashes. Adultery calls for beheading the man and stoning the woman. Whips drive a man caught drinking around the market place in disgrace, his drinking bowl tied around his neck.

While the faithful are enjoined to return to the simplicity of earlier times, the Mahdi applies a less stringent standard to himself. He accepts gifts of wives and concubines from powerful chiefs, and revels with them in the seclusion of the harem—or so it is rumored. Although he never touches wine, he becomes addicted to a popular Sudanese beverage made from date syrup and ginger, which he quaffs from a silver cup looted from the Roman Catholic mission.

THE ILL-FATED EXPEDITION

In 1883, the Egyptian government dispatches William Hicks to put down the Mahdi's rebellion.

Hicks Pasha

A retired Indian Army colonel with a thick mustache and goatee, Hicks at fifty-three is an impatient, obstinate soul. Under his command, Egyptian conscripts, the most demoralized and untrained malcontents imaginable, have tried every conceivable means to avoid being sent to the Sudan. His force also includes eight European staff officers—but only one, a Major Farquhar, is of real help. With them also are a surgeon, two German orderlies, two newspaper correspondents, and an artist for the *Illustrated London News*. (For information, the British government relies on the newspapers, whose reports from special correspondents arrive by telegraph ahead of the official dispatches that are delivered by courier.)

The rank and file comprise six thousand infantry—many of them serving prison terms—and five hundred irregular camel cavalry of Bashibazuks, described by Hicks as "swaggering bullies...galloping their horses about the country and taking whatever they want." Armed with two-handed swords and lances, some wear suits of chain mail, and their horses are equipped with large copper head-guards and quilted blankets to protect them from lance-thrusts. The Bashibazuks' brutal tax-gathering methods have estranged them from the local population, whose best chance of survival lies with the government, so its loyalty in battle is assured.

A Muslim in command is preferable since a Christian in charge will only fan fanaticism. So Hicks requests that "a high Sheikh or Priest of the Mohammedan religion, a holy man with green turban, a descendant of the Prophet" be sent with him to preach against the Mahdi. Instead, he must make do with Suleiman Pasha Niyazi, aged seventy-five, who despite instructions to defer to Hicks, pays little attention to this understanding, and difficulties inevitably arise. His frustration eventually reaching a limit, Hicks throws his sword on the ground and telegraphs to Cairo, "My being here is of no use, and I beg that I may be recalled." Her Majesty's government, however, replies that the responsibility for the campaign is Egypt's, and the khedive instructs him to "accomplish the reduction of Kordofan—the crown of the Sudan." So Hicks is left to carry on as best he can.

This would be a difficult enterprise even if there was time to mobilize and train this assorted bundle of incompetents. However, Hicks is impatient. He wants to complete the job and leave the Sudan as soon as possible. First, he must wait until rains fill the ponds along the route and then start off before crops are harvested. Otherwise, there will be inadequate water and forage for the horses and mules which consume twenty thousand pounds a day.

His spirits fluctuate, but he is no defeatist. "If my army will only behave well, I ought to give them a good thrashing. I shall have six thousand men, and they are estimated at forty-five thousand, but my men are incomparably better armed, and can sweep any number off the face of the earth if they will only keep their heads and hearts and fire steadily." His army has Remington rifles, Krupp howitzers, brass mountain guns, and some Nordenfeldt machine guns operated by a crank, capable of firing a thousand rounds a minute—so long as the operator's arm holds out. However, he doesn't seem to appreciate that the Mahdi's victories have put rifles in the hands of men who know how to use them. His enemy can't be so easily dismissed as fanatical, half-naked tribesmen but as soldiers with prior military experience.

Hicks's army on the march

Little is known about routes into Kordofan and water sources along the way. Intelligence is abysmal, slowing his advance. Will the first desert wells, fifty miles away, be sufficient to supply the soldiers as well as the camels, horses, mules, and donkeys accompanying the expedition? After that, the wells at some halting places will be able to supply no more than seven hundred men, and at El Obeid water is so scarce that at times it sells for a dollar a flask—"the price of claret" Hicks ruefully reports. Can a line of communication be maintained with sources of resupply on the Nile? How should the advance be organized and nightly bivouacs be managed? Should the front side of the zeriba open up in the morning and each regiment pass through, followed by guns and camels to form a square outside, or should the square march out together? Transport animals of course must be inside the square when the enemy is engaged. "No other arrangement does for the Egyptian troops. If there were an ordinary baggage guard and the baggage were attacked, the troops would run away." But with six thousand men it will be impossible to form a square large enough to contain five thousand camels, plus horses, mules, and guns, as well as all the supplies.

So, with precious little information on enemy strength and the whereabouts and availability of water, Hicks's so-called "Victorious Army" and its two thousand camp followers leave the security of the Nile at Dueim, one hundred and twenty miles south of Khartoum, on September 27, 1883 and lumber into Kordofan through waterless scrubland. They proceed through grass taller than their height, past villages all but deserted except for women and children. The men have gone over to the Mahdi after abandoning their lands and closing up the wells. Hicks's soldiers fear that they are advancing to almost certain annihilation. Vizetelly of the *Illustrated London News* makes his sketches and O'Donovan of the *Daily News* maintains his diary, but who will send their reports to those anxiously awaiting news at home?

The people of El Obeid look forward to the arrival of "the gallant hero, Hicks, his army and lion-like cavaliers," to defeat the Mahdi and re-occupy the country. They say, "It was Ramadan when first we heard that an army was being prepared against us and that the name of its leader was Hicks and that great stores of dried meat and biscuits and water skins were being collected. And in Hicks's army were Jaaliyin and Shaigiya and Blacks but most were Egyptians. They had much artillery, long Krupp guns and machine guns, not with one barrel but with five, and there were many horses for the cavalry and thousands of camels for the water and provisions, and so Hicks came to Dueim and started thence against El Obeid, where lay the Mahdi."

The camels in the square present a forest of heads and necks for bullets to strike. They must be made to lie down during an attack and their legs tied so that men can fire over them. Some are killed, of course, but there would be total confusion otherwise. Asked for his thoughts, Hicks replies, "I am like Jesus Christ in the midst of the Jews."

Hostile Mahdists harass the column as it slowly advances. At night, they surround Hicks's bivouac at night and beat empty tins so that his men can't sleep. The Mahdists always stay close behind, occupying campsites as they are vacated. Along the route in front of them, scattered proclamations from the Mahdi warn that it is hopeless to fight against the soldiers of Allah. But the ragged, thirsty, demoralized square pushes onward from one watering hole to the next, never knowing more than one day's march ahead if there will be water, or if the wells will be filled in or polluted by livestock.

Eating lubia beans worsens the soldiers' thirst. For the Bashibazuks wearing chain mail tunics and iron helmets, the summer heat is unbearable. In addition to his rifle and ammunition, each soldier carries a caltrop of four iron spikes to throw down on the sand in front of the charge of the barefooted enemy. With the temperature in their tents over one hundred degrees, the European officers suffer from prickly heat and boils, and their faces become raw and cracked. Their water bottles empty, soldiers leave the ranks and wander outside the square in search of water, and sometimes find melons to assuage their thirst. Riding his white horse around the square, Hicks orders the officers to keep the men in hand and lectures on the folly in becoming easy prey of the enemy.

The route follows a riverbed that flows briefly in the rainy season until absorbed in the porous soil. Along its course are three shallow lakes. A more direct tract would have been via Bara—and safer, too, by passing through country controlled by the Kababish nomads, who have not joined the Mahdi. But Hicks chooses a more circuitous route offering better prospects of finding water. Guides are called in and questioned about what lies ahead. Either deliberately or through carelessness, even the guides lose their way. Hicks's officers quarrel over the conflicting advice in which they have little confidence. Bashibazuks are sent out to reconnoiter a few miles to the front. Colonel Farquhar consults his compass to find the shortest way through almost impenetrable forest. He decides to plunge ahead to the other side, but it takes several hours, troops and transport becoming hopelessly entangled. Soldiers grumble, "Is this what they call the skill of the English to lead us blindly against advice of our guides into a dense bush?" Darkness approaches, the bugler sounds assembly, and eventually the army is collected.

Differences arise between Hicks and Alal-Din Pasha, the governor-general, who is accompanying the expedition and speaks neither French nor English, while Hicks speaks neither Arabic nor Turkish. They disagree over the deployment of the irregulars: Alal-Din wants them on the flanks, Hicks wants them in the square, since they are not trustworthy. When Hicks changes the next day's marching orders, the governor-general, wanting to let things stay as they are, remains in his tent. Complains Hicks: "Now here I am ready to confer with him and he is asleep. The result will be that our march will be delayed and all owing to His Excellency."

The villages they come across are deserted, the wells filled in. The inhabitants have fled, taking all the food and anything else of use. Circling above, carrion vultures accompany the expedition, a grim harbinger of its fate. Dervishes have driven their cattle into the waterholes, leaving behind only muddy puddles. When a small stream is reached, the troops lunge forward in a confused mass. Enemy scouts cut down any soldier who strays from the square in search of water. Unable to forage outside of the square, the camels eat the straw pads of their saddles; the wooden frames chafing their haunches gall them into a pitiable state. A cavalry patrol goes out with a guide. On its return, the guide, remembering that he has left his rifle behind, goes back to the well. The next day they find him sitting under a tree with both hands cut off.

Gustav Klootz, one of the German orderlies, deserts to the Mahdi. When he says that he is prepared to turn Muslim, the Mahdi gives him the name Mustafa because it sounds to him like "Gustav."

At Rahad, the army camps inside a large zeriba. A letter comes in from the Mahdi, urging surrender: "He who surrenders shall be saved but if you trust in guns and powder, you are to be killed." But Hicks is "full of courage and like an elephant…I am Hicks; my arm is an arm of iron and my army carries an army in its belly. If the heavens fall, I will hold them up with my bayonets, and if the earth quakes I will hold it fast with my boot."

Merchants accompanying the expedition have had enough. They break out of the zeriba and make their way back to the Nile.

Early each morning, the troops march out and form three squares in a triangle, each with its own transport and ammunition in the center. Hicks with his staff lead the way, followed by the four guns of artillery, the marching band—to preserve an illusion of normality—playing in a futile attempt to boost morale. Cavalry covers the exposed flanks, and a detachment of horsemen brings up the rear.

When the Arabs attack from the rear, a few of them penetrate the square. The battalion at the front wheels around in support. Egyptian soldiers cry out, "Oh, our Lady Zainab, now is your time to help us." To which the Black troops give their mocking reply, "This is the expected Mahdi." Some soldiers and camels inside are killed. When those carrying waterskins fall outside, the waterskins can't be recovered.

With devastating effect, the Mahdi is allowing the country and the climate to fight for him. He waits until the right moment before striking, dispatching one force to attack from the front while the rest fall upon the rear. He tells his followers that twenty thousand angels will attack the unbelievers when the battle is joined. Rising from his prayer mat, he draws his sword and shouts three times: "Allahu akbar; you need not fear for the victory is ours."

A guide leads Hicks's men into the valleys, leaves them there, and escapes to the Mahdi. "I have brought Hicks and all the infidels to the middle of Shaykan, and they did not have water for three days...It was a route that no man but the Devil could cross."

On come the squares, bayonets fixed. The thick trees hinder the horses and the march of the square. The lead square reaches a wooded depression where, led by the emir Wad Nujumi, the Dervishes spring up like a swarm of bees, yelling fiercely. Their horsemen ride down upon the square. When their horses go down under them, riders pick themselves up and charge on foot. The lead square is broken, and in the confusion, the flanking squares fire wildly on one another, on friends as well as enemies. Men cry out, "I'm hit! I'm hit! O God, the Merciful, the Compassionate, help me!" Frightened horses and mules neigh and bray, oxen and camels bellow as they are hit and trample one another. Hicks fires his revolver until it is empty. When his horse is hit, he dismounts and fights on foot with his sword, until at last he also falls. As one of his officers is dying, he hamstrings Hicks's horse, saying, "No other shall ever ride on you, either."

In a quarter of an hour, it's all over. Ten thousand soldiers and camp followers, along with thousands of camels, horses, and other livestock have perished. Seventeen hundred rifles, one million rounds of Remington ammunition, seven Krupps, six Nordenfeldts, and twenty-nine mountain guns are captured. Less than three hundred of Hicks's force survive. His severed head, identified by Klootz, the German defector, is sent to the Mahdi.

One of the survivors is Hicks's cook. Seriously wounded and dragged from a thicket, he finds Arabs plundering the medical stores. He stops them from eating some ointment and applies it to his wounds. He tells them that he is a cook—hard to believe by Arabs whose women do the cooking. Brought before Nujumi, he stays with him for five years as chief doctor of his force.

The Mahdi's triumphant return to El Obeid is a scene of dusty, barbaric splendor: tribesmen carrying the many-colored flags, followed by massed thousands of Dervishes intoning "la Ilaha ilallah"—there is no god but God—while others dance out of the ranks and shake their blooded spears. Next come the three khalifas and the cavalry. Every now and then, a halt is made. A number of riders dash forward at full gallop, poising their lances for the thrust before returning to the ranks amid the applause of the others. After the cavalry come the wretched remnants of Hicks's army, many of them naked, and after them, the captured guns drawn by wounded mules. Last of all, the Mahdi appears, mounted on a white camel. Spectators are ecstatic, throwing themselves on the ground and kissing the dust. (It is a sad irony that within a mile of the spot where the thirst-stricken troops were overwhelmed, a large pool of water could be found.)

Frank Power, the *Times* correspondent, is indeed lucky. He went to the Sudan for the express purpose of attaching himself to Hicks's army, but on the third day of the march, he comes down with dysentery. He is so weak that he has to be led on a horse with two soldiers holding him on. The Syrian physician with the expedition sends him back to Khartoum as unfit for another day's march. Drinking large amounts of milk and lemon with sugar and water, he recovers, at least enough to put on a sun helmet with a crimson silk pugaree and a crimson cummerbund—to prevent another bout of dysentery—and goes out in the early morning to sit in the big square under the palm trees and watch the street life.

A cloud of smoke on the horizon signals the return of the long-awaited steamer that has been sent up the Nile to obtain news of Hicks's expedition. It is only then he learns that the "Victorious Army" has been completely destroyed. A general panic seizes the people. Thousands of Egyptians, Syrians, and Europeans leave for Egypt. But among the Sudanese, the annihilation of Hicks's expedition is greeted as a great victory.

Power wrote the *Times*: "You see, this dysentery that I cursed and swore at so much saved my life. A Greek merchant told me that after the battle, each sheikh was shown Hicks's body and permitted to plunge his spear into it; so that they might say they assisted at his death."

SLATIN TO DARFUR

The novelty of Gordon's appointments lay in choosing Europeans, and Christians at that, to positions of authority over the Muslim population of the Sudan. Gessi is appointed governor of Bahr al-Ghazal with the rank of pasha. Darfur is offered to Richard Burton, the famous traveler-explorer and Arabist, who turns it down: "I could not serve under you, nor you under me"—referring to Gordon—as if anyone could ever conceive of two such willful personalities working together. Instead, it is given to a young Viennese officer, Rudolf Carl von Slatin, whom Gordon has recruited and trained. Among the others he picks up is Eduard Schnitzer, a German doctor who adopts Islam, changes his name to Emin—the faithful one—and is appointed governor in Equatoria. "This motley of expatriates was not a happy family," Slatin's biographer writes. Giegler is not above taking bribes. Gessi is always speculating in some commodity or another. Others are suspected of slave trading. Personal animosities invariably underlay these allegations. Still, Gordon is justified in writing, as he does later, "No man could lift his hand or foot in the land of the Sudan without me."

Twenty-one is a young age for Slatin to be appointed governor of Dara in southern Darfur. He has been a sub-lieutenant in the 19th Hungarian Infantry before coming to the Sudan in 1879. Gordon had sent him a telegram telling him to meet him between El Obeid and Tura al-Hadra on the White Nile. There, he finds Gordon sitting under a tree, exhausted after riding from El Obeid and suffering from sores on his legs. Slatin has brandy with him. Before long, Gordon is back in the saddle and, true to form, dashing on ahead. While being rowed out to Gordon's steamer, Slatin is sitting in the stern next to Yusuf al-Shallali who has been traveling with Gordon—the same one who is later killed near Jebel Gedir. Slatin asks him to dip the cup that is next to him into the river and give him a drink. Gordon turns to Slatin, saying, "Are you not aware that Yusuf Pasha, in spite of his black face, is very much your senior in rank?

Young Slatin

You are only the mudir of Dara, and you should not have asked him to give you a drink." Slatin apologizes, and Yusuf, also with a smile, responds that he is only too pleased to oblige anyone to whom he can be of service.

On board the steamer, Gordon and Slatin discuss the situation in Darfur. Seeing him over the side, Gordon says, "Good-bye my dear Slatin, and God bless you; I am sure you will do your best under the circumstances. Perhaps I am going back to England, and if so, I hope we may meet there." On reaching the riverbank, Slatin waits for the steamer to start. He hears the shrill whistle and the anchor being weighed. In a few minutes, Gordon passes from sight.

On the way back to his Darfur post, Slatin arrives unexpectedly at a village ahead of his escort. The villagers are sweeping the area and spreading out mats in preparation for the arrival of the new governor. They ask him what sort of man is this governor, not realizing that he, who they are talking to, with his boyish face, soft and gentle features, and only a haze of a mustache, is himself the governor. "Is he brave and kind-hearted? Is he like Gordon who was indeed brave and never ceased to distribute money and presents? When the fight was at its worst, Gordon found time to light a cigarette, and when he divided the spoils, no one was forgotten."

That evening, having arrived at the garrison town of Dara, his mud village capital, Slatin is eating dinner with his sub-governor, Zughal, when he learns that Harun, the putative sultan of Darfur, is preparing to attack an outpost three days away. He wastes not a minute in assembling his troops and telling them that he will share every hardship with them. Then they set off, each man with a rifle, ammunition, and a goatskin bottle of water. Villages along the way supply them with sorghum soaked in water, pressed, and mixed with tamarind fruit, the normal fare while campaigning. Each village sheikh is given a receipt for remission of taxes equivalent in value to the food he has provided. At this, the sheikhs are astounded, it being the practice of other "Turkish" officials to simply requisition food without thought of compensation and, in addition, to expect gifts of horses and women.

Some weeks later, Slatin is watching women drawing water at a well. A few Bashibazuks ride up to water their horses and ask the women for their buckets. The women refuse. "We shall first fill our jars and then you can use the buckets." To which the Bashibazuks contemptuously respond, "This is the result of bringing liberty into the country. Were not Slatin with you, you and your vessels would soon be our property." Pleased with what he heard, Slatin allows himself a flicker of a smile, and quietly rides on.

When Slatin is made governor of Darfur in 1881, the rising tide of Mahdism is already being felt. The Mahdi had sent Madibbo Ali, nazir of the Rizaigat Baggara, back to his tribe with the title of emir to raise Darfur against the Turks. Slatin must deal with him without help from outside because the telegraph line with Kordofan has been cut. Secret communications must be sent in the soles of boots or sewn in clothing. (Once Slatin hides a message by wrapping it in a piece of goat's bladder and concealing it in an incision in the shoulder of a donkey.) To deal with Madibbo, he must depend on his small contingent of Bazinger regulars and Bashibazuk irregulars—"whose somber purpose was to protect the tax collectors at their grisly work."

A series of bloody skirmishes with Madibbo take place. When attack is imminent, Slatin's men build a thorn zeriba, dig trenches if time allows, and run out the mountain gun to the rear face of the square where the Arabs will most likely attack.

Slatin's Blacks

Emissaries from Madibbo call on him to surrender: "I have eaten bread and salt with you, and therefore I will not deceive you. If you surrender, you need have nothing to fear." When these appeals are ignored, the Rizaigat horsemen charge, lances in the right hand and bundles of small throwing spears in the left. As long as Slatin's troops stay inside the zeriba, they are safe, although their horses and camels can suffer a lot.

At night, he sends out skirmishing parties, sometimes joined by tribal enemies of the Rizaigat. Together they steal within a few hundred yards of a Rizaigat village. The bugler sounds "Commence firing," creating panic among Madibbo's Bazingers who flee, some leaving their guns behind. Horses break their tethers and bolt in all directions. Slatin's men set the huts on fire, throwing abandoned saddles and ancient matchlocks into the flames but keeping the Remingtons for their own use.

Slatin sends a message—hidden in a dry pumpkin gourd—to Frank Lupton who has succeeded Gessi as governor of Bahr al-Ghazal, telling him to attack from the south, but Lupton is unable to help. His ammunition is in such short supply that slaves are being traded in the markets for ammunition, a boy for three packets of cartridges, a girl for five, two girls for a Remington. So Slatin casts bullets out of salvaged cartridge cases by melting down musket balls, percussion guns, and the bracelets and anklets bought from local women.

When the ponds dry up, his troops subsist on melons or a kind of juicy radish they avidly suck. Coming across a shepherd, they seize his sheep. Slatin tells the shepherd that his life will be spared if he will guide them to water. He leads them to a nearby grove. Fearing an ambush, Slatin advances cautiously, but as soon as the pool comes into view, his thirsty troops can't hold back. They rush forward helter-skelter and plunge into the water. At that moment, the Rizaigat attack. Slatin drives them off, losing only one horse. He tells the shepherd that when he next comes to Dara, he will give him the value of his sheep.

Slatin's men build a zeriba and kill the sheep for their dinner. While they are eating, a lone Rizaigat horseman blunders into their midst. Realizing his mistake, he cries out, "Allah is great! I have killed myself!"

Working their way through dense bush, Slatin's Bazingers are out on the flanks with buglers to warn of an attack. The rear guard goes back to look for camels that have broken down and for stragglers who have strayed or deserted. The bugle signals "Lie down," and the square prepares for another attack. Slatin jumps off his horse to show that he is ready to risk his life along with that of his men. Half of his right forefinger is almost amputated by a bullet. A soldier standing nearby takes a sword and hacks off the dangling part.

Now in boggy land, Slatin's men are trying to free horses sunk in the mire when Rizaigat again attack. The enemy is upon them before his Bazingers can reload their double-barreled muskets and his Egyptian regulars, who are armed with rifles, have time to fix their bayonets. After the battle, drums are beaten and bugles are blown so that anyone who has fled or been stopped by the swampy ground will know where the others are. Slatin looks for his orderly, an intelligent boy of sixteen, whose duty it was to guard one of his horses.

"Isa, where is Morgan, who was leading my horse Mubarak; he is an active fellow and perhaps mounted the horse and has managed to escape?"

"I found him not far from here, lying on the ground, a spear wound in his chest…When he saw me he smiled and whispered, 'I knew you would come and look for me. Say goodbye to my master, and tell him I was not a coward. I did not let go his horse, and it was only when I fell down stabbed in the chest that I cut the bridle to which I clung. Show my master this bit of the bridle that is still in my hand, and tell him that Morgan was faithful.'"

"Tell me, Isa, what was the end?"

"He was thirsty, and I took his head in my hands, and in a few seconds he was dead. Then I got up and left him. I had other things to do, and there was no time to cry."

One of Madibbo's slaves appears, waving a white cloth and bearing a letter calling again on Slatin to surrender. "If he is really an adherent of the Mahdi and desires the pleasures of paradise promised him, let him come here tomorrow morning" is Slatin's reply. "We shall wait for him." Laughing, some of the wits in his midst beg the messenger to give Madibbo their complements.

Slatin sets off again after Madibbo, who narrowly misses capture by jumping on his horse bareback. But Slatin captures his copper war drums, which in the Sudan is regarded as a grievous humiliation.

He obtains his best intelligence in the brothels of Dara where merisa is brewed and tongues wag freely. An officer he particularly trusts tells him that his men remain loyal because they are paid regularly and receive a fair share of the plunder, but they are tired of the fighting.

"The idea has gotten around that in this religious war you, being a Christian, will never be able to gain a victory," the officer says.

"Suppose that I turned Mohammedan, would my men hope for victory?"

"But will you change your faith from conviction?"

"In this life one has often to do things which are contrary to one's persuasions. Whether others believe me or not is a matter of indifference to me. Keep this conversation entirely to yourself. Good night."

The next day, Slatin calls the troops together and announces: "I have shared your joys and your sorrows. My life at such times is of no more value than yours. While I am a foreigner, I am not an unbeliever. I bear witness that there is no God but Allah and Muhammad is his Prophet."

The soldiers raise their rifles, shake their lances, and shout their congratulations. The officers step forward and shake his hand. He tells them that he will attend prayers with them and that he has chosen the name Abdul Qadir—the servant of the All-Powerful.

With the annihilation of Hicks's army in November 1883, the tide of Mahdism takes possession of Slatin's men and capitulation becomes unavoidable. So the young Austrian rides out of Dara to surrender to Zughal—his erstwhile sub-governor at Dara—now named Ibn Khaled, the Mahdi's emir of the West. Afterward, Madibbo follows Slatin back to Dara and tells him: "If you are really a brother to me, then, in token of our friendship, accept my favorite horse, the finest and handsomest animal owned by the tribe."

"I do not require it. I shall not want to ride much now."

"Who knows? You are still young. Be obedient and patient. Allah is with the patient. He who lives long sees much."

"You may be right, Madibbo, but now will you accept this token of friendship from me?"

Slatin's servants bring out the copper war drums that were captured earlier and place them before Madibbo. His eyes light up and face breaks into a smile. Madibbo orders his men to carry them off and, making farewell salutations to Slatin, joyfully departs, his earlier humiliation now entirely dispelled.

With Frank Lupton, another of Gordon's young protégés, is Zenuba, a beautiful Abyssinian girl, who has been a servant of Martin

Hansel, the Austrian consul, in Khartoum. Lupton is serving as first officer on a cargo ship in the Red Sea when he is hired by Gordon to become governor of Bahr al-Ghazal. But he never has the support he needs. His sub-governors in the outlying districts were mainly Danagla, prone to follow whoever permits the trading in slaves that was their lifeblood.

Lupton Bey

His predecessor, Gessi, had placed almost blind confidence in the Dinka whom he stirred up against everything Arab. He called on them to hunt down Jellaba who had taken refuge in the bush, and the Dinka hailed him as a savior. Once Suleiman was out of the way, Gessi reduced the size of his forces, allowing many of his disbanded troops to keep their arms—creating a more serious problem later for Lupton.

With their villages, fields, and cattle ravaged by government and Jellaba, Dinka turn to the Mahdi. They long had intimate contact with the Arabs to the north and were alienated by the abuses of influential merchants, sub-governors, and slave traders like Zubair and his son. They associate the Mahdi as a holy man with their own spirit of rain. A Dinka chief sends the Mahdi one of his daughters, and in battle, Dinka frequently carry the green Dervish flag sent to them by the Mahdi. His victory against Hicks's army in 1883 raises the Mahdi's prestige to new heights and dooms Lupton's administration in Bahr al-Ghazal.

At first, the Dinka see the Mahdists as liberators, but, in due course, their revolution degenerates in their eyes. With many of the Bazingers—who have been in both the government garrisons and in the private armies of slave merchants—now fighting for the Mahdi, the Dinka see little difference with the regime that had exploited them in the past. The Mahdi's adherents—Ansar—invaded with the same objective as the Jellaba, and full-scale slavery returns. "It was the Mahdi who destroyed the people. His people called Ansar were the people who came with destruction. They said, 'La Illah, ila Allah, Mohammed Rasul Allah' while they slaughtered and slaughtered and slaughtered. They also captured our people and treated them like slaves."

Threatened by treachery on all sides, Lupton in Bahr al-Ghazal is cut off entirely. Steamers no longer arrived at Meshra al-Rikk. The slave route to Shakka has been reopened. Slaves are being bought and sold for ammunition while Lupton is running short of bullets. The last steamer to arrive with a load of arms and ammunition also brings Juan Maria Schuver, the intrepid, hearty Dutchman—Abu Kalb. He is headed for the government garrison sixty miles deeper to the southwest, despite warnings that the road is not safe. Only after Schuver can show that the government has given him permission to go wherever he likes does the Sudanese official at Meshra al-Rikk let him go, providing an interpreter and five Jihadiya as guards. But the following day, his luck runs out; the reckless adventurer is killed at the village of a local Dinka chief.

The countryside is now in open revolt, and Lupton's situation becomes truly precarious. No news from Slatin, so Lupton can't expect help from that quarter. Assaults against outlying government garrisons are erupting everywhere. Lupton has only twelve hundred regulars, four companies of Bashibazuks, and a main force of Bazinger irregulars he can no longer depend on. In his last letter to Emin, his nominal superior in Equatoria, he writes: "The Mahdi's army is now camped six hours march from here. Some Dervishes have arrived here and want me to hand over the Mudiriya to them. I will fight to the last. This is my last letter to you. My position is desperate, as my own men have gone over to them in numbers. The enemy is armed with Remingtons and has four or five companies of regular troops with them. Slatin wrote me two lines; he only said: I send you this man Hajji Mustapha Karamullah to you. Slatin is now Emir Abd al Qader. It is all up with me here…I am perfectly alone."

In April 1884, Lupton's garrison goes out to surrender. The Dervish cavalry with Karamallah, a Dungolawi trader by origin, at its head, dashes forward, shakes their swords in the air and gallops back. This they do three times. When the dust has settled, Karamallah dismounts, and Lupton and his officers do the same. Karamallah calls on Lupton to renounce his faith and to assume the name of Abdallah, which the Mahdi has said he should be called. Lupton replies that he has already adopted Islam. Karamallah asks him to confirm this by repeating after him, "There is no God but Allah, and Muhammad is the Prophet of Allah." Then, Karamallah's emirs shout in one voice: "Hold to your faith, you are now one of us as we are of you."

Lupton has done everything in his power to defend Bahr al-Ghazal. After capitulating, he is leaning despondently against the stockade of his fort. Reflecting on the futility of the last three years, he is smoking his last cigarette. A Dervish approaches him and strikes him on the face. "The Mahdi does not allow smoking." Lupton remains silent. Later, he ends up in Omdurman where he dies in chains in 1888.

MAHDI MOVES TO RAHAD

Now summer, the fever season, water is scarce, and El Obeid is a pestilential place. Amid the thousands of tattered shelters, myriad camels, horses, donkeys, sheep, and goats in the Mahdi's sprawling camp, filth piles up and dead animals remain unburied. Stench and dust fill the air, swarming with flies. The captive missionaries, suffering from diarrhea and fever, lie in chains on their palm mats. Two nuns and a lay brother have died, but slaves don't remove and bury their bodies. When Ohrwalder, the Austrian priest, asks if he can return to his mission in the Nuba hills, the Mahdi tells him to wait until after the fall of El Obeid and, in the meantime, wear Arab dress to obviate the taunts of his people.

After the fall of El Obeid, the Mahdi moves his whole camp to Rahad, a two days' journey to the southeast, where water is more abundant. The elephant's tusk trumpet emits its enormous sound, and the copper war drums boom the signal for departure. Green, red, and black flags rise over the multitudes as the khalifas appear, followed by the army, glistening and proud, and in its wake, throngs of men, women, and children, heavily laden camels, donkeys, flocks of sheep, and Baggara riding oxen. The sun beats down on the procession. In the heat and dust, animals fall, children cry for lost parents, and slaves search for lost masters.

Assigned as a camel driver, Ohrwalder shares the meals of his master's horse and begs a drink from a slave. His feet are blistered from the burning sand and his legs swell. The nuns suffer as much. Although presumed to be more tractable than the priests, they also won't renounce their faith, and they are paid for their recalcitrance by having to carry loads barefoot over the hot sands. One of them is suspended from a tree and the soles of her feet beaten so badly that the toenails drop out—but they are never sexually violated.

At Rahad, the Mahdi's quarters are set up between two large trees where Ohrwalder waits until after noonday prayers. Still wearing drawers and jibba of rough cloth, girth, and turban, the Mahdi seems to be a lot stouter. He asks about Christian prayers, and Ohrwalder recites the Lord's Prayer in Arabic to the amazement of those sitting around. "I know that you Christians are very good people, and that you feed the hungry." When, out of nowhere, a dwarf appears, the Mahdi asks about his tribe and whether he is married. When he learns that to possess a wife is the dwarf's most heartfelt desire, the Mahdi orders that he be provided with one. He then turns to Ohrwalder and gives him permission to leave.

Several days later, Slatin and his servants arrive at Rahad. The plangent wail of the ombaya signals that the Khalifa is coming out. Across a broad, open space batches of horsemen with poised lances gallop at full speed toward Slatin, shake their spears in his face and shout, "For God and His Prophet." They tell Slatin to gallop toward the Khalifa and likewise caracole, displaying his own horsemanship. He is guided to a "rakuba," a rectangular straw shelter, and served dates and a gourd of honey and water. The Khalifa, limping from a bullet wound in his thigh at El Obeid, appears. Two years older than the Mahdi, he is of middle height, with a long, prominent nose, full beard, and slight mustache. His dark brown face is pitted by smallpox and his hair is beginning to turn gray. Smiling, his glistening white teeth and shrewd eyes convey a ruthless charm. Wearing a jibba and a skullcap wrapped by a turban, he settles down cross-legged on an angareb and indicates to Slatin to sit lower down on a palm mat. He can neither read nor write. He asks Slatin if France is a tribe.

The Mahdi leads afternoon prayers, his sheepskin spread out in front of the vast congregation ranged in closely packed lines. He asks Slatin in a quiet tone, "Are you satisfied?"

"Indeed I am in coming so near to you I am most happy."

Taking the oath of allegiance and kissing the Mahdi's hand begins a long habit of flattery that wins Slatin a unique place among the Mahdi's prisoners. Others sprinkle themselves with ashes or don the yoke to show submission, but Slatin has taken Madibbo's simple counsel to heart: "Be obedient and patient, Abdul Qadir. Allah is with the patient. He who lives long sees much." Soon after surrendering to the Mahdi, he is awarded the status of "mulazim," a kind of servant-courtier-bodyguard.

One day a Frenchman arrives. About forty years old, with sunburned face, fair beard and mustache, wearing a jibba and turban but speaking no Arabic, he has taken the name Yusuf. He claims that he has come to offer his assistance to the Mahdist cause, but his real purpose is to bring back a scoop for the Paris newspaper, *Le Figaro*.

Olivier Pain

"My name is Olivier Pain. Since I was quite a boy I sympathized with the Sudan and its people. In Europe, there are nations with whom we are at feud, and one of these is the English nation. I have come to offer you my assistance and that of my nation."

"I do not count on human support," is the Mahdi's reply. "I rely on God and His Prophet. Your nation are unbelievers, and I shall never ally myself with them." What assistance could he expect from this mysterious stranger who has traveled so far for the sake of friendship?

Unable to digest the food that is given to him, Pain becomes despondent. Slatin tells him that he shouldn't despair, that he is being put through a test of patience and faith. But with a fever that turns to typhus, Pain weakens. Sending him five Egyptian pounds, the Mahdi wishes him a speedy recovery. Tears roll down his sunken cheeks as Pain asks Slatin to tell his wife and children that his dying thoughts were of them. An angareb is tied to the saddle of the camel for Pain to lie on, but he is too weak to hold on and falls down heavily and does not revive. Whether or not he is still breathing when his body is wrapped in a cotton shawl and covered with sand is debatable. "If Yusuf dies here, he is a happy man," the Khalifa says. "Allah in his goodness and omnipotence has converted him from an unbeliever to a believer." But Slatin expresses little sympathy for this "ass of a French journalist."

Among the other misfits and misguided whom the Mahdi inspires is an errant American named Harrington, in transit in Egypt, who embraces Islam and declares himself a mahdi. A doctor hired by the U.S. consulate general advises that this drifter is suffering from a mild form of religious mania and should be deported. There also is fellow named Shubert, who plans to send his reports on the Mahdi to European papers. He shares a house in Sennar with the trader, Giuseppe Cuzzi, and buys the whole stock of wine consigned to the local Greek merchant. After two pleasant months together, he leaves to join the Mahdi, and Cuzzi never hears from him again. Even in the U.S., the Mahdi's cause stirs feelings. With its loathing of the English, many in the Irish community welcomed the Mahdi's victory and considered sending an Irish brigade to the Sudan to support him.

The Mahdi dispatches emissaries to all parts of the Sudan. One of them is Osman Digna, born in Suakin on the Red Sea to a large and prosperous family that trades in cotton, ostrich feathers, and slaves. Trade with the merchants on the Arabian coast thrives until the late 1870s when the British take active steps to curb it. Digna makes his way to El Obeid and is welcomed by the Mahdi: "I send you Sheikh Osman Digna of Suakin as your emir, in order to revive the true religion. On his arrival, join him and obey his orders, advance against the Turks, and drive them out of your country."

Digna has little success in promoting Mahdism until he enlists the support of a venerable Sufi sheikh named Tahir al-Majzub, who gives up his silk and satin clothes and adopts the coarse garments of a herdsman. He calls on the Hadendowa—the renowned "Fuzzy Wuzzies" with their bushy "Afro" hairstyles—to give Digna their allegiance, and thus he musters from the arid hills a fanatical and devoted tribal army. The Hadendowa, who have a contract to transport stores for Hicks, have received less than what was agreed for each camel load and are ready to join the rebellion.

Magnificent fighters, armed with sword and spear, shield and camel-stick, they approach stealthily down the twisted ravines of the

Red Sea hills to fall upon the enemy. Against them, the hollow square of Egyptian levies—the convicts and "sweepings of Cairo streets"—doesn't have a chance. At El Teb, they famously "broke the British square." In their ferocious rush against well-armed troops paralyzed with terror, the Hadendowa achieve an almost mythical status as immortalized by Kipling: "So 'ere's to you, Fuzzy Wuzzy, at your 'ome in the Sowdan; you're a pore benighted 'eathen but a first-class fightin' man; An' 'ere's to you, Fuzzy Wuzzy, with your 'ayrick 'ead of 'air—You big black boundin' beggar—for you bruk a British square."

GORDON RETURNS

Hicks's defeat in the west and the battle of El Teb in the east send Khartoum into panic. "In three days, this town may be in the hands of the rebels," Power writes at the end of December 1883. The telegraph poles have been pulled down all the way to Sennar on the Blue Nile. The wealthier families are fleeing down the Nile towards Egypt. The Khartoum garrison is demoralized. The Mahdi's proclamation that he will take Egypt, then Mecca and Jerusalem, spreads the ferment of revolt. Placards posted in Damascus call on the people to drive out the Turks. Even unflappable London expresses alarm. *The Pall Mall Gazette* writes that while England may not be able to send a regiment to Khartoum, it can at least send Gordon to treat with the Mahdi. He can relieve the garrisons and do something to save whatever he can from "the wreck of the Sudan."

In England, Gordon is staying at the home of the vicar of Heavitree, near Exeter. Traveling one day in the vicar's carriage, he is urged by Sir Samuel Baker to go back as governor-general. Although Gordon says nothing, his eyes flash and an eager expression passes over his face. Late that night, Gordon enters the vicar's room.

"You saw me today?"

"You mean in the carriage?"

"Yes, you saw me—that was the self I want to get rid of."

A week later Gordon meets with Lord Wolseley and four wily Cabinet members who are more concerned in perpetuating England's economic hold on Egypt than in any humanitarian purpose in the Sudan. They ask Gordon if he understands what they have in mind.

"Yes, they would evacuate the Sudan."

"Would you go?"

"Only too delighted."

"When?"

"Tonight."

So Gordon writes to his sister: "I leave for the Sudan tonight. I feel quite happy, for I say if God is with me, who can or will be hurtful to me? May He be glorified, and the world and the people of the Sudan be blessed, and may I be the dust under His feet."

And to the people of Khartoum he writes: "Don't be panic-stricken, you are men, not women; I am coming."

So great is his belief in himself as the instrument of God's will that he impulsively relies on intuition. His deeply held faith invests his decision with a divine sanction. When he writes about the future, he appends the letters D.V.—Deo volente.

At Charing Cross, finding that Gordon had only a few shillings in his pocket, Wolseley presses into his hand his own spare cash, his watch and chain, and bids him Godspeed. So, less than five years after his resignation as governor-general, Gordon is sent back into the maelstrom of the Sudan to report on the situation and advise on evacuating the garrisons. Illiterate in Arabic and with a command of the spoken language meager at best, he agrees to go, even without the aid of his former secretary, Berzati Bey, who has perished with Hicks. Berzati had been able to sense the gist of Gordon's erratic thoughts and arguments. He could untangle the stumbling dictation in Arabic and write in several ciphers without looking at the keys. Gordon misses him dearly. "He was my most intimate friend for three years, and I can say that, in all our perils, I never saw him afraid."

Gordon faces an almost impossible task: tame a fanatical leader who had already destroyed two Egyptian armies led by English officers, withdraw twenty-seven thousand men in the teeth of that enemy, and set up members of the old reigning families as rival powers to the Mahdi. Conducting an inglorious retreat is a task for which he is unqualified. He chafes under discipline and is aware of his own unfitness. "I know that if I was chief I would never employ myself, for I am incorrigible." Incapable of subtle management and tact, he is being thrust into a situation that calls for finesse and diplomacy. He deludes himself in believing that he can ride off to see the Mahdi, reason with him, and persuade him to disperse his tribesmen, leaving behind some sort of government. He plans to restore the country to its traditional leaders by setting up Sudanese sheikhs as independent rulers, like the maharajas in India. This is wishful thinking. The once-influential old families are now powerless. Khartoum, Dongola, and Kassala are new towns that have no traditional authority, and it is not clear how the Mahdi's government will take up the slack.

The conduct of Emir Abdul Shakur, heir to the Darfur sultans, provides a mocking commentary on the impracticability of Gordon's plan. Attired in a splendid uniform, he is sent up the Nile with Gordon. Extra rail carriages are put on to accommodate his twenty-three wives and concubines and mountains of baggage. By the time they reach Aswan, he has been drinking heavily. Drowning his self-doubts in hot rum and water, he gets only as far as Dongola before turning around and, with all his entourage and baggage, returning to Cairo.

Before leaving Cairo, Gordon chances to run into Zubair, against whom he has struggled for years and whose son Gessi had executed. By coincidence, they meet face to face at one of the ministries. Zubair refuses to shake his hand. An angry Gordon asks why.

"Because, it is the hand of the man who signed the death-warrant of my best-loved son. How can I shake the hand that is stained with the blood of my son?"

"It was not I but you, Zubair, who was responsible for your son's death. You wrote to him from Cairo urging him to rebel against the government."

"I did no such thing. Send for the proceedings of the court martial that sentenced him to death, and if my letter is there, then you can put me to the sword for I do not wish to live."

The proceedings are sent for, and the letter isn't there.

"Of course it isn't there," says Zubair, "for the very good reason that I never wrote such a letter."

Only then does Gordon realize that his interpreter had misinformed him. He was led to conclude that Suleiman was guilty of the murder of two hundred Egyptian soldiers, and, for this, he was justly put to death. Zubair explains, however, that he wrote to his son telling him to surrender. Gordon looks straight into Zubair's glowering countenance, holds out his hand, and apologizes. Only then does Zubair relent, "We are friends again. I give you my hand upon it. I am your slave for life and will do anything you wish."

With this reconciliation, an inspiration runs thorough Gordon's mind. He is seized with a "mystic feeling." What if he should make Zubair an ally? With his prestige, his presence in Khartoum would paralyze the Mahdi. He could be the center around which the tribes could rally. He could take over after the Egyptian garrisons are evacuated. Men like Zubair may be villains, but they know better than the Turks how to govern the country. And, whatever his past faults, Zubair is a man of great energy and resolution. As a pasha, he will get at sources of information and supply Gordon with reliable news. Without him, Gordon would have to rely on the tender mercies of Greek merchants and other Christian informants to find out what is going on. But uncertainties still tumble in Gordon's head: "Will Zubair ever forgive me the death of his son? I have been told he bears me the greatest malice, and one can't wonder at it, if one is a father." On the other hand, what would he gain from hurting him? So, in the end, Gordon asks for Zubair.

Sir Evelyn Baring, the British consul-general at Cairo, seeks the advice of Nubar Pasha, the prime minister. But Gordon is impatient. "What the two decide, I do not know. I am precious tired of long wearisome talks." Baring distrusts "mystic feelings." So also do the abolitionists in England who would never agree to return the greatest slave raider of all to the Sudan. They don't realize that, with regard to the slave trade, the Mahdi will be ten times worse than Zubair.

On January 26, 1884, Gordon leaves for the Sudan, traveling up the Nile to Kurusku—just beyond Aswan—and then across the desert to rejoin the Nile at Abu Hamid. He has already decided on the three most senior appointments of his administration: the chief of the Shukriya tribe, which has remained loyal to the government; an old adherent of Zubair named Said Bey Husain; and Ibrahim Bey Fawzi, an Egyptian who had been with Gordon in Equatoria. They are to be made pashas and keep him informed of public opinion. Gordon will clear out all the Egyptian officials, who will not be missed at all by the local population, and will replace them by a purely native administration.

Crossing the desert, fearfully cold at night and fearfully hot by day, he covers over a thousand miles and arrives in Abu Hamid on February 8. "I have ignored the existence of any rebellion, and I hope to meet many of the chiefs of the Mahdi's army at Khartoum," he writes. "We are going to have a big conclave at Khartoum on 25 Feby. I hope that the country will be quiet in a month." So great is Gordon's confidence and expectations.

"I got a fresh camel near here, a bull-necked brute, and off he went full speed with me. I was in a state of mind, not for my bones, but had I fallen, it would have been a very bad omen and done much harm with these superstitious people. I am glad to say I kept my seat, and I shall indulge in no more of these displays."

Berber

On February 12 he reaches Berber, a collection of squat mud huts and an occasional house of European style in a superb setting of majestic palms, tall acacias, and cool gardens. A battalion of regular infantry of Blacks and an irregular cavalry of Bashibazuks are drawn up to meet him. However, Gordon's small entourage—composed of only two adjutants, Col. J. D. H. Stewart and Ibrahim Bey Fawzi, and a few orderlies but no soldiers—inspires little confidence at a time when government forces have been crushed by Osman Digna at El Teb and the overall military situation is so bleak. Most Sudanese are convinced that the Mahdi is invincible.

The Berber sheikhs seem to be still holding out—just barely— and Gordon realizes that he must do something to dissuade them from going over to the Mahdi. He publishes a proclamation sanctioning domestic slavery until 1889—after which, under an Anglo-Egyptian Convention, all slaves should be freed. Then, he recklessly goes one step farther, revealing to them a secret firman proclaiming Egypt's intention to abandon the Sudan. The Jaali sheikhs, who have made their careers as slave dealers, had expected that Gordon's arrival will herald the return of the Egyptians and the resumption of trading as before. They are dismayed to learn that his purpose is to evacuate the country. Gordon acknowledges that he didn't fully understand the firman which was written in Arabic. His intention had been to stiffen their resolve and spur them to organize an independent government, but the effect is just the opposite. The fact that he has no force at his back convinces the sheikhs, already wavering in their allegiance, that the safest course would be to declare for the Mahdi.

Gordon has sympathy for the people he's now among, and his intentions are noble. But he has opened a Pandora's Box by proclaiming the divorce of the Sudan from Egypt and appointing Sudanese officials to every important post. In Berber, he is confronted by ranting crowds with charges against the governor, but Gordon can't persuade them that the governor, a Circassian, has already been sacked. Clearly, he has miscalculated the extent of his own influence in this climate of uncertainty and conflicting loyalties. He had been popular with the Arabs of Kordofan, but they now have a Mahdi whom they adore. Can he convince the Nile valley tribes, which he is now among, that the Mahdi is in no position to help them? Can he, who crushed so many of their Jellaba relatives, assure them that the government has noble intentions? The unclear mission of this lone Christian convinces them that the Sudan will be evacuated and given over to the Mahdi. As Gordon later confesses, "I have laid the egg which the Mahdi has hatched…Everything has sprung from that."

In Berber, everyone presses around with petitions, which he accepts without so much as glancing at them. To each petitioner he gives a gold coin. Some fall to their knees to kiss his hands and feet. He invites Giuseppe Cuzzi, a trader originally from Sennar, to dine with him. After the meal, Gordon produces letters in Arabic and in French appointing him his representative.

The following morning Cuzzi is on the quay where he describes Gordon's leave-taking: "Weeping and crying loudly, and waving their hands vigorously, a crowd of men and women followed the boat along the bank, while Gordon stood on the bridge and waved good-bye with a kerchief. Soon, he had disappeared from our sight—disappeared for ever."

On a clear, crisp morning, a few days later, Gordon reaches Khartoum, having made the trip from Cairo in eighteen days, the shortest time on record. "Gordon—sword and Bible—travels like a whirlwind," writes Power, who is fattening a turkey and a tame ostrich for that joyous day of his arrival. "It is wonderful that one man can have such an influence on two hundred thousand people. He is indeed, I believe, the greatest and best man of this country."

Gordon is given a splendid reception. Thousands crowd to the river landing, shouting and waving to greet "Our father." Military and civil officials, religious notables, and consular agents are there to meet him. Six elephants under the control of their Indian mahouts salute him, raising and lowering their trunks three times in succession. When he walks to Government House the crowds press forward and try to kiss his hands and his feet. Women ask him to touch their children to cure their ills. Gordon reassures them all, "I come without soldiers, God on my side, to redress the evils of the Sudan. I will not fight with any weapons but justice. There shall be no more Bashibazuks." He is back in his element. As Lytton Strachey describes in *Eminent Victorians*: "The glare and the heat of that southern atmosphere, the movement of the crowded city, the dark-faced populace, and the soldiers and the suppliants, the reawakened consciousness of power, and glamour and the mystery of the whole strange scene ... He was among his people— his own people and it was to them only that he was responsible—to them and to God."

The Mahdi sends a message of welcome, and Gordon orders that all hostilities against him should cease. He sends him a red robe of honor, a fez—a hated symbol of alien authority in Mahdist eyes!—and a letter offering to make him sultan of Kordofan. He forms a council of twelve notables. He declares that the gates in the ramparts be kept open so the people can pass freely, that taxes be cut, and duties on food entering the town be abolished. He orders his deputy, Colonel Stewart, to strike the irons off the legs of debtors and prisoners of war and destroy stocks, whips, branding irons, and other instruments of torture. Some of these measures "may have passed the narrow line which, in some cases, divides religious exaltation from lunacy," according to *The New York Times*.

He astounds his audience—and appalls abolitionists—when he announces: "Today, I desire you to recommence with perfect freedom the traffic in slaves, and I have given orders that public criers shall make this known to all, that they may dispose of their domestics as they see proper, and no one in the future shall interfere with the commerce." By making this announcement, Gordon erases any lingering traces of credibility that may remain among officials in London and Cairo and the support they might provide to him later on.

Gordon releasing the prisoners

Amid the jubilation, three messengers in Dervish uniforms are shown into his presence. Standing with hands on their swords—not in keeping with Arab courtesies by the way—they hand him a bundle and a letter from the Mahdi: "I have no need of the sultanate, nor the kingdom of Kordofan or elsewhere, nor of the wealth of this world and its vanity. I am but the slave of Allah ... With this message I am sending a suit of clothes, consisting of a jibba, ridaa, sirwal, imma, takiya, keraba, and sibha. This is the clothing of those who have given up this world."

Gordon flings these humble items of dervish garb on the ground and tramples on them. Appalled by this sacrilege, the startled messengers beat a hasty retreat. Gordon has badly underestimated Ansar religious fervor, with tragic consequences. The solution is not merely in ending oppression and installing a just administration; the problem is deeper than that.

He turns now to the people of Khartoum for support. He reads to them the Mahdi's summons to surrender. They exclaim that this is the false mahdi and that they will put their trust in the governor-general. A learned sheikh draws up a theological statement showing how this Mahdi does not fulfill the requirements as prophesied. They note that the true mahdi was born in the year of the Prophet 255, from which it follows that he must now be 1,046 years old!

Conciliation is now out of the question. As a soldier, Gordon can't brook the idea of retiring before the Mahdi. He again asks for Zubair and for two hundred Indian troops to "smash the Mahdi." The ever-loyal Stewart, who earlier had his doubts, now agrees: "Even if we could sneak away, I am convinced Gordon is the last man in the world who would do so. Hence I see no option but Zubair." But Gordon is not so sanguine, as he writes to his sister: "I expect that my asking for Zubair to come up was the last drop in the cup, and henceforth I am a complete pariah." His sanctioning of domestic slavery has provoked a new wave of protest among British abolitionists. So it comes as no surprise when, again, he is overruled.

Officials in London and Cairo believe he is largely driven by fancy. His impulsiveness is reflected in the telegrams he sends whenever an idea strikes him. He doesn't deliberate before making a proposal. Telegrams pile up each morning on Evelyn Baring's desk in Cairo, twenty or thirty at least, often delayed in transmission and out of sequence. "What a queer fellow Gordon is." His messages include jokes and appeals to Isaiah and a whirl of contradictory policies. Writes Baring: "A man who habitually consults the Prophet Isaiah when he is in difficulty is not apt to obey the orders of any man; besides, he is too flighty and changes his opinions very rapidly." In Baring's view, a more unfortunate choice could scarcely have been made to carry out official policy and evacuate the Sudan. Gordon is too hotheaded and swayed by emotion. "He that would govern others first should be the master of himself."

Gordon asks for two hundred Indian troops to be sent to Wadi Halfa, then for "five hundred red-blooded Englishmen under capable officers." If they also aren't available, then four thousand Turks—"and see that they get well paid." When the government refuses this request, he announces that he will hold on as long as he can. And if unable to suppress the rebellion, "I will retire to the Equator and leave you with the indelible disgrace of abandoning the garrisons of Sennar, Kassala, Berber and Dongola, with the certainty that you will eventually be forced to smash up the Mahdi under great difficulty if you would retain peace in Egypt."

Bright sunny mornings with a nip in the air give way to steady blazing heat. The garrisons become Gordon's obsession: eight thousand men in Khartoum and garrisons in Darfur, Bahr al-Ghazal, and Equatoria. For their fidelity, would he abandon them to their fate? How could they retire to the frontier of Egypt? Boats could take only a few. Where would he get the camels to take them? Would the Mahdi supply them? The thought of thousands of Egyptians with their wives and children escorted by demoralized troops trailing day after day across waterless desert is too appalling to contemplate. "They will be plundered to the skin." The choice, as he sees it, is either to surrender absolutely to the Mahdi or defend Khartoum at all costs.

In early March, four thousand Arabs swoop down on the Nile near Halfaya, immediately to the north of Khartoum. With the telegraph line cut and access from the north blocked, messages have to be sent out on strips of paper concealed on anyone willing to venture through enemy lines. Persuading someone to carry messages into beleaguered Khartoum is even more difficult. The siege has begun. Twenty-five thousand civilians and eight thousand soldiers—who are not very reliable at that—are completely cut off. Meanwhile, the daily life of the town drags on, muted and fatalistic, its inhabitants reduced to eating donkeys and horses, dogs and rats, gum, and the pith of date trees.

"You ask me to state cause and intention in staying at Khartoum knowing government means to abandon Sudan," Gordon answers. "I stay in Khartoum because Arabs have shut us up and will not let us out." Not really, for he can escape, but he will not leave his soldiers behind. With him are Stewart, his second-in-command; Frank Power, whose company he enjoys and for whom he feels genuine affection; Herbin, the urbane French consul whom he admires; Hansel, the Austrian, for whom he has lesser regard; the Greek consul; and a number of other Europeans.

The town is protected on the north by the Blue Nile and on the west by the White Nile. Each branch is half a mile wide at low water. Gordon's artillery comprises a few antiquated bronze cannons and one Krupp field piece. Fortifications consist of a deep ditch to the south of the town, extending for nearly four miles between the Niles, and inside, ramparts reinforced by three bastions and pierced by two gates. Vulnerability lies principally along the White Nile. As it recedes, an expanse of river bottom between the ramparts and the riverbank is more exposed, enabling the enemy to easily cross over to the town. Hansel regularly takes a morning walk along the riverbank until two cannon balls strike the water nearby, and he decides to give up the habit.

Gordon never succumbs to despair. He keeps up his usual whirlwind of activity, reinforcing the ramparts with wire entanglements and laying down primitive landmines, "crow's feet"—caltrops—and broken bottles in the sand to deter barefooted Dervishes, and spreading out in long sloping lines hundreds of yards of cotton cloth dyed the color of earth to deceive the enemy. To keep up morale, he distributes to both men and women decorations made of silver and pewter and inscribed "Siege of Khartoum." He searches out private stores of food and buys up unripe grain to be laid out in the sun to mature before being threshed. The more hopeless the situation, the more energetic and cheerful he seems. He suffers privately, of course. Frank Power attests that he hears him "walking up and down his room all night (it is next to mine)."

The treasury is nearly empty and the pay of officials and troops three months in arrears. Of the £100,000 that Baring sent him, £40,000 disappeared in the pockets of the tribes that provided transport; a high official returning to Egypt appropriated the rest. When funds dry up—not one piaster from Cairo—he issues his own banknotes in £1 and £10 denominations—which the Egyptian government refuses to honor.

Shaigiya tribesmen hold the surrounding country. Nominal allies of the government, they become one of Gordon's main worries, "a dreadful lot continually feathering toward me or toward the Mahdi. I expect both sides despise them equally." From captured spies, they learn of an impending attack but make no move to defend themselves. Twenty-three of them are taken prisoner—one is killed and one wounded, in addition to the loss of five women, eight slaves, seventeen cows, three donkeys, seven horses, and twenty-four Remington rifles. Their chief, commanding the fort on the other side of the Blue Nile, is sleeping in town that night and, therefore, not at his post when the attack takes place. "They shut themselves in their houses about seven p.m. and don't go out again until broad daylight…The Cairo Turkish Bashibazuks, the Shaigiya, and the Fellahin soldiers, I will back against any troops in the world for cowardice," Gordon writes in his journal.

Standing with Power one day on the palace roof, he watches his troops attack enemy forces massed near Khartoum. His Egyptian cavalry enter the woods at the base of some sand hills. Their five principal officers, who have been riding ahead, suddenly dash back, breaking through their own ranks, pursued by sixty Dervish cavalry who rush out at full gallop from behind the hills. His troops break up without firing a shot. Dervish horsemen, armed with lances and swords, cut down the fleeing men. Infantry, hacking at the men disabled by the cavalry charge, follow them up. The rout confirms that Gordon can't count on his Egyptians, Bashibazuks, and any others wavering in their belief that the Mahdi is vulnerable.

— Chapter 6: The Siege —

Closing the Noose

In late April, the Mahdists take Fedasi, between Khartoum and Sennar on the Blue Nile. In May, they take Berber, at the critical junction between the Nile and the Red Sea coast where Giuseppe Cuzzi is the English consular agent. Originally a trader in Sennar, he has been sent to Khartoum by his company. The commercial life of the town at a standstill, he spends sociable evenings with a compatriot named Lombroso, the French wholesale merchant Albert Marquez, the Syrian physician Georgi Bey—who will accompany Hicks—and the Austrian consul general Hansel. They meet in each other's house and often invite the European officers of Hicks's army to join them. On September 8, 1883, "at the last banquet these unlucky men were to have in this world," they raise their glasses in a toast to the success of Hicks's mission.

After the annihilation of Hicks's army, Cuzzi is told by his company to close down his agency and go to Berber and there await further developments. With him are his faithful slave and now wife, Usna—freed "so that she would never become the slave of another man"—and their five-month-old daughter. On passing through Berber, Gordon appoints him Britain's agent. When the wires to Khartoum are cut, Cuzzi forwards to Cairo by telegraph Gordon's messages, written on small slips of paper sewn in the garments of spies.

On March 23, 1884, Cuzzi sends his last telegram: "Khartoum is encircled. The situation is getting more and more serious." Baring replies that he is going on leave and Cuzzi is free to leave his post if he wants. So Cuzzi hires some camels and prepares to flee to Egypt with his family. "My wife had only just recovered from a serious illness and was still very weak. I therefore got a bed fixed onto a specially tranquil camel and provided it with a canopy and flanks for protection against the sun, to make the journey for her as little strenuous as possible. As I had a great deal of luggage, I took ten extra camels."

Not many miles out of Berber, they are intercepted by a band of Jaaliyin Dervishes armed with wooden clubs.

"You are Giuseppe Cuzzi, the English Consul in Berber?"

"Yes"

"You were at the same time the representative of Gordon Pasha, your brother, who is now in Khartoum?"

"I was Gordon's representative, but he is not my brother."

Told to embrace Islam in order to spare his life and that of his wife and child, Cuzzi is persuaded "to play the farce...though with a heavy heart." He is taken to the Nile to be washed. Assured that crocodiles never take hold of orthodox Muslims and after being thoroughly scrubbed, he is given the name Muhammad Yusuf. "You have joined the true religion, you are therefore one of us. You will now go to Khartoum to hand over our letters and to report on our successes. Do not let yourself be tempted by the unbelievers to stay with them, but return to us as soon as possible!"

Cuzzi does as directed under a flag of truce and is met by Stewart. Ever the consummate professional, Stewart agrees that Cuzzi must keep his promise "even if it were to show our enemies that we Europeans have only one word." He urges Cuzzi to eat and take a rest, but Cuzzi demurs; he cannot eat with unbelievers, but he will avail himself of a glass of wine.

But Gordon will have nothing to do with someone "who had abjured his faith to save his skin." Also, he suspects that Cuzzi may have betrayed Berber to the Dervishes. How else could his favorable treatment be explained?

This is nonsense—Cuzzi could never have betrayed Berber since he left the town before the siege began. Still, Gordon is adamant. He dismisses out of hand any mediation by such a "vile traitor" and admonishes the Mahdists accordingly: "As you may be aware, the Mohammedans who are with me do not want to surrender. Could you therefore demand from me, the Christian, that I should be the first to do so? Whenever in future you have to send messengers to me, do not send Europeans but your own people."

En route to Kordofan to see the Mahdi, Cuzzi's health deteriorates. No relief is obtained from swallowing magic blessings on scraps of paper and being bled from his neck by a feki. He is reduced to a skeleton, too weak to move, his eyes swollen and filled with pus. He later wryly notes in his memoirs: "In view of my imminent journey to the next world, my kind guards could certainly not be blamed for appropriating my few earthly possessions." However, he miraculously recovers and reaches Rahad. There, the Mahdi tells him, "I shall capture Khartoum, then conquer Egypt, depose the Sultan from his throne, and then defeat Europe. Italy will be one of the first countries I will attack. I shall defeat her and appoint you the first emir of Italy. The old world must be demolished and out of its ruins I shall create a new one."

When Cuzzi departs, the Mahdi gives him farewell presents: "two camels, fifty dollars and—truly Sudanese!—a slave-girl." Once again, Cuzzi tries to see Gordon, but with no better luck than before. "Although I knew of Gordon's often unjustified mistrust...I felt deeply hurt, as I was conscious that in the task with which he had entrusted me, I had certainly done my duty." Returning to Berber, Cuzzi learns that his child has died of hunger. Devastated with grief, he seems to the local citizens to be mentally deranged.

Umm Dubban

At Umm Dubban, within easy striking distance from Khartoum, Sheikh Wad Badr continues to vacillate in his allegiance. He doesn't reply to the Mahdi's several letters urging him to join the revolt. He believes that Muhammad Ahmad, while a Sufi, has lost his way, that he has not reached the higher stage of inspiration needed to become the Mahdi. The defeat of Hicks convinces him of the rebellion's ultimate success, and he decides to give his support. Thus, his headquarters at Umm Dubban becomes a threat to the government in Khartoum.

Exposed to this new danger, Gordon dispatches Muhammed Ali Pasha, the Egyptian officer he most admires, up the Blue Nile to drive away the Dervishes. Despite being told not to leave the protection of the steamers, the "fighting pasha," as Gordon refers to him, pursues Wad Badr into the interior, where he is ambushed and killed. When facing death, Muhammed Ali places the sheepskin from under his saddle on the ground and, not moving from the spot, awaits the inevitable. This is the heroic way to die in the Sudan. Muhammed Ali Pasha meets his fate in this way, and Gordon, who so admires him, is devastated.

At the end of the Ramadan fast, the Mahdi announces that the Prophet has told him to lay siege to Khartoum, and he sends proclamations for one and all to join him. The end of the rainy season, when the earth has dried enough to hold water in pools, is a favorable time to begin the greatest wholesale migration ever seen in the Sudan: a multitude of men, women, children, "the blind carrying the crippled," and thousands of their livestock.

The war drum booms the signal for departure. The Mahdi is mounted on a fine Bishari camel; his feet, hanging from the front of the saddle, rest on the shoulders of mulazims walking alongside. This great assemblage proceeds toward the Nile. Camel-owning tribes stick to the north and Baggara with their herds of cattle to the south, where supplies of water are more plentiful. Progress is slow, but having starved El Obeid into surrender, the Mahdists are in no hurry to attack Khartoum. In any case, it is better to wait until the Nile has fallen at the end of the year. The ranks swell as others join in. They live off the land and are welcomed at the temporary markets of Jellaba where they buy meat, dates, onions, and salt.

Ansari Warrior

With the Mahdi are Slatin and all the Europeans, including the Catholic missionaries who haven't changed their religion. Slatin, eager to join Gordon, writes to him to explain how he had no choice when his demoralized troops refused to fight any longer. "Does Your Excellency believe that to me, as an Austrian officer, that surrender was easy? It was one of the hardest days in my life." But Gordon is unyielding. He won't deal with these apostate foreigners: Slatin now Abdul Qadir, Lupton now Sheikh Abdallah, Cuzzi now Muhammad Yusuf, Klootz now Mustafa. Because he has acted dishonorably, "I will have nothing to do with Slatin's coming in here to stay unless he has the Mahdi's positive leave. His doing so would be the breaking of his parole, which should be as sacred when given to the Mahdi as to any other power and it would jeopardize the safety of all those other Europeans, prisoners of the Mahdi." So he doesn't respond to Slatin's appeal and remonstrates to the ulama of Khartoum on the degeneracy of the faith, when Christians become Muslims to save their lives and Muslims become followers of a false prophet to save their property. "When it is a question between Allah and their goats, they will be inclined to look after their goats."

Slatin writes to Gordon in French and in German—for Hansel to translate—which draws further suspicion that he is sending secret messages to the enemy. He is told to sit on the ground with legs outstretched while his feet are placed in two iron rings joined by a thick iron bar, and the rings hammered closed. Another ring is placed around his neck and a chain attached to it, making it hard for him to move his head. Not allowed to speak to anyone, he occupies himself by counting its figure-of-eight links, always keeping in mind Madibbo's advice: be obedient and patient.

Again, the war drums boom. Tents are struck and baggage loaded on camels. With the iron chain wrapped around his body, Slatin is lifted onto a donkey and held in position by someone on each side.

Finally, the palm trees of Khartoum move into view. How Slatin longs to join the garrison in the defense of the town! Instead, he must sit in a tattered tent, surviving on food of the vilest description. Passing by, the Khalifa Abdallahi asks, "Does Abdul Qadir think we are going to fatten him up here, whilst his uncle, Gordon Pasha, does nothing but fire shells all day at our master? If he had made his uncle submit, he would not now be in chains."

The Mahdi has with him fifteen thousand head of cattle, which he plans to drive into the Omdurman fort to explode the mines. Rockets from the fort push them back, and forty-one of the beasts—worth £20 a head by Gordon's reckoning—are captured. Humiliated by the capture of the cows, nineteen Dervishes come along the right bank of the Nile and seize a donkey. This insult infuriates some Shaigiya, who sally out to engage the Dervishes in what transpires to be an inconclusive fight.

Deserters arriving at the palace under a white flag provide Gordon with intelligence, much of it suspect. He sends out courier-spies to

Dongola with £10 each and a promise of another £10 on reaching their destination. They are entrusted with letters and gifts for Dervish chiefs. Spies coming in report—probably falsely—that they get nothing before returning. Messages from the Mahdi's camp are treated with skepticism. But when one of the Mahdi's emirs complains that he has no soap, Gordon sends him some.

Some reports are almost too good to be true: Dervishes returning to their homes in Kordofan, and the Mahdi sending out troops to bring them back; slave troops escaping if given half a chance or being kept on short rations and promised full rations only if they fight; Dervish commanders impounding rifles each night and returning them in the morning because so many of their soldiers are deserting. When camels are hired to bring grain to the Mahdi's camp, their Arab herders often abscond—with the animals and the money—into the interior.

Deserters filtering into the government lines are turned into government soldiers. One, a "dreadfully itchy escaped soldier," is ushered into Gordon's office where he is astonished to see his face in a mirror and asks who it is. Similarly, a black mother with two sons comes in and, seeing her image "grinned and smirked" at the reflections. Asked why they deserted, they answer, "Why, the Arabs give us nothing," prompting Gordon to remark, "So it is true that the belly governs the whole world."

He learns that a strange Frenchman in Dervish dress has come up from Dongola to salute the Mahdi. Perhaps it's Ernest Renan, author of *The Life of Jesus,* whom Gordon had met earlier in the Royal Geographical Society, where he told him that he was taking leave of this world. Gordon wanted to see him again. But, alas, the mysterious Frenchman was Olivier Pain whose fate has already been sealed.

The rainy season ends, and the Nile is rising. Gordon places most confidence in his "Thames penny steamers," paddleboats that can engage in a running fight along the river provided they keep to midstream. He sends them up the Blue Nile to Sennar and Down the Main Nile to Berber to attack the enemy and collect grain and cattle. He has seven of them, all inherited from Baker. Each is fitted out with a rude wooden turret, bulletproof but not shellproof, and open at top, and a nine-pounder brass howitzer up front. At the foot of the turret is the cooking area where slave girls spend most of the day baking bread—miraculously not setting the ship on fire! Aft of the turret is a fore hold and a gangway on each side for landing; a foremast to which a birdcage—a sort of iron bucket—is slung for a lookout; the midship turret between the paddle boxes with another nine-pounder on top; the funnel, riddled with bullet holes; the boiler, protected by logs placed over it, the hatchway of the main-hold; and, farthest aft, a saloon or deck-house, on top of which is the wheel where the helmsman needs to be protected to the extent possible. Sheets of boilerplate over which men can fire protect the sides of the ship. Gordon puts Egyptian soldiers on the steamers when in action—he says because "they cannot run away."

Gordon places great stock in these steamers: "I never feel anxious about any of the fights, except when the steamers are involved, and then...I am on tenterhooks, as long as they are out." He is building another one, which people in Khartoum want to name after him, but he refuses. "I have put most of you in prison and otherwise bullied you, and I have never to fear of your forgetting me." Instead, he names it Zubair "even though the Anti-Slavery Society will be furious."

The Arabs are agog at the sight of these steamers, belching smoke as they come chugging down the Nile. Running the gauntlet of fire from the banks is always hazardous. The boats must avoid rocks and shifting sandbanks, where they are especially vulnerable to enemy guns. Merely stopping for wood to feed the boilers can involve danger, so captains are instructed to take wood only from isolated spots and are warned against anchoring near the bank. It is safer to remain in mid-channel and exchange musketry fire from there, even though the expenditure of ammunition is considerable. Holes made by the Krupp shells can be repaired, but mountain guns leave two-foot holes in the hull that are hard to fix. "My beautiful steamers, which used to be comparatively sweet, now stink like badgers. As for the swell Ismailia, she is a cesspit."

In early September, Gordon sends the small paddle steamer, Abbas, downriver with urgent dispatches asking for aid. Her shallow draft gives her a better chance of getting through the cataracts. Despite the considerable risk, Stewart, Frank Power, and the French consul, Herbin choose to go along. The only European remaining with Gordon is Hansel, the Austrian consul for whom he has little use. But he will greatly miss Power, who has been an enjoyable guest at the palace. He could use Stewart's support in these perilous times, but he also can willingly forego the sullen reserve of this regular officer whose main concern is his career. Gordon will face the impending battle alone.

Does he harbor a subconscious wish for solitary martyrdom? At least, death will free him from the memories of erecting forts on the Thames, when he took in young boys and washed them with his own hands, fed them and clothed them and taught them before sending them on their ways. He loved these boys. Will death free him from these apparent lusts of the flesh, which most recently were aroused when a little boy with large limpid, black eyes was brought in from the Arabs and given work to do in the palace kitchen? In Gordon's mind, to kill himself would be a crime before God, but death at the hands of the Mahdi would provide him with welcome escape from these thoughts.

A letter from the Mahdi arrives. The Abbas has been disabled and captured, and Stewart and the others on board have been killed. According to Hussain Bey, Stewart's interpreter, the Abbas was proceeding downriver with two escorting steamers. After passing Berber, they return to Khartoum, contrary to Gordon's instructions. The Abbas strikes a rock at the entrance of the fourth cataract at Monassir and can't be dislodged. Stewart orders the boxes of spare ammunition thrown overboard. After spiking the gun, he throws it also into the river. Local people, who have come down to the bank, shout, "Give us peace and grain."

Stewart sends the captain ashore, promising peace. Summoned also to come ashore, Stewart, who has little admiration for the Sudanese, mistakenly believes that "the Arabs could not dare to do anything." Unarmed and without escort, he, along with the two consuls and Hussain Bey, their interpreter, goes ashore. They enter the house of a blind feki who arranges with Suleiman wad Gamr, the principal sheikh in that part of the country, for camels to take them to Merawi, further down the Nile.

Suleiman says that Stewart is a guest and therefore under his protection. If he will pay him a visit and provide half the price of the camels, the balance can be paid on their safe arrival at Merawi. Leaving their guns behind, except for Stewart who conceals a small revolver in his pocket, they are cordially received at Suleiman's house and given dates and coffee. After they have taken refreshments, Suleiman goes outside and, with a copper pot, signals to his people, who split into two groups. One group enters the house, ordering "surrender," the other rushes down to the shore where the other passengers from the Abbas have gathered. They throw themselves into the water, where they are killed or drowned. Ordered to surrender, Stewart gives up his pistol and fights with his fists but is easily overcome. Power and Herbin are also killed and their bodies thrown into the river.

When he gets the news, Gordon is devastated. "Stewart was a brave, just, upright gentleman. Can one say more? Power was a chivalrous, brave, honest gentleman. Can one say more? Herbin I liked very much. He was a most agreeable and gentlemanly Frenchman, and very sharp ... though naturally with a French bias. If Stewart, Power, and Herbin died because they would not change their religion, they are as much martyrs as Peter and Paul."

THE RELIEF EXPEDITION

With increasingly strident public opinion and after months of procrastination, Gladstone finally accedes to General Garnet Wolseley's insistence that an expedition be sent—and soon—in support of the isolated Gordon. In early October 1884, the relief expedition begins a sixteen hundred-mile journey up the Nile to Khartoum. It becomes a desperate race against time. A month later, it reaches Dongola at the great bend of the river. Its leader, Wolseley, sends a message to Gordon asking at what point he would be in serious difficulty.

Gordon's Relief Expedition

Gordon finds this question absurd, "as if a man on the bank, having seen his friend in the river already bobbed down two or three times, hails, 'I say, old fellow, let us know when we are to throw you the life-buoy.'" The relief force, he replies, should be prepared to relieve the whole of the garrisons, his "beautiful black soldiers" as well as the "worthless Egyptians;" it would be "shabby" to do otherwise. To rescue him alone is out of the question; he will not be "a rescued lamb." On November 9, he writes with emphatic underscoring: "I declare positively...I will not leave the Sudan until everyone who wants to go down is given the chance to do so...If any letter comes up here, ordering me to come down, I will not obey it, but will stay here, and fall with the town, and run all risks."

On November 22, he is even more adamant: "If the expedition comes here before the place falls (which is doubtful), and if the instructions are to evacuate the place at once, and leave Kasala and Sennar too, I will resign, and have nothing more to do with the Govt of this place, or of the Sudan."

In the meantime, he pours out advice: Small parties that can move rapidly and attack just before dawn are what are needed. The strength of the rebels is their horsemen who won't fight in the dark. Medical officers will not be needed since there will be no wounded, "for Arabs give no quarter." If you go to help their wounded, they will try to kill you. You are only pretending to help them in order to kill them afterward...and "they will enter Paradise if they kill an infidel." A handful of redcoats will suffice. When they arrive, the Mahdi will lose heart, his followers will return to their villages, and the siege will collapse. On December 14, he sets his deadline: "Now Mark This, if the Expeditionary Force, and I ask for no more than two hundred men, does not come in ten days, the town may fall; and I have done my best for the honor of our country. Goodbye. C. G. Gordon."

On leaving Egypt, the Relief Expedition's route traces the Nile from the second cataract at Wadi Halfa to the third cataract at Dongola where Nubia ends and the Sudan proper begins. At that point, the river curves sharply, enclosing the Bayuda desert, peopled by tribes that rear sheep, goats, and camels. A line of wells extending across this desert provides a shorter route to rejoin the Nile in the vicinity of Metemma, and from there, past the sixth cataract and on to Khartoum.

The logistics are staggering: eight hundred whaler boats thirty feet long to carry military equipment, supplies, and forage. The boats' shallow drafts, flat bottoms, and large rudders are better able to navigate the shallows and avoid the rocks. Each boat is steered by two Canadian Indians and, in slack water, rowed by Sudanese. British soldiers on camels track them from shore and haul them by means of rollers and levers across the rapids between banks strewn with the ribs and planks of wrecked boats. When one of them goes on the rocks, the boxes and bags are tossed overboard, and a hundred days' provisions go "floating merrily down the Nile."

Whaler Boat in the Cataracts

Before setting out, native guides must be hired, four hundred riding and baggage camels purchased, and ten thousand umbrellas ordered from London to shade the troops from the desert sun. Egyptian subordinate officers are charged with portaging the stores from one station to the next, filling the water skins and bottles, and watering the camels. The British soldiers are taught how to handle the surly animals. "The novice soon learns that a camel is not a pleasant beast to ride. The camel is always in a state of extreme mental depression. He whines and groans incessantly, and never, apparently, like other animals makes friends with his master. He trots along all day with an air of hopeless misery, which nothing seems to alleviate. Only the kurbash—a hippo- or rhino hide whip—has any effect on him." Besides, the jolt of its gait is most unpleasant—unlike a smooth-riding dromedary, which can carry the experienced rider at a gentle jog for hours. Given these discomforts, the British camel corps is provided with saddles on which men sit astride as on horseback, whereas the native habit is to sit with legs crossed on rugs and blankets laid on top, with a prop behind to lean against. Special instructions are prepared for the neophytes: "Before engaging the enemy in battle dismount, but only after getting the camel to lie down in order to avoid rupture when jumping from such a height." When expecting attack, form a square outside the camels and tie them down by the heads and knees to prevent a stampede.

Special correspondents and artists from the London press accompany the troops. Not allowed to travel on government boats, they, too, make their way along the banks by camel. Why, they grumble, is an Egyptian clerk or officer's native servant allowed passage on a boat while the representative of an English newspaper must travel by camelback? Why must they dine on a dinner of cold bully beef, sleep under a moon amid the creaking of water wheels and surrounded by curious natives who gather to observe them in their bizarre bivouac? Serious doubts regarding their real purpose arise when they come across villagers who have not even heard of the Mahdi, much less that there is an expedition to relieve that fellow, Gordon.

On approaching the great bend of the river and the grazing lands of Bayuda, messages urging submission are sent out to the Arab tribes along the way: "You know that you are quite unable to oppose our troops. Do not therefore be obstinate but come down and yield and seek security, for we are merciful. But, if you do not come at once but remain far away, we will consider you as rebels and great evil will befall you. The word of the English is true and their promises are kept."

Meanwhile, Gordon is secluded in his palace while the Mahdi tries to persuade him to surrender and avoid bloodshed. Each day Gordon perambulates the ramparts to see that sentries are properly placed. He bucks up the soldiers who are sullen and numb with hunger and fatigue. He walks through the town's dusty, stinking streets, smiling at the people, who sit in silent groups and stare at him. He assures them that relief is on the way. In his office, he sits at his desk, a tin of cigarettes at his elbow, scribbling furiously in his journal, spattering blots of ink because of the tension in his hand. He sleeps little and takes his frugal meals alone, his only companion a mouse, which has taken Stewart's place at the table and eats from Gordon's plate.

He does not give way to despondency but turns more frequently to the brandy decanter. It is on the far side of his office so that, at night, he has to walk from his bedroom to reach it. He monitors the antics of his favorite turkey cock in the courtyard and the hawks flying by along the river and wonders whether they are destined to pick out his eyes. He quotes in his journal, "The eye that mocketh at his father, and despiseth to obey his mother, the ravens of the valley shall pick it out, and the eagles shall eat it." When the turkey cock kills two of its chicks and becomes rambunctious, he puts its head under its wing and rocks it to and fro until it falls asleep.

Hours are spent on the roof with a telescope pointed to the north fort on the other side of the Blue Nile, the direction from where relief will come—if ever it does come. When a donkey grazing near the fort explodes one of the mines, it amuses him to see that the donkey, angry and surprised, is able to walk off unhurt. When a large woman squawks about how she was pushed into the river and lost the only two dollars she had to buy sorghum, he gives her the money, "to comfort her black soul."

Gordon begins his journal in September after Stewart and the others have left on their fateful journey. In it, he seems happier than he has been since his arrival in Khartoum. He is now alone and entirely dependent upon himself. In the solitude of his palace, with ruin closing around him, "he let his pen rush on for hour after hour in an ecstasy of communication, a tireless unburdening of the spirit ... addressed more to himself than to anyone else."

Marginal notes, deletions, underlining, neat little maps, and biblical references fill the pages, providing a revealing self-portrait of his hopes and anxieties, biases and fits of conscience, all leavened with lighthearted excursions into the trivial, the antics of his turkey cock, and the idiosyncrasies of the Arabs. "If the Arabs are not eating, they are saying their prayers; if not saying their prayers, they are sleeping; if not sleeping, they are sick. You want to send an immediate order and there is your servant bobbing up and down, and you cannot disturb him ... Not one of my subordinates, except the chief clerk and his subordinate, appeared today. I had to send for them. It is Friday and unreasonable to expect us at the office, is what they say ... I boxed the telegraph clerk's ears for not giving me the telegram last night but then, as my conscience pricked me, I gave him five dollars. He said he did not mind if I killed him—I was his father…."

Gordon is unconstrained in expressing his prejudices: Blacks are "patient, enduring, friendly and wonderfully clean;…the Egyptian fellaheen and Turkish Bashibazuks are cowardly, cruel and effeminate;… my Bedwin Arabs…are fine handsome fellows who do not 'loll about, or spit, or smell,' while the English are 'the cream…but we will not exist on two dates a day, as these others do without a murmur.'"

Gordon's unshakable serenity might be seen as evidence of exceptional spiritual, mental, and physical resilience. However, a sign of the mental strain is the constant reference in his journal to the fate of two Egyptian officers whom he had put to death after their defeat at Halfaya. On further thought, Gordon convinces himself that they were "judicially murdered."

Similar fits of conscience and vacillation have arisen in the past. Ibrahim Fawzi serves Gordon faithfully in the early days and is promoted eventually to governor of Equatorial provinces with rank of "miralai"—colonel. On being told that Fawzi is implicated in the slave traffic, Gordon dismisses him and claps him in irons. However, after leaving the Sudan, Gordon comes to realize that he has been overly harsh and arranges that Fawzi should be attached to him as his aide-de-camp with rank of pasha. He also gives him a present of ten £10 notes, and, in the end, Fawzi accompanies Gordon on his last journey to Khartoum.

THE SIEGE OF KHARTOUM

In September 1884, Khartoum learns that General Wolseley's force has reached the bend of the Nile. Relief is on the way! Pervasive gloom gives way to rejoicing, and a salute of 101 guns booms renewed defiance from the ramparts. Actually, Wolseley won't reach Korti, where the Nile loops back to the northeast, for another two months. There, he makes his headquarters, and his soldiers celebrate Christmas with music, burlesque orations, "nigger dances," and patriotic songs. He divides his army into two columns, one continuing to follow the river and the other proceeding directly across the Bayuda desert to Metemma. Since the wells along the desert route can't support such a force, supplies must be brought forward and stored in advance. The double journey with insufficient camels further delays the advance.

Gordon sends three steamers to meet the desert column at Metemma. They encounter hostile fire from the riverbank. Two of the steamers go downriver on a foraging expedition and bring back grain, Near Metemma, however, one of them takes a shell near its engines and has to be towed.

In the Bayuda desert, ten thousand Dervishes are prepared to block access of the column to the Abu Tulaih wells, twenty miles before Metemma. Arriving too late in the day to attack, the British encamp on a ridge and listen to the beating of war drums throughout the night. At first light, they advance in square formation. As Venus begins to rise, five thousand of the best of the Mahdi's cavalry, under the command of Musa, brother of the khalifa Ali wad Hilu, sweep down on the rear of the square and force their way inside by sheer numbers.

What has been a source of weakness now becomes strength. The rear face is forced right up to the line of camels to form a living traverse that breaks the rush. The troops on the other side of the square turn and direct a devastating fire upon the advancing enemy, which is attempting to follow up the success gained by the leading horsemen. In the hand-to-hand fighting and the din of battle, commands cannot be heard. Each soldier has to act on the impulse of the moment.

Battle at Abu Tulaih

Sir Charles Wilson, who is destined to lead the first contingent into Khartoum, is amazed at the fearlessness of the Mahdists advancing over bare ground in the face of tremendous fire: "I saw a fine old sheikh on horseback plant his banner in the center of the square behind the camels. He was, at once, shot down, falling on his banner. He turned out to be Musa wad Hilu of the Dighaim. I had noticed him in the advance with his banner in one hand and a book of prayers in the other, and never saw anything finer. The old man never swerved to the right or left, and never ceased chanting his prayers until he had planted his banner in our square. If any man deserved a place in the Moslem paradise, he did."

The battle over, eleven hundred Dervish bodies are strewn about the perimeter of the square where seventy-four British also lie. Although the Mahdi had prohibited expressions of grief for those who enter paradise, the loud keening of women continues for hours when the news reaches Omdurman. On hearing the wailing in the Mahdi's camp, Slatin knows that the enemy has suffered a serious defeat. Though overwhelmed, the Mahdi orders a salute of one hundred and one guns to convince Gordon that it was the British, not the Dervishes, who suffered most gravely. However, from the roof of the palace, Gordon has already been observing through his telescope the paroxysm of lamentations that are taking place in the enemy camp.

The Mahdi makes his headquarters on the west bank of the White Nile. In early November, the shelling of Khartoum on the east side of the river begins. Little harm is done, but the effect is unnerving. Gordon writes in his journal: "November 12: One tumbles at 3 AM into a troubled sleep; a drum beats—tup! tup! tup!—The hope arises that it will go away. No, it goes on and increases in intensity…up one must get and go on to the roof of the palace; then telegrams, orders, swearing, and cursing goes on till about 9 AM. Men may say what they like about glorious war, but to me it is a horrid nuisance. The Arabs are firing across the river at the Mogrim fort, which is answering by Krupp and rockets. Is the European who is reported to be directing the guns the Frenchman who came from Dongola and might be Renan? The skyrockets puzzle the Arabs. The Arabs never seem to bother to aim the Remingtons. Their shells fall short: You can see with your telescope them aim at the fort and then hear the thud in the water. The buglers sound their calls and a renegade Dervish bugler replies."

Omdurman fort and the troops under Farraj Bey are now cut off from Khartoum and the river. Gordon can still communicate with bugle signals, but the Mahdi's bugler knows the signals. On January 15, 1885, Omdurman capitulates, its supplies exhausted. Farraj Bey is well treated—an inducement for the Khartoum garrison to join the Mahdi.

The Mahdi's principal emir, Abdul Rahman al-Nujumi, has brought up his Krupp and mountain guns. That his precious steamers now have to face enemy cannon as well disturbs Gordon more than the rifle bursts and the tac-tac-tac of Nordenfeldts and other nuisance fire. Nights are deadly silent except for random enemy shots across the river and the croaking of bullfrogs on the mudflats. At dawn, women gather below. Having long ago sold their jewels for food, they cry out for grain. Mercifully, some hoarded stocks are found in town. When Gordon tries to buy more from merchants, they say they haven't any for sale. But he does persuade Ibrahim Bordeini, a monstrously fat and rich Sudanese merchant of Syrian extraction, and, through him, a few others to release some of their stocks of sorghum and biscuits.

By the end of December, supplies have run out entirely and every living thing—donkeys, dogs, monkeys, and rats—has been eaten. Only palm tree fiber and a kind of gum that contains little nourishment are left. Conditions become desperate. Officers are robbing men of their rations, and the storekeepers are giving short weight. Soldiers are sick from eating gum, strips of hide from angarebs, and the crushed cores of palm trees. In the streets the dead lie in hundreds. If the majority wishes to go over to the Mahdi, it will be an immense relief. So Gordon issues a proclamation that they can do so, and many avail themselves of the opportunity.

Time acts as an advantage as long as the sandbanks are covered at high Nile and Gordon's steamers can still inflict damage on the enemy. But time has run out. The Nile has ebbed back from the crumbled ramparts and the ditch is filled with sand, leaving a broad path for those who dare to cross.

On January 21, a lookout on the steamers that Gordon sent to Metemma sees the English cavalry approaching the town. Flags are hoisted, and the music on board begins to play. One of officers on the boat hands Gordon's final journal, written up to December 14, to the arriving British, along with a note the size of a postage stamp in Gordon's hand—to fool the enemy if intercepted: "Khartoum all right, can hold out for years."

The arrival of redcoats has a decisive psychological effect on the Dervishes. Gordon had said, "If only a couple of English soldiers of the advancing force could be paraded about the lines of Khartoum, I should not fear an enemy attack." Therefore, under the command of Wilson, a twenty-six-man "flying squad" wearing sun helmets and scarlet tunics will proceed immediately to Khartoum, still a hundred miles away. But

Wilson approaching Khartoum

Wilson delays for two-and-half days because his naval colleague is suffering from boils and doesn't want to miss the historic adventure. Some of Wilson's men are dressed in the heavy, highly unsuitable red garb that the Guards had been carrying in their kits. On January 24, two little steamers pull away, heading for Khartoum. At the sixth cataract one of them, the Bordein, strikes a rock. The other, the Talahawein, remains behind to help, and more time is lost. On January 28, Khartoum is sighted in the distance. It seems, at last, that help for Gordon is at hand.

Gordon, approaching fifty-two, is worn to a shadow. Although still determined and totally fearless, deep in his heart he yearns for death. "I would that all could look on death as a cheerful friend, who takes us from a world of trial to our true home." To his secretary, Giriagis Bey, he says, "Go and collect all the people you can on the lines and make a good stand. Now leave me to smoke these cigarettes."

Another letter arrives from Nujumi, who again calls on him to submit and save the lives of the inhabitants of Khartoum.

"If any people want to go over to the Mahdi, they are at liberty to do so," Gordon concludes. "Reliance for succor from other than God will bring you nothing but destruction...I am here like iron and hope to see the newly arrived English ... It is impossible for me to have any more words with Muhammad Ahmad, only lead."

To sustain the hope that rescue was imminent, on Thursday, January 22, he tells his troops and the people of Khartoum: "The English will be here tomorrow." Though no English come.

On Friday: "They must be here tomorrow."

On Saturday the people are saying, "Gordon himself despairs, he tells us lies."

The merchant Bordeini, a devout Muslim—although he never turns down a glass of brandy and a cigarette whenever he comes to see Gordon—finds him sitting disconsolately in his office, smoking. Gordon pulls off his tarboush and throws it across the room. "What more can I say? The people will no longer believe me. I have told them over and over again that help would be here, and it never came, and now they must see that I tell them lies. If this, my last promise, fails, I can do nothing more."

Sunday, January 25, comes and goes, but still no English arrive.

Time means little to the Mahdi. He is in no hurry to crush the Khartoum garrison. After his abortive attack on El Obeid, he dreads a frontal assault on earthworks. Better to starve out the enemy. In delaying, he also has an ally in the river, which is receding over the long flat slope on the Khartoum side. A traitor named Omar Ibrahim steals across to his camp and informs him that there is the strip of land and shallow water at the end of the ramparts near the Muslimaniya Gate over which an attack can easily be launched. With that, the Mahdi decides to take action before the British arrive. The Prophet has assured him in a vision that God has put the lives of the garrison in his hands. His men should fear nothing; they are fighting a jihad and should have no fear of death.

"The Mahdi, prayers and peace be upon him, gathered all the army and, mounted on his camel, harangued us. He said that the enemies of God had dug a wide and deep ditch surrounding Khartoum and placed in it iron teeth, each with four iron spikes, three on which it stood, leaving the fourth spike upright to pierce the feet of men or the hooves or horses. Then he said, 'Swear allegiance to me unto death.' The whole army with one voice shouted three times, 'We swear allegiance to you unto death.'"

In Khartoum, on the evening of January 25, a brass band plays some jolly airs to relieve the despair that hangs over the city. After dining in solitary gloom, Gordon goes to his wing of the palace, there to write until well past midnight before putting out the light.

There is a story of how Gordon spent his last night in Khartoum. No doubt apocryphal, it still bears on the essential character of Gordon. It tells of how a young soldier named Willie Warren, who had been befriended by Gordon when he was working on forts on the Thames, had escaped through the lines and managed to reach the palace. He carries the message that the British forces had reached Metamma and that Khartoum would be relieved before dawn on the twenty-sixth. Gordon is elated and asks for every detail. He presses on Willie food, brandy, and cigarettes. He has a bed prepared for him in his bedroom, remembering how, years earlier, he had given him a bath and put him to bed and how much he loved him. To avoid thinking about him and to purge erotic impulses from his mind, Gordon, drinking heavily, forces himself to sit at his desk and keep writing until the wee hours of the morning in his last journal—which will never be seen. As dawn is breaking, benumbed by fatigue, he lies down on the leather sofa in his office to try to get some sleep.

Under a bright moon, the Mahdi and the three khalifas make their way by small boat across the Nile to a tree where Nujumi and his emirs are waiting. The Mahdi calls upon them, in the name of the Prophet, to launch the assault. "God is most great. Advance, advance, with God's blessing…Slay not the man Gordon, brethren, but take him alive and bring him to us, for he is a man of great worth among his own people. Do not kill him because his capture, alive, will be very useful for us. We want to exchange him for two fine men—al-Zubayr and Urabi"—who led the nationalist revolt against British and French in Egypt in 1882.

An hour before the dawn of January 26, the Ansar creep forward, skirmishers in front, the main force following with spears, swords, and rifles. The cavalry is on the rear flanks. Nujumi leads the way. Although he is Jaali, he is somebody in whom the Baggara recognize warlike qualities similar to their own: a thin, dark man, stern, hard, ascetic, "withal a spice of madness," who had devised the stratagem that annihilated Hicks. Nujumi and his fighters spend the night before the ramparts repeating over and over, "La ilaha illa llah…allahu akbar." Then his barefoot soldiers inch silently through the shallow mud. Suddenly, one of his emirs jumps up and shouts, as if possessed, "Companions of the Mahdi! Do you not see the houris of Paradise as they glide there gracefully, waving to you with their white kerchiefs."

Gordon's troops, spaced along the ramparts at intervals of four or five paces, are too exhausted to provide effective resistance. In the pandemonium an officer tries to rally them, kicking them and shouting at them. Another officer, preparing to die, has shaven all the hair from his body. The commander of the whole line, Faraj Pasha, throws civilian clothes over his uniform and flees through the Muslimaniya Gate.

Past the trench and first line of defense, Nujumi's men dash into the town and split up. One group heads straight for the palace. In his dressing gown, Gordon only has enough time to hurry to his bedroom and slip into a white uniform and seize his sword and revolver before the assailants are inside. At the top of the staircase, he meets four tall, swarthy Dervishes with swords drawn and spears flourishing. A deadly pause, then one of them shouts—some say it was Taha Shahin, a Dongolawi—"O cursed one, your time is come" and plunges his spear into Gordon's body. He falls, and the spears of the other assailants hack him to death.

There are other accounts since the exact details of Gordon's death remain obscure. Nobody admits to killing him or explaining exactly how he died—disobedience to the order to take Gordon alive could bring swift retribution, but there is today a plaque on a wall of the palace marking, as near as possible, where he died.

It was a party of Nujumi's men who killed him. When Nujumi comes and learns this, he is furious. He orders the body dragged down to the garden where Gordon's head is cut off and taken to Omdurman to display before the Mahdi. The rest of the body is left in the garden all day where it is jabbed by the spears of passing tribesmen—and then flung into a well.

Wrapped in chains, Slatin lies wide-eyed in the silent darkness, his head humming with a tumult of thoughts as he listens for the clamor of battle. Sleep has become a kind of helpless tumbling through blank space for him. He drifts off before dawn, but is awakened by the crash of muskets and rifles and the boom of cannon. It lasts only a matter of minutes. Then, except for the occasional rifle shot, all is quiet again.

A band of light appears on the eastern horizon. Hearing distant shouts, Slatin crawls stiffly from his tent. The purplish light takes on an orange hue. The clouds above, tinged with gold, turn red as the scarlet disk of the sun appears. Soon it blots out the horizon and bathes the Mahdi's camp in a harsh light. A crowd has collected before the quarters of the Mahdi and the khalifas. Slatin then sees the beginning of movement in his direction. A crowd advances toward him, three Blacks in the lead. One of them, a former slave named Shatta, is carrying something wrapped in a bloody cloth. He stops in front of Slatin's ragged tent and unwraps the cloth.

Dervishes showing Gordon's head to Slatin

It is Gordon's head, the blue eyes half open, the hair and short whiskers almost white except as stained with blood. "Is this the head of your uncle, the unbeliever?"

"What of it?" asks Slatin. "A brave soldier who fell at his post. Happy is he to have fallen; sufferings are over."

The grisly trophy is taken to the Mahdi who asks, "What is this?"

"This is Gordon's head."

"What deeds are these? Why did you disobey my orders? Why have you mutilated him and cut off his head? What is the use of it?" The Mahdi's eyes darken in anger, for he respects Gordon to whom he has written eleven letters—a respect that is mutual. Still, Gordon is the enemy, so the Mahdi orders that his head be fixed between two branches of a tree at the southern end of Omdurman, that all who pass may stone it. Thus, "by those for whom he lived he died."

Sixty hours pass before the British arrive. At last, their steamer has cleared the rapids. During the afternoon of January 27, a man on the left bank shouts out that Khartoum has fallen and that Gordon is dead. Nobody believes him. The next day, though, they sight Khartoum in the distance above the trees with palm groves scorched and houses wrecked. The palace stands out plainly, but no flag is flying.

Plundering Dervishes ransack Khartoum and then raze it completely. They leave only the palace and the Austrian mission church standing. To reveal where jewelry and money are hidden, they flog merchants and wealthy householders. They imprison those thought to be infidels. They take men and women across the river to Omdurman and herd them into compounds. Starvation and smallpox will later take care of the rest. All loot that has been recovered is placed in the public treasury to be shared according to each man's status and reputation in battle. Gordon's notes and papers are publicly burned or left in the streets for goats to eat. Martin Hansal is killed by one of his orderlies, who had been on bad terms with him. The Greek consul has his hands cut off and is then beheaded. Ibrahim Fawzi is bound to a palm tree for several days and flogged until he tells where his valuables can be found. Lupton and Slatin are put with other prisoners in an immense zeriba, given uncooked sorghum to eat and locked up at night in a common cell called the "house of stone," swarming with scorpions and vermin.

After the trashing of Khartoum, the Mahdi makes Omdurman his capital. Now in his late thirties, he abandons himself to a soft life. Grown fat, his body is anointed each day with sandalwood oil, his eyes painted with antimony. He trades his patched jibba for drawers and a shirt, which are scented before he puts them on. In his house in Omdurman he reclines on pillows of gold brocade with thirty women to take care of him: pitch-black Nile women, copper-colored Abyssinians, and little Turkish girls, barely more than eight years old, fanning him with ostrich feathers and massaging his feet and hands.

A month later, on June 22, 1885, the Mahdi dies, whether from poison—as alleged by some—or, more likely, from typhus, as Slatin and Ohrwalder say. Like Gordon's, the exact details of his death remain a mystery. He leaves behind the four wives permitted in Islam and fifteen concubines, the same number as the Prophet Muhammad. Before dying, he designates Abdallahi his successor.

The bond between the Mahdi and the Khalifa is like that between the Prophet and his successor, Abu Bakr: "He is of the Mahdi…and the Mahdi is of him…The Khalifa Abdallahi is the Commander of the Faithful, and is my khalifa and agent in all religious matters. Therefore, I leave off as I have begun—believe in him, obey his orders, never doubt what he says, but give all your confidence to him and trust him in all your affairs. May God be with you all. Amen."

Despite the Mahdi's deathbed wishes, heated disagreement breaks out almost immediately within the council of notables. Leaders of the riverain tribes and many Sufis are opposed to the Khalifa Abdallahi, who remains silently apart. Ultimately, one of the notables takes his hand and swears loyalty. Others follow and lastly, reluctantly, the ashraf, who are the Mahdi's closest relations and the least disposed to accept a Baggara as their leader.

A public oath of allegiance takes place in the open mosque outside the room in which the Mahdi's body lies, and proclamations are sent out ordering the provincial governors to administer the oath to their troops. Clansmen or clients of the Khalifa soon replace all of them, except Osman Digna. Thus, power passes uneasily from the relatives of the Mahdi and the Nile tribes who supported them to the Taaisha of the western Sudan and their clients. But at the subordinate and clerical level where literacy and administrative skills are prerequisites, the awlad al-balad, the riverain people, retain their posts, maintaining that illiterate and unsophisticated nomads from the western Sudan, whom others jeeringly refer to as "Our lords the Taaisha," are unqualified to replace them.

– CHAPTER 7: THE KHALIFA –

THE KHALIFA'S RULE

THE KHALIFA NEVER LEAVES OMDURMAN. STILL wearing his greasy jibba, he lives grandly with his bodyguard and retinue of eunuchs in a two-story house furnished with carpets and curtains taken from Khartoum. Each day, he arises at dawn to go to the mosque.

The Khalifa

Since he is now quite fat, he depends on Abu Takku, reputedly the most powerful man in the Sudan, to lift him onto his horse. Women fall on the ground behind him and embrace his footprints in the hope that they will cure their illnesses or ensure a quick and painless delivery of their babies. After prayer and a nap and a conference with his emirs, the Khalifa rides out once again, black flag in front and his escort behind, to review his soldiers. Midday prayers, then he is back behind the walls of his house. After sunset prayers and announcements at the mosque, his day ends with a fifth and final meeting for prayer and an evening meal before retiring to his harem and his seventy wives and concubines—"mothers of the faithful"—who wear jewelry and ornaments, and dress in silk. Theirs is a privileged position, as one recalls: "Once I was a young and beautiful girl. When the Khalifa came to Metemma, I hid in a date palm, but the Khalifa's men saw me, and dragged me forth, taking me to the Khalifa himself…I was taken to his Harim, and I found favour in his eyes. So now I am a wealthy woman."

No one can look at his face. Anyone wanting to talk to him approaches on all fours, eyes fixed on the ground, addressing him as "Ya Sidi," and when leaving, head still bent, retires backwards. (A former Egyptian soldier, who out of habit addresses him "Effendim," the Turkish mode of respect, is beaten so severely for this indiscretion that he dies a few days later.) At the mosque, when the Khalifa mounts the pulpit, everyone keeps his head lowered and eyes downcast while he is speaking.

His most trusted adviser and commander in chief of his troops is his half-brother, Yaaqub. A short stout man, very dark, face pitted by smallpox, with high projecting cheekbones, deeply set eyes, slight mustache and beard, he has taken one of the Mahdi's daughters as his wife. More educated than the Khalifa, he can read, write, and recite the Koran. He is wholly devoted to his brother, standing all night at his door, not wanting to disturb his sleep as he waits for him to come out at dawn to pray. When the Khalifa is near death, he reaches for his sword, which is hanging beside him, and places it across his knees to indicate that should he die he, Yaaqub, will carry on his mission. The Khalifa opens his eyes, reaches across for the sword, and says, "One will never succeed me because the Mahdiya will die at the time of my death."

His army is composed largely of Jihadiya, who receive regular rations of grain while ordinary citizens remain near famine. Also they are exempted from attending the prayers that take place in the large open space adjacent to the Mahdi's tomb, roofed over by mats and set aside as a mosque where each day thousands assemble. Female slaves brought from Kordofan serve as their wives. Having formerly been the troops of the old Turco-Egyptian army, they are mistrusted by most ordinary citizens, resented for their privileges, and generally regarded as a public nuisance. The Khalifa doesn't punish them or curtail their arrogance since they are armed with rifles. More trusted are the Arabs coming from different tribes, who keep arriving in Omdurman and serve as the army's swordsmen and spearmen. Having earlier counted their wealth in flocks of goats, they are now drawn to the town by dreams of leading armies into battle and taking over whole provinces. They come also to visit the tomb of the Mahdi with its eighty-foot dome, which is deemed holier than going to Mecca.

Omdurman has a population of one hundred and fifty thousand and spreads out in a honeycomb of flat-roofed huts and narrow streets stretching six miles along the Blue Nile. On market days, fifty or sixty women and rather fewer men, their bodies rubbed with oil and their owners touting their pedigrees, are offered up for sale, ten to twenty pounds the going rate for a pretty young concubine. When one of his governors asks how to handle people who claim dire poverty, the Khalifa tells them they should be given slaves from the bait al-mal—the treasury.

Wanting Baggara to be the backbone of his army, he sends an emir to induce them to migrate to Omdurman: "If you rely on delaying in your land, and if your wealth and children and homes are dearer to you than God and His Apostle and the holy war for His sake, then Allahu akbar, Allahu akbar, Allahu akbar. And prepare to fight." Taaisha and Habbaniya begin coming to Omdurman in large numbers, but not the Rizaigat and Humr. The Khalifa's emir is ordered to burn the crops of these recalcitrants and foment discord, and each tribe is told to take the property of the other because they are corrupt.

The Khalifa's open reliance upon the Baggara deepens the rift between him and the riverain people who have been the Mahdi's principal followers. At their center are the Mahdi's kinsmen—the ashraf—who are told to give up their war drums and slave troops and plant their flags in front of Yaaqub's quarters as proof of their new allegiance. Although the ever-loyal Yaaqub does what he can to make peace with them, they never acquiesce. Their leader, Muhammad Sharif, tries to poison the Khalifa and winds up in chains. The Khalifa is plagued by rebellions. Some are religious in nature, such as that of the followers of a rebel leader who claims to be Jesus Christ. Others are fueled by tribal jealousies, past injuries, and unsettled wrongdoings. When they refuse to pay taxes, sixty-seven of the Batahin are arrested and brought to Omdurman where some are hanged, others decapitated or have their right hand and foot hacked off. Among those who openly defy the Khalifa is Madibbo of the Rizaigat. Denied authority over southern Darfur, his tribal homeland, he rises against the Khalifa and is executed. He is the same man who, a few years earlier, counseled Slatin on the importance of obedience and patience.

NUJUMI INTO EGYPT

Al-Nijumi, "the star child" in Arabic, has been with the Mahdi from the very beginning. He plans the defeat of Hicks and leads the Ansar in the final assault on Khartoum. He is driven by a mystic faith in the power of Mahdism, the natural outlet for his wild temper. But his virtues—fearlessness, fanaticism, asceticism, and single-mindedness in his devotion to the Mahdi—can blind his judgment. Setting fire to his house in Omdurman, he vows not to return until he has conquered Egypt, which had been the Mahdi's firmest resolve. He is deluded into believing that the people of Upper Egypt—particularly the village of Binban known to be a nest of Mahdist sympathizers—are waiting for a sign to rise up and join him.

When Nujumi is ready to embark on his quixotic campaign, the Ansar emirs stretch out their hands toward Cairo, calling out, "Allahu Akbar" three times, as the Khalifa exhorts them, "O Ansar, the whole land of Egypt will fall into your hands." (Like the Prophet Mohammed, who died before he could take Syria and other parts of the world, it was not necessary for the Mahdi to live until his vow had been fulfilled.)

Nujumi sets forth with a mixed force of five thousand Baggara, Jaaliyin, and Shaigiya—and a like number of the women, children, and other camp followers. No one believes that he can successfully undertake so wild a project. To advance over hundreds of miles of waterless desert in summer is madness. Babikr Badri, who goes with him, writes: "My father said that al-Nujumi was a fool to set off to invade Egypt without supplies; but my mother told him not to speak ill of Nujumi, who she said ought to be the fourth of the khalifas. She would take my father's cheek between her finger and thumb and say, 'Hey, don't prophesy defeat for the faithful of the Mahdi.'"

Nujumi's army passes through Nubian villages too poor to support so large a force. Camp followers survive on powdered date seeds and the core of date palms. Once he reaches the borders of Egypt, there is no relief from harassment by an enemy that controls the Nile. The Egyptian government isn't strong enough to attack the invaders, but it can deny them access to the river. Nujumi's letters to the Khalifa tell how gunboats shadow them and prevent them from drawing water and gathering dates along the banks, how the number of his camels and other livestock has declined, and how some of his army have deserted to the enemy. Nevertheless, he labors on, rejecting the advice of his emirs to fall back until supplies can be replenished. Foremost in his mind is the disgrace that awaits him in Omdurman if he retreats. "No, by God, I will retreat only as a cold corpse. If we are hungry and thirsty, we are after all fighting in a holy war. Let us endure in patience until we triumph either with victory or with martyrdom."

Proceeding parallel to the river but keeping well in the desert, he can't prevent parties from sneaking down to the river after the exhausting night marches. Babikr Badri describes the risks they take: "I took the two water skins and the two donkeys to the river. Seeing that the steamer was there in the middle of the river, I tied the mouth of one of the water skins to my neck, put down my spear and lay down on the ground and rolled over and over until I reached the water. When the skin was soft and pliable I filled it, holding its mouth downstream for fear that, if the water entered too quickly, the soldiers on the steamer would hear the bubbling sound and fire at me. Returning to the camp, I would sell six cups of water for six riyals and buy green dates and foundered meat to give my family for the only meal of the day ... Twenty-seven days without the taste of bread left my body very weak ... When I had performed my ablutions without water and was praying, my 'God is most great!' was just a moan. Yet, if they had brought me a Koran, I would have sworn upon it that we would still conquer Egypt. What a spirit was this!"

Grenfell Pasha, the commander-in-chief of the Egyptian forces, sends messages to Nujumi that his campaign was hopeless and urges surrender: "You intend to reach Binban whose people you think are inclined to you. But you do not know that between you and it are hundreds of leagues, filled only with sands and rocks and without water. Suppose you arrive there—and this is a stroke of fancy—you will find only English and Egyptian armies, long trained and dreaming only of shedding the blood of their enemies. They await your coming, hour by hour, to drink your blood and send you to destruction."

On the morning of August 4, 1889, near the village of Tushki sixty miles inside Egypt, heavy fighting takes place, much of it hand-to-hand. No ground is better suited for disciplined and well-armed troops: undulating desert of hard, shingly sand, over which infantry, cavalry, and artillery can move easily and where modern arms can work with deadly effect. Nujumi's men charge again and again with desperate bravery—until finally forced to retreat. They take up a second strong position against which a Sudanese regiment under British officers advance with drums beating and bugles blowing. Before long, the Dervish army is in full retreat.

Galloping over ground strewn with drums, swords, spears, and chain-armor, a solitary rider tries to rally the dispersed Dervish troops, until his horse is shot out from under him. His bodyguard places the wounded rider on a rough camel-litter to carry him to the rear. Again fired on, the camel falls. The bodyguard risks their lives in defense of Nujumi's revered corpse. One of Nujumi's sons, aged five, lies dead beside the camel. Of the fifty-seven hundred fighting men and eight thousand camp followers who have crossed into Egypt, only one thousand soldiers and two thousand camp followers return to their homes in the Sudan.

Ohrwalder and Slatin Escape

Back in Omdurman, the greatest problem Father Ohrwalder faces is food. He tries various ways to earn a living. He goes into soap making with Lupton; then makes hooks out of telegraph wire, and, after that, ribbons on a small loom. The mission sisters with him eke out a precarious livelihood by needlework. They have witnessed the full horrors of the famine in 1889 when dead by the hundreds lay in the street, and men and women were reduced to eating boiled leather and grinding up skins and bones to make bread, tearing open the bowels of donkeys to eat the intestines, or stealing children to eat.

In 1891 Ohrwalder escapes with Sisters Venturini and Chincarini and a little black girl named Adila, who was born in the mission house in Khartoum. The moment of departure is the most fraught with risk because the camels are restive and anxious to be off. The two nuns are each mounted behind an Arab, and Ohrwalder takes Adila behind him on his camel. With a guide, they leave Omdurman under cover of darkness. The well-fed camels glide away quickly, softly passing cooking fires where people are sitting around gossiping. In the darkness, they skirt villages where the barking of dogs has given them warning, and they avoid being seen. They pass by some Jellaba on donkeys. Their guide stays behind to exchange greetings and news. Before daybreak, they leave the regular track altogether to avoid villages, and, at length, dismount, eat some biscuits, drink a little water, and cinch up their saddles. Then, it's up and away again. Ohrwalder's eyes are so red and swollen he can scarcely see. One of the nuns falls to the ground, exhausted, and is knocked unconscious. She is revived, lifted back up, and tied to the saddle. Some shepherds, tending goats, ask questions of the guide, who purposely remains behind out of earshot.

When they dismount to eat dates and drink some water, Ohrwalder's legs are so stiff that he cannot stand up straight. But after feeding the camels a little sorghum, they are off again. Seeing some camel men in the distance, they hide in a bushy ravine. Reaching the Nile, they give two dollars to a boatman who kisses their hands and wishes them a safe journey. They water the animals, fill waterskins, mount, and again set off. Antelopes, about twenty paces off, prick up their ears and look inquisitively at them. The sun beats down, and the horizon swims in mirages. Traversing a stony place they hear a hissing, which alarms the Arabs who regard snakes as an evil omen, and the lead camel swerves suddenly before resuming its pace. The high fat hump and thick necks of their once-healthy camels have by now shrunk to half the size. At the start, it was difficult to hold them back; now they must be constantly whipped. Ohrwalder is totally exhausted and tries every means to keep awake, talking loudly to his companions and startling himself awake by giving a sudden jerk. Instinctively knowing when their riders are asleep, the camels fall into an even slower pace. Ohrwalder's head nods and sinks down onto his chest, until, with a jerk, equilibrium is recovered and sleep momentarily vanishes.

Seven days' travel brings them in sight of the fort that defends the wells at Murat. They fire their rifles, and the small garrison answers their salute by discharging their guns in the air. The little caravan has covered a distance of five hundred miles.

As for Slatin, life in Omdurman is going from bad to worse. In prison a heavy iron bar with rings weighing eighteen pounds is hammered onto his ankles. One of the wives of the principle jailer takes pity on him and boils the only food—sorghum—he receives. At night he lies on the ground, a stone for his pillow. After he finds the discarded lining of a donkey saddle, he sleeps—"like a king." And in the morning the door is opened. He hobbles down to the Nile to wash and defecate before assembling with the other prisoners—some eighty Greeks and other Europeans—for prayers. Lupton's Abyssinian wife, Zenoba, sometimes comes with her little daughter to see him. And Slatin can talk to Lupton, whose hair and beard have turned white. One day, the Khalifa visits him and asks with a smile:

"Abdul Qadir, are you well?"

"I am well, Sidi. I have sinned and I repent before Allah and His Prophet. I lie here patiently on the bare ground waiting for the time when I may receive pardon."

"As you are a foreigner, I spared your life. However, if your repentance is real and true, I will pardon both you and Abdallahi—Lupton."

He tells the warden to take off Slatin's chains. He also gives him a wife, described by Slatin as having "an ugly black face, two little eyes, a great flat nose and enormous blubber-shaped lips, which when she laughed, were in danger of coming in contact with her ears." When Slatin complains, the Khalifa feigns indignation, but that evening Slatin finds a younger girl in his hut.

After months in chains, he can walk only with difficulty. As a "mulazim," a kind of courtier or bodyguard, he sits at the door of the Khalifa's house and cross-legged before him in the mosque. Cramps are one of the severest trials he has to face. He accompanies the Khalifa when he goes out, trotting along beside him when he is riding, but later is given a donkey of his own to ride. At heart, the Khalifa likes Slatin, who takes great interest in Sudan affairs, and enjoys talking to him. He is also flattered to have a former high government official under his control. "See, this is the man who was formerly our master; now he is my slave."

Poor Lupton, however, has a sad ending. After a while, he gets work in the dockyard repairing steamers and then making ammunition and percussion caps with another prisoner named Hasan Zaki, who had previously been a doctor in Khartoum. An explosion seriously damages Lupton's eyesight, and his health deteriorates rapidly. Ill with meningitis, he asks Slatin to look after Fanna, his daughter, and Zaki to look after his wife, Zenuba—whom Zaki later marries. In 1888, at just thirty years of age, he dies. Slatin arranges for his body to be washed, wrapped in a shroud, and carried to the mosque for the customary prayers.

In 1895, Slatin is able to follow where Ohrwalder has gone. With the help of Ohrwalder, who is then in Suakin, British officials arrange for his escape. After months of waiting for clandestine meetings with mysterious intermediaries who would take him in hand, Slatin finally makes his move. He tells the Khalifa, "I am ill, and I intend to take a purgative before the arrival of the month of Ramadan." A boat will be waiting for him at the pier, so he tells his servant, "I want to go to Abu Ruf jetty to buy some sorghum." That night he crosses by boat to the east bank. On the camel that has been brought for him he races into the desert, hides in caves, and subsists on sorghum and dates.

Slatin escapes

171

He takes his camel down to river settlements to feed and water and searches for the guide who will handle the next stage of his journey. The Khalifa, deeply angered by Slatin's escape, alerts villages and ferry crossings along the way to be on the lookout. In some villages, Slatin's guides have kinsmen who warn of dangers and offer asylum and food. His guide for the final stage of his flight asks what he will earn by taking him to Aswan.

"On the day of my arrival, I will pay you there one hundred and twenty Maria Theresa dollars, and in addition, a present, which I shall calculate according to the manner in which you accomplish your duties."

"I accept. Allah and the Prophet are my witnesses that I trust you. I know your race. A white man does not lie. I will bring you to your own folk across untrodden mountain ways known only to the fowls of the air. Be ready. After the sun is down, we start."

They have but one camel between them. The route takes them though difficult, mountainous country. The guide, an old man, suffers from the cold mountain air and becomes sick, so Slatin gives him his jibba. Slatin's feet are badly bruised and cut, and his camel can hardly walk. At last, with Slatin and the camel limping after the elderly guide, they descend into the town of Aswan.

Some British officers are sitting in the officers' mess. Addressing one of them, the waiter says:

"There is a man outside who asks to see your Excellency."

"Tell him he can wait till I have had lunch."

"The man insists. He begs in Allah's name to be allowed to see Your Excellency."

"I'm damned if he can't wait. Who is he? What does he want?"

"He is a wretched, poor man, and he is dirty. He is squatting outside."

Such conduct is most unusual, and the British officer becomes mildly intrigued; so the man is brought in.

"Who are you?"

"I am Abdul Qadir."

"Have you any other name?" Then remembering Slatin's Arabic name, the officer exclaims, "Good God above! Are you Slatin?"

"Yes, I am Slatin."

BATTLE OF OMDURMAN

March 18, 1896—to the music of Scottish pipes, English flutes, drums, and brass, a force of more than twenty thousand with guns and gunboats and a column of camels and horses, sets forth to avenge Gordon's death.

Gunboat in the Cataracts

An army of Egyptian, Sudanese, and British officers under the command of the sirdar, Horatio Herbert Kitchener, presses slowly up the Nile via Dongola, Abu Hamed, and Berber.

Months later, at Atbara, they storm the zeriba of the emir Mahmud wad Ahmad, the Khalifa's cousin and principal agent in the west. He has collected tribesmen in Kordofan and Darfur to confront the invaders, and at Atbara two thousand Dervishes die. Mahmud, awaiting death on his sheepskin, is taken prisoner and brought before Kitchener in chains. Kitchener, on horseback, asks, "Why did you come here to burn and kill?" Mahmud stares proudly before him and answers, "I obeyed my orders as you obey yours." As he is dragged away, he adds, "You will pay for this at Omdurman. Compared to the Khalifa, I am but a leaf."

On September 1, 1898, the Anglo-Egyptian troops see the dome of the Mahdi's tomb looming above the blurred horizon. When their gunboats are within range, shells begin to strike the shrine itself. The Khalifa cries out, "They fear not God but have destroyed the qubba… We built the qubba from mud…we will rebuild it with mud."

The Khalifa deploys his army in battle formation on the plains of Karari immediately to the north of Omdurman. A long line, four miles from end to end, comprising hundreds of banners and fifty thousand Dervishes, at the center of which are twelve thousand Jihadiya with rifles and thirteen thousand spearmen under the command of Yaaqub and the Khalifa's bodyguard of two thousand. On the right wing two thousand Dongolawis under the khalifa Sharif and seventeen hundred Hadendowa under Osman Digna, and on the left wing, the khalifa Ali wad Hilu with five thousand warriors. An hour before dawn, they pray together for the last time and, to shouts of "Allahu Akbar" attack straight into the British artillery fire. Their cavalry is formidable, the muzzles of their rifles press against the flanks of their horses as they swing their heavy swords. But courage is not enough against the Maxim automatic machine gun, which is being used for the first time in a major campaign. G.W. Steevens, the war correspondent, writes from the battlefield, "Our men were perfect, but the Dervishes were superb—beyond perfection. It was their largest, best and bravest army … and it died worthily of the empire Mahdism won and kept so long. Their riflemen, mangled by every kind of death and torment that man can devise, clung round the black flag and the green, emptying their poor, rotten, home-made cartridges dauntlessly. Their spears charged death at every minute hopelessly … A dusky line got up and stormed forward; it bent, broke up, fell apart, and disappeared. Before the smoke had cleared, another line was bending and storming forward in the same track."

A blind sheikh, Abdul Rahman Ahmad, waiting on horseback after the initial attack, asks, "Where is Yaaqub?"

"He's gone ahead of the enemy."

"Where are the infidels?"

"They are in front of you."

He asks that his horse be turned to face them, then unsheathes his sword and dashes forward, colliding with the front ranks of the enemy where horse and blind rider fall to the ground.

Yaaqub learns that the emir Khalil of the black standard has been killed. He raises his spear: "Ansar, look at us now! Young men like Ibrahim al-Khalil have gone to their eternal resting place. Here we are still on horseback...A tabaldi tree has fallen. A tabaldi has fallen on the infidels. Raise your banners aloft and let your horses charge."

Yaaqub with thousands of the black flag behind him leads a last desperate charge until struck down by machine-gun fire. Still clutching his spear, he falls from his horse.

Yaaqub and the Black Flag

Amid a tempest of bullets, two horsemen dismount and raise his body to take it to the rear, but they, too, fall victims to the Maxim. When the Khalifa learns that his devoted Yaaqub had been killed, "he lost interest in the course of the battle. He suffered from a shock that was never to leave him. All he wished was to seek martyrdom on his farwa."

Within two hours, ten thousand Dervish bodies lay strewn on the desert, while Kitchener's casualties are but four hundred. When British bullets hit Dervishes, they fall, for the British are using soft-nosed dum-dums that inflict gaping wounds. "It was not a battle, but an execution."

Seeing the corpses pile up on the battlefield, Kitchener orders, "Cease fire! What a dreadful waste of ammunition!" He adds the Khalifa's black flag to his own, and—after a break for lunch—rides into Omdurman. He disregards the ongoing plunder of grain and the destruction of the Mahdi's tomb, and considers impassively the damage done by the three hundred, fifty-pounder shells that had been poured upon the city: the dead and dying, the cries of the wounded, and the smell of rotting carcasses lying in the afternoon heat. Many of the wounded have now been killed—and often not necessarily to put them out of their agony. Some of them remain on the field exposed to the sun, crawling a few yards each day toward the Nile in quest of water. Others lay under small bushes and are kept alive by women who slip out after dark to bury their dead and bring food and water. "The quiet hills each night listened to the wails of the bereaved digging graves." Kitchener orders the release of some thirty prisoners and walks in the palace garden below the stairs where Gordon had been killed.

Slatin, who had accompanied the army, rushes up: "The Khalifa has left the city."

"When?"

"Two hours ago."

"In what direction?"

"To the south."

Accompanied by members of his family, one of his wives, his most faithful followers, and some of his emirs and Jihadiya, the Khalifa flees to the southwest. They hack their way through the forest until they reach Umm Dibaykarat in the Nuba hills. Ali wad Hilu approaches the Khalifa and says, "I remember, ya Khalifa al-Mahdi, what the Mahdi, peace on him, said when we passed by this place coming from El Obeid. He said that both of us would lie in this place."

Deciding that it is here that he will make his final stand, Abdullahi addresses those around him: "You have been with me throughout the bloody conflict between the enemy and myself. I lost more than half my army at Omdurman. I have now decided to face the enemy and seek martyrdom here. I release you from your allegiance to me. Whoever wishes to leave now, before the enemy's assault, let him do so. I absolve everybody. I am satisfied with you all."

He spends the night receiving allegiance anew. Drums and cymbals beat. Two hours before dawn, on November 24, 1899, astride his charger, he deploys his forces. At first light, Col. Reginald Wingate, commanding the "flying column" of Egyptian troops that had been sent in pursuit, orders cannons, machine guns, and riflemen to open fire. The Khalifa and his followers dismount, face Mecca, and roll out their sheepskins. Abdallahi places one of his khalifas on his right and the other on his left. Their emirs sit around them unflinchingly and silently wait. But khalifa Ali wad Hilu cannot bear the pressure. He unsheathes his sword, rises slowly, and limps forward. Abdallahi calls him back to meet his fate—the last words the Khalifa uttered. Three balls hit him in the chest, one penetrating his heart.

— Chapter 8: The Legacy —

The Legacy

The Mahdi inveighed against moral decline, earthly vanities, and social inequities. He called on people to be more self-consciously Islamic and on jihad to implement Islam in one's personal life and in society. Deviating from orthodox belief in the direct relationship between God and the individual Muslim, he proclaimed himself the Mahdi of Allah and representative of the Prophet. His message became the unique heritage of the Sudan. It was an entirely internal development. It provided an alternative to a remote and impersonal government. It promised to rid the Sudan of a heavy-handed foreign authority of "Turks" and Christians and arrogant Bashibazuks who looted with abandon. And he told the people of Egypt he would do the same for them.

Jihad is not present in popular Islam, but with Mahdism it became a valid response to autocratic authority and foreign mercenaries. The Mahdi's message fulfilled a need for guidance amid the confusion that stemmed from Gordon and Gessi's zeal in suppressing the slave trade in a land where keeping slaves was not a crime. What he preached provided a way out of a world of tribal rivalries, competing sects, and regional jealousies. It united a mixed population behind an overarching religious purpose: the concept of the Islamic "umma"—community— as a unifying force. His commitment was to the unity of the Sudan, bridging tribal divisions. Arab tribes married within kinship groups, but Mahdists could marry across tribes. Maqbula herself, a wife of the Mahdi and mother of Abdul Rahman, had a Darfur father and a mother from the south. Even though he was from the Nile valley, Muhammad Ahmad was able to enlist the loyalties of the western Sudanese. Dinka and other Nilotics who had been in the thrall of the zeribas, assisted in the spread of his revolution—at least for a time. Many of the Mahdi's emirs were from the south, where they had been slave soldiers under Zubair. Everyone became a potential Ansar. Whoever accepted Muhammad Ahmad as the Expected Mahdi—as the reincarnation of the Prophet—and read his "ratib," a simple prayer book, was Ansar. All others were "unbelievers," whether Muslim or non-Muslim. Devout Sufis could marry into Ansar. They could become Ansar without giving up their Sufi rituals. Islam became part of the Sudanese culture. It brought people out of the fourteenth century and into the nineteenth century. They were no longer content chasing after cows.

The Mahdi urged people to arise from their lethargy and regain their God-ordained heritage and identity. He united the four Muslim rites in a ritual accessible to all. He urged the common people to espouse the ratib, with which they could identify. It enabled them to understand what before had been accessible only to the clergy. He affirmed the Sufi concept of "zuhd"—self-denial—as epitomized by the patched jibba, and purged Islam of its faults and accretions. He introduced new prohibitions against adornment, music, extravagance, tobacco, and wine, and he reduced the amount of the bride price the groom must pay. He said that women are the key to change in society. He prescribed punishments against theft and other crimes. He made visiting Omdurman equivalent to the onerous obligation of pilgrimage to Mecca. He gave practical meaning and expression to ideological traditions that have spawned Islamist movements across the Muslim world.

His advent is not found in the Koran. References to the Mahdi appear in the "hadiths"—the statements of the Prophet. However, the Mahdi did not entirely fulfill his prescribed role. He did not conquer Jerusalem or fill the world with justice. Some believe that his "hadras"—assemblies with the Prophet—were largely speculation. What he did achieve, though, was through his baraka, charismatic leadership, and his military success against better-armed forces sent against him: Abul-Suoud at Aba, Hicks and al-Shallali in Kordofan, Valentine Baker in the Red Sea hills, Slatin in Darfur, and Gordon in Khartoum. He made Omdurman his missionary capital, the soul of the Sudan. Racial attitudes persisted, but there was intermingling of tribes and intermarriage of ethnicities. Physically, Omdurman was linked to the western Sudan and to Egypt where his next battle lay. It represented the first authentic attempt against tribalism. The Sudan was united by religion, whereas elsewhere nationalism was the unifying force.

His successor, Khalifa Abdallahi, mobilized the people of the western Sudan behind the Mahdi. He convinced Muhammad Ahmad to move to Jebel Gedir and engage the support of Baggara Arabs and Tijaniya Sufis from the western Sudan. The concept of an Expected Mahdi had always been a part of their beliefs, and this Sudanese Mahdi promised to fulfill that expectation.

But the Khalifa was unable to inherit the spiritual force needed to sustain this unity. He was unable to overcome the inherent distrust existing between Nile dwellers and Arabs from interior regions. He did what he could to achieve reconciliation and make his rule popular, but, in the end, he couldn't check the erosion of authority that began almost immediately after the Mahdi died.

The Anti-Slavery Society in Europe spread fresh accounts of the Khalifa's brutalities. Slatin and Ohrwalder wrote first-hand descriptions, which were heavily edited by Wingate to convince British public that the "reconquest" of the Sudan—ostensibly on behalf of Egypt—was unavoidable and could be carried out without difficulty. The Khalifa was portrayed as a debauched beast, cruel and vain—the Sudan, as hell on earth. With accounts of atrocities, such as inflicted on the Batahin, and, smarting from the failure of the Relief Expedition and the humiliation of Gordon's death, England was bent on vengeance. The Khalifa was the archenemy, a barbarous despot from whose tyranny the Sudanese would be released by the British-led invasion.

Overlooked in most accounts were the Khalifa's efforts to restore order in the backwash of the Mahdi's revolt. He extended Mahdist rule to Sennar, Blue Nile, and Kassala in the eastern Sudan, governing an area twice the size of Europe. His task was made more difficult because of the uncertain loyalty of the Ashraf and Nile dwellers from which the Mahdi had drawn his ruling elite. Nor was he ever fully in command of his provincial officials. He had to contend with localized revolts and intermittent war with Abyssinia. Overlooked also were his efforts to establish norms pertaining to the status, transfer, and treatment of slaves. He forbade their export—but the principal slave-producing districts of southwestern Sudan were no longer under his control.

To make his rule more popular, he lightened the burden of taxes. His tax of "zaka"—alms tax—was less onerous than government taxes had been before. No European captive was put to death. After the defeat of Nujumi's army, the threat of Mahdist expansion into Egypt was dispelled. Rumors of tribal backing, particularly on the part of the Shukriya and Jaaliyin that had been most clamorous for outside intervention, proved unfounded. Caught up in the drumbeat of jingoism, the British failed to appreciate the breadth of support for the Khalifa that existed at that time.

In the final showdown, forty thousand Sudanese from diverse tribes and different parts of the Sudan rallied to his banner against the infidels. They fought with extraordinary bravery and, despite staggering losses at Kerari, there were no mutinies among them afterward. The emirs who survived the massacre were among the eight thousand who went with the Khalifa to Umm Dibaykarat where others joined to make yet another stand. But modern bolt-action rifles, Maxim machine guns, and dum-dum bullets gave the British every advantage against the aging breechloaders, elephant guns, and homemade ammunition of the Mahdists. Even so, the final battle against fanatical resistance ended only with the death of the Khalifa on November 24, 1899. Only then was Wingate able to declare, "Now and only now the Mahdiya is over." Gordon's death, at last, had been avenged.

The overall conduct of the victors was less than heroic. Kitchener often seemed a heartless tyrant. His army killed outright twelve thousand Dervishes at Kerari and dispatched an additional sixteen thousand of the wounded, many of whom would have probably died anyway from untreated wounds. In some cases, finishing off the wounded may have been justified to prevent them, before dying, from taking more infidel lives. Still, Winston Churchill would conclude "that the victory of

Omdurman was disgraced by the inhuman slaughter of the wounded and that Kitchener was responsible for this." The desecration of the Mahdi's tomb, sacred to all who worshipped Allah, was an act of raw vengeance and nothing more. Kitchener toyed with the idea of using the Mahdi's skull as an inkstand or drinking cup or sending it to the museum of the College of Surgeons in England. This suggestion produced a howl of rage—"even the Queen expressed shock."

The Mahdist state would not have lasted as long as it did if it had been governed solely by greed and inhumanity. Life was no worse than under the Turkiya, and, toward the end of the Khalifa's rule, there was no mass exodus of refugees. A coherent Islamic state—albeit a turbulent one—had been established and lasted for a decade and a half. At a terrible price, however: A population of seven million prior to the Mahdist revolt dwindled to a bare two million afterward—though there are no records to confirm these numbers.

Wars and slave trade destroyed thousands each year. Smallpox and syphilis were endemic. Plagues of locusts blocked out the sun and turned croplands into desert overnight. An acute viral disease called rinderpest wiped out whole herds of cattle. Entire tribes migrated to Omdurman, forsaking normal cultivation and husbandry. The horrific famine of 1889—at the height of the Khalifa's reign—was as much due to dislocation as to drought. By the end of the Mahdiya, hundreds of miles of Nile banks were as desolate as at the time of Baker's expedition three decades earlier.

The defeat of the Mahdists ushered in a period of suffering and hardships for the families of the Mahdi and the Khalifa and their emirs. Held captive in Egypt and in northern Sudan, many died from food shortages and disease. Slatin, newly awarded a knighthood and appointed inspector-general, seemed to have forgotten the kindness that had been shown to him by the Khalifa. The British prohibited visits to the Mahdi's cave on Aba Island, which had become a shrine, and did not respond to the appeals of his descendants for better treatment. They feared that Sufi ceremonies would lead to a revival of religious fanaticism. They imagined hordes of dervishes "waving blood-stained swords, as they hack their way through the forces of 'unbelievers' to the cry of Allah Akbar." A ban was placed on Sufi practices, their mosques, religious schools, and prayer meetings. Wearing the patched jibba could result in being pressed into a work gang. Only with the beginning of the

World War I and the resignation of Slatin—as a citizen of Austria, now an enemy power—did the government relent in its vindictive policy and recognize the depth of Mahdist sentiment.

PRESERVATION OF THE MAHDIST LEGACY

The Mahdi's youngest son, Abdul Rahman, was born twenty-two days after his father's death. He went to a khalwa and, by the age of eleven, had memorized the Koran. Forbidden to live at Aba, he settled on El Fil Island, a hundred miles from Omdurman on the Blue Nile. He was given a paltry allowance of five pounds and third-class travel warrants on government steamers and railways. He could not use the title "imam," and the expression "on him be peace" could not be appended to his name. Being addressed as "sheikh" was acceptable but not as "sayyid," the honorific title accorded to a Muslim holy man. Regarding the Ansar as still a threat, the British prohibited mass gatherings and public recitals of the Mahdi's ratib. Hardly a year passed without a feki declaring himself to be the Mahdi or the Nabi Isa—the Christ—who would return and kill the Antichrist and fill the world with justice. These millennial impulses were most prevalent in the western Sudan.

Nearly a century before the Mahdi's time, people in Nigeria thought Usuman dan Fodio (1754-1817)—a pious Fulani who led a holy war to reform Islam in the north—was the Mahdi. He didn't deny it at first, although later he told them that the Expected Mahdi would appear in the East, and an eastward migration of the Fellata began. According to eschatological authority, the Mahdi would appear at the beginning of the fourteenth century and it was then, in the year 1301 A.H.—year of the Hejira—that Muhammad Ahmad declared himself the Mahdi. Alarmed by the influx of holy men from the west, the British labeled Nigerian fekis as undesirable. To forestall a resurgence of fanaticism, they took harsh measures against overzealous mystics. As a further precaution, they recalled from Cairo the leader of the Khatmiya, the only Sufi sect to openly oppose the Mahdi.

Turkey's entry into World War I did much to remove the stigma of Mahdism. Implacable foes of the Turks—and indeed the name "Turk" was synonymous with infidel—Mahdists became allies of sorts when the British most needed allies. Hadn't Mahdists always despised the Turks?

After a time, British paranoia began to wane. Abdul Rahman was given property on Aba and permission to build a waterwheel and farm the land. He toured the region on the government's behalf, conducting a quiet campaign to revive Mahdism as a religious brotherhood. Ansar arrived at Aba to cultivate his fields, and, through them and pilgrims returning from Mecca, his influence penetrated deeper into Kordofan and Darfur where the Mahdist legacy was most keenly felt. By then the resurgence of Mahdism was no longer seen as a revolutionary threat. Why shouldn't simple people have the same right as other Sufi sects to pray according to a ratib? If Abdul Rahman could calm incipient revolts by bringing Tijaniya and other potential militants to Aba, wasn't it in the government's interest? Soon gatherings at the end of Ramadan were being attended by thousands of pilgrims, armed with swords as in the old days. Abdul Rahman arranged for the education of their children in Aba's khalwas. As Imam of the Ansar and heir to the baraka of the Mahdi, Abdul Rahman also reached out to the lesser Sufi orders, which had been denounced by his father, and invited them also to participate.

He was given permission to build his own mosque in Omdurman. He was allowed to join the delegation of religious and tribal leaders sent to England in 1919 to affirm their loyalty to the British throne. In London he presented the Mahdi's sword to King George V—which the king returned to him "that he might better defend the British Empire." How times had changed!

During World War II, rivalry between Ansar and Khatmiya sects led to the emergence of two political parties: Umma and Ashigga. Umma advocated an independent Sudan; Ashigga pressed for union with Egypt. The Umma regarded the fight for independence as a natural continuation of the Mahdi's jihad. In the last free elections, held in 1986, the Umma got forty percent of the vote: One and a half million against one million for the Khatmiya and eight hundred thousand for the fundamentalist National Islamic Front (NIF).

Today, Mahdism is enshrined in the family of the Mahdi, hence in the Umma Party. The baraka of the Mahdi passed down to its present leader, Sadiq al-Mahdi, great-grandson of the Mahdi and Imam of the Ansar. His illustrious name alone assures him legitimacy, respect, and political influence. Ansar are committed to him through a personal oath of loyalty. This allegiance is especially intense among the Baggara of the western Sudan, who were the backbone of the Mahdi's rebellion, and the Fellata, who migrated from Nigeria. They were mainly farmers and herders and poor peasants, constituting some eight million out of the twenty-five million Sudanese.

In 1970, viewing the growing influx of Ansar with alarm, Sudan's then president, Jaafar Nimeiri, threatened to attack their center on Aba Island. Al-Hadi, one of Abdul Rahman's sons, was Imam at the time. He cancelled the celebration at the end of Ramadan, but thousands of Ansar still showed up. Prepared to meet death, they arrived with swords and white shrouds for their burial. When the air attack and shelling began, they streamed into the Imam's palace. Nearly a thousand of them, representing sixty-five tribes, were killed. Imam al-Hadi was forced to flee and was later tracked down and killed.

Aba remains an Ansar center and preserve of the Mahdist legacy. Thirty-five miles long and three miles wide, with a population of some ninety thousand, the island has seventeen mosques, the most important being Masjid al-Qawn—"Mosque of the Universe"—founded by Abdul Rahman. Fields of wheat and sorghum surround its many hamlets. On holidays, urban Sudanese picnic in the lushly shaded gardens at its southern tip. Except for the mosques and Abdul Rahman's palace— now a university—a hospital, schools, and local government offices, the town proper consists of a spread of unadorned, one-story mud-brick houses. A modest dwelling on the riverbank protects the cave where the Mahdi had his first audience with the Prophet. The entrance to the cave is filled with sand, which kneeling women reverently stroke to absorb its baraka. Visitors can see where the Khalifa told the Mahdi to hide his wound so as not to dishearten his followers, where Abul-Suoud peed his pants when the Mahdi angrily expostulated, "I am not to be ordered, and if the Hikumdar wants war, I am prepared for it." A large khalwa with a dormitory for boarders from all parts of the Sudan is located not far away. A pupil from faraway Darfur proudly showed me a verse inscribed on his wooden tablet. Every day, the local Ansar association provides food for the pupils.

With the Friday call for prayers, men in sparkling white robes and turbans, wrapped in the Ansar style—a tail hanging over the shoulder—

and women in colorful "tobes" issue from houses and make their way to the mosque to perform their ablutions. Young boys, many also wearing turbans, join them. Women and girls pray in a room adjacent to the main hall of the mosque. Beginning his sermon, the Imam refers to recent events in Iraq. Afterward, the several thousand devotees stand and join in prayer. Once the service is over, the congregation meanders about, exchanging salutations and blessings. To the uninitiated, the sense of brotherhood is palpable.

Aba is almost entirely Ansar but for a few recent university graduates who are Islamists—members of the National Islamic Front or the Ansar al-Sunna, which, like the Wahhabis of Saudi Arabia, are strict fundamentalists. Every Ansari is Umma. They are not Sufis, but Sufis belong to Ansar. It is a complicated tapestry of religious and political strands, and, when questioned, villagers argue among themselves over the correct answers.

Since the death of al-Hadi more than thirty years ago, who is rightfully now the Imam? Some say the title belongs to Ahmad as the oldest son of Abdul Rahman. Others say that al-Hadi designated Sadiq as successor to prevent Ahmad from becoming Imam. Since baraka is transmitted to the Imam, however he might be chosen—not necessarily through primogeniture—Sadiq's baraka is as authentic as any claim made by Ahmad. Furthermore, Sadiq himself has always said that being Imam is not an inherited right; only the Ansar community can choose its Imam. The dispute over succession is not just a theological matter between traditionalists and pragmatists but one largely driven by political rivalry. Sadiq's objective, some say, is to strengthen his position in the Umma while Ahmad's is to fulfill the formal functions of Imam: giving speeches, attending funerals, paying condolences, inviting Ansar to banquets on holy days, and suchlike. Sadiq, a secularist at heart, argues that Islam is a culture and shouldn't be confused with politics. So now Ahmed, by inheritance, and Sadiq, elected by his supporters, both claim legitimacy. Their followers assemble on Fridays in separate mosques and belong to separate Ansar associations. The dynastic controversy has now spilled over into the Umma party, one faction allied with the government while the other, under Sadiq, in opposition. Two imams and two Umma parties: is this what is left of the legacy of Mahdism?

When asked about this legacy, Sudanese say that Ansar today are like a Sufi brotherhood: the sheikh dies and his son or brother succeeds him. But with the spread of education and the media—and there are now more women than men in universities—the Sufi model has less appeal. Young Sudanese are no longer willing to be hostage to tradition. They are no longer content being part of a flock shepherded by a sheikh, docilely accepting their fate. They are leaving the land and moving to towns where they may find a job. As Mahdist traditions lose relevance, other ideologies take hold. Communism once offered an attractive alternative, but since the Soviet collapse, they have turned to Islamism and its emphasis on institutional structures rather than dynasties and give their support to the Islamic Front.

Although the Mahdist legacy has weakened over time, it still has resonance in areas away from the Nile and the political center where citizens feel neglected and outside of the mainstream of development and social change. Friction points exist along the boundaries where different ethnicities rub against each other, where government mediation and customary controls are weak or non-existent, and where pastoral and sedentary needs come into conflict. This is especially true in times of famine, when cattle-owning Arabs, who would normally cross into Dinkaland for grazing rights, exchange the security of livestock for food in the seasonal markets of southern Kordofan and Darfur—with Jellaba merchants taking an active part in this commerce, as they have for generations.

EROSION OF THE LEGACY

After the Mahdiya, the Ngok Dinka moved permanently from Bahr al-Ghazal into southern Kordofan and established good relations with Baggara Arabs. A blood-brotherhood pact existed between them. During the lean season, the Dinka awaited the arrival of the Arabs with their surplus millet, which they preferred to their native sorghum, and the Arabs benefited from a favorable exchange of their millet for livestock. Entry points into each other's territory were agreed upon, and cultivation within the immediate vicinity of nomad wells was prohibited. At the end of the grazing season, intertribal meetings dealt with disputes, the return of hostages taken in raids, and the settlement of blood-money claims. When government veterinary services didn't cover the Baggara, the Dinka, fearing the reintroduction of disease among their own herds, invited the herdsmen to bring their cattle down to be vaccinated. That is now history. The increase in livestock that came with peace and stability in the 1950s and 1960s put pressure on grazing. Baggara had to give up some of their customary access to Dinka pastures and change their transhumance routes. Instead of returning north peacefully, they began to attack Dinka villages and cattle camps. Prolonged drought and famine in the mid 1980s made matters worse. One million cattle were lost. Baggara began their southward migration earlier than usual. Spending more time in Dinka country, they over-fished streams, cut down trees to provide forage for their goats, decimated large and small game, and overgrazed rangelands. No longer welcomed, they were harassed by Dinka, and in Darfur, they encroached on the cultivations of the sedentary Fur.

Bygone conflicts were generally sporadic and at low levels of violence. However, in the late 1980s, the long-festering separatist controversy between Khartoum and the Southern Peoples' Liberation Army—SPLA—exacerbated intertribal relations. Arabs on the borders with the SPLA were given arms, since the government was unable to provide protection. Suspecting that Dinka, being largely Christian or animist, were supporting the SPLA, the government mobilized the Baggara, who had always been Ansar and Umma voters. They were given arms and enlisted into militias as a proxy force. They were also allowed to keep what they captured as legitimate booty. Given this opportunity to replenish their herds, Baggara rampaged through Dinka settlements. The level of violence escalated sharply and, with it, memories of conditions during Turkish and Mahdist times. Dinka spears and hippopotamus skin shields were no match against AK-47s.

"Murahaleen," as the young men who accompanied livestock in seasonal movements ahead of the rest of the tribe were called, came on horses, donkeys, on foot, and in Toyota pickup trucks with machine guns. They put their horses on the train—which proceeded at little more than walking speed, supplying government garrisons in the south—and brought them out to use on raids. Spreading around a village, they burned the papyrus grass that Dinka used for building their huts. They plundered everything they could lay their hands on, sugar and pieces of cloth, even the clay pots used for carrying water. They set fire to the huts and the grain in the stores. They chopped down mango trees and contaminated wells so that Dinka would not return later. They captured women and children, who were driven, along with pillaged livestock, across the Bahr al-Arab where they were distributed among clans and sold. Only breast-feeding children were allowed to stay with their mothers. Thus, they acquired cattle, grazing land, and water, as well as field hands and domestic labor. The sale of Dinka animals and women became a means of getting rich. Abductions provided hands for tending livestock, clearing land for agriculture, drawing water from wells, and building zeribas. They did what in Arab eyes was considered as degrading work, fit only for slaves.

Dinka called them Jellaba because Arab depredations recalled Egyptian and Mahdist times, when slave abductions were used to terrorize African populations. "Where are the cattle that that God gave the Dinka at Creation to be the noblest form of wealth and food known to man; they are gone!" Cattle supplied not only milk and meat but also were the major source of wealth. In times of shortage, farmers could sell or barter their animals to obtain food. Without livestock, Dinka went hungry. They fled their wasted villages and settled on the outskirts of towns to the north, seeking relief. Young virgins were made "women" of the Baggara, and older women were employed in collecting firewood, brewing beer, or cutting the yellow thatching grass, which was woven into long mats and sold to traders. Adolescent boys cared for the goats and cows of the nomads. Impoverished Dinka would leave their children with Baggara families to herd cattle in return for money and the promise that they could retrieve them later when they returned south.

If they so feared the Arabs, why did Dinka flee to the north and not in the other direction? Part of the answer is found in the stories they tell: "The Arabs want to occupy our land…When they came the children scattered and I also ran…When the SPLA arrived, the Murahaleen left, taking the cows, goats, and sorghum they had looted. When I found them a few days later, they were still on the road. They were riding on horses. My four daughters and other captives were on foot, tied by their hands together. 'Give me my children, if you refuse, I will go with them, and if you won't let me, you should kill me here…I told them they already took four children, and I wanted my last four back. They relented and gave me the four girls. Our area is totally destroyed and we are very hungry."

Twenty thousand displaced Dinka were living in the town of Daein in southern Darfur. They built a church, which became the focus of animosity on the part of the Rizaigat Baggara who talked of "ridding Daein of Dinkas." In early 1987 when some Rizaigat insulted Dinkas, calling them slaves and beating them, verbal violence led to physical violence and retaliation followed just as surely. Rizaigat ambushed some young Dinka, torturing and killing them. The cycle of retribution escalated. Officials moved many Dinka to the railway station to take them to the provincial capital for safety. Policemen demanded protection money from each Dinka on the train. "Leave the Dinka to us," said the Rizaigat, who torched the railway carriages and reduced two hundred Dinka to ashes.

In the Nuba Mountains of Kordofan, counterinsurgency was carried to extremes through vicious raiding by Arab militias, abetted by government military intelligence. The Nuba are a collection of non-Arab peoples, distinct from their Arab neighbors in appearance, culture, and way of life. A source of slaves in the past, they suffered neglect and exclusion, and in the 1980s young Nuba rose in revolt. Central to their rebellion was an assertion of their cultural distinctiveness. In the SPLA, they found allies who adopted their cause in its confrontation with the Muslim government in Khartoum. But Khartoum's response went beyond suppressing revolt and became an effort to create an Islamic state by force. While reports are selective, truth was not far behind: there was a government policy of "tashteet"—literally combing or ethnic cleansing by any standard—to depopulate areas under SPLA control.

For generations, Baggara nomads had been coming down after the rains and making their camps near Nuba villages. "They used to share our water and...seek boys to work with them as cowherds." They soon took over some wells and let their cattle graze on Nuba farms. "What is your farm? Let the cows eat," the Baggara said. In the past, they had only a few ineffectual old guns, and the ethnic balance radically changed when the government began arming them. With automatic rifles and army backing, Baggara militias began a systematic campaign of pillage, rape, abduction, and burning of houses and churches and books written in the local languages, driving the Nuba, bereft of their livestock, into the hills. Whole villages were forcibly relocated to barren areas, euphemistically called "peace camps." Even Muslim villages under SPLA control were not immune from attack. "The soldiers burned the whole village including my mosque...They burned the Holy Koran...[and] took fifteen sacks of sorghum that was part of zakat." Does Islam exist only in areas controlled by the government? "We are not kufar, we are Muslims."

A comparable pattern of escalating violence erupted in Darfur. In the 1990s the Rizaigat, who had raided across the Dinka frontier to the south, turned their modern weapons against their predominantly "African" neighbors to the north—Fur, Masalit, and Zaghawa—with whom they had many ancient quarrels over pasturage and water. Again, echoes of Mahdist times.

In 1874, Zubair destroyed the Fur sultanate, opening the pastures and cultivations to the Baggara. Madibu of the Rizaigat—enemy, then friend, of Slatin—saw this as an opportunity to place contested lands under the control of his kinsmen. When the British destroyed the Mahdist state, Ali Dinar, heir to the title of sultan, had spent much of his reign driving the nomads back. His success lay mainly in heavy cavalry with imported horses and chain mail, but he was unable to impose his will on the Arab tribes for long, though not for want of trying. After independence Darfur became a bastion of the Mahdist religious movement and a stronghold of its political wing, the Umma Party and Darfurians gave its leader, Sadiq al-Mahdi, victory at the polls.

Under its policy of indirect rule, the British gave a "dar"—a homeland—to each major tribe, including the Rizaigat Baggara, and a paramount chief was appointed with authority to allocate land. But the camel-owning tribes in northern Darfur, including sections of Rizaigat, did not benefit. Their migration routes traversed the lands of settled African communities. Their herds grazed wherever there was grass and rain. Their camels pastured on harvested fields, fertilizing them, and they helped villagers transport their grain to market.

With drought in the mid-1980s and expropriation of large tracts of land for mechanized agricultural programs, pasturage became increasingly scarce. Suffering major losses of livestock, impoverished

Zaghawa—non-Arabs—fanned out across Darfur and Chad in search of land and economic niches. Rizaigat camel-herders became interlopers on African lands and complained that the sedentary Fur, Masalit, and other non-Arabs enclosed unfarmed lands and burned grasses to stop them from passing through. Denied their customary access, they attacked the villagers who, in the absence of an effective police force, formed their own militias. Periodic skirmishes degenerated into repeated assaults, and the political gap widened between those identified as "Arabs" and those identified as "Africans." Conditions were ripe for ethnic cleansing.

Neglect and discrimination against groups in remote Darfur and the privileged position of the central Nile Arabs contributed to the mounting unrest. Ethnic and cultural prejudices had persisted since Mahdist times between the people of the Nile—"awlad al-bahr"—and those of the west—"awlad al-gharb." The elite of Nile riverain tribes, whose authority extended only nominally to the periphery, continued to dominate the government. The indigenous population in the west spoke of them prejudicially as Jellaba. Emanating from the Nile, they were not that different from the petty merchants of the past. Discrimination against the "Africans" became rampant. "When we harvest our crops and take them on donkeys to market, the government takes money from us…If you have no money your daughter or son cannot go to school; the teachers will send them away.…" A disproportionate number of Sudanese soldiers were from the non-Arab or African farming population, while the officer ranks were recruited from among the Nile tribes.

The Islamist regime that came to power in 1989 made matters worse by interjecting the perception of Arab and Islamic cultural superiority. Transformed into a political force, Islamism was used to suppress opposition. "Non–Arabs" were denied the right to assert their existence as a people with their own language and culture. The National Islamic Front was in the forefront while sectarian leaders of the opposition were loath to repeal Allah's laws and risk being accused of apostasy.

In the face of marginalization, non-Arabs mounted insurgencies against the government. The Sudan Liberation Army, drawing on Fur "self-defense militias" and using rocket-propelled grenade launchers, machine guns, and satellite phones, attacked police stations and army garrisons, and in April 2003, took control of the airport in El Fasher, Darfur's capital. With its own troops—largely Darfurian of uncertain loyalty—unable to control the situation, the government turned to freebooting Arab militiamen called "Janjaweed"—Murahaleen under a different name—to put down and terrorize the rebels into submission. Many of these proxy forces were from the camel-owning branch of the Rizaigat who had not been given a dar and found themselves excluded from customary sources of grazing and water. They had a tradition of banditry and camel theft and could easily obtain arms from neighboring Chad. This policy of "counter-insurgency on the cheap" enabled Khartoum "to deny that there was a civil war in the Sudan at all."

A parade of human suffering has been left in the wake: villages burned, men castrated or beheaded, ears cut off, women raped, children abducted, livestock seized, wells poisoned, schools, clinics, and underground grain stores torched, more than 2.5 million people displaced, two hundred thousand of them seeking refuge in Chad. Sudanese soldiers were followed by hundreds of menacing Janjaweed on camelback and horseback, wearing turbans around their heads and mouths, so that only their eyes were visible and carrying "hijab"— tiny leather boxes containing Koranic verses—to keep them safe from bullets. They cut down fruit trees and destroyed irrigation ditches as a way of eradicating farmers' claims to the land and ruining livelihoods. Ethnic cleansing in Darfur, they said, meant clearing the land for "good Sudanese Arabs."

Human rights groups have described the details: "The Arabs and the government forces arrived on both sides of the village, with vehicles, on horseback and on camels, and armed with big weapons. The Arabs cordoned the village with more than a thousand horses. There was also a helicopter and an Antonov plane. They shelled the town with more than two hundred shells. We counted one hundred and nineteen persons who were killed by the shelling. Then the Arabs burnt all our houses, took all the goods from the market. A bulldozer destroyed houses. Cars belonging to the merchants were burnt and generators were stolen."

Many who fled their villages lived off of wild grasses and toxic berries, which had to be soaked in water to become edible. Eventually most of them gathered in barren refugee camps. The makeshift shelters of twigs, cardboard boxes, and plastic bags provided little protection from sandstorms, rain, and scorching heat. The camps became breeding grounds for cholera, typhoid, and hepatitis. The displaced ask, "We die here or we get shot outside. What is the difference?" It is said that the death toll from hunger and disease "surpassed the numbers killed by violence."

When Janjaweed seize women and children, they say, it's because "you are black, you are like slaves." Is this the rebirth of slavery with all its most reprehensible connotations? Or is it just the way slavery is done in a culture where redemption is always possible? In hard times, a poor family pawns a child to a richer family, and when times improve, the parents buy the child back. Didn't Gordon have his "voluntary slaves?" The Dinka mother says to the police: "I found my son with someone. They had taken him from me, and then they dug a hole. They wanted to kill me and bury me in that hole. I escaped...I came to you to bring my child back to me." A policeman records the case in a ledger and tells her to come back with a court injunction, for parents can ransom back children at double the original price.

What is happening—officially at least—is abduction, and abduction is not the same as in the past when two million Blacks were taken north and sold as slaves. Today, there is no market for slaves. Abduction, on the other hand, stems from a time-honored tribal custom: hostages seized in raids are returned when blood money is paid. Today, intertribal committees identify abductees and government mediates in blood money settlements. But should a Dinka woman, seized fifteen years ago and now living quite happily with her Baggara husband, be forced to return to her original community? That sort of question still arises.

Suppression of the slave trade, but not domestic slavery, was a factor in uniting the people against Turco-Egyptian rule. During Mahdist times, the trade revived. Slaves were conscripted into the Khalifa's army as Jihadiya. The contrast between army life and the drudgery of farm labor lured slaves away from the land. The result was labor shortages, and agricultural production suffered. After the demise of Mahdism, colonial ambivalence regarding slavery stemmed from this experience. Kitchener wrote to his governors, "Slavery is not recognized in the Sudan, but as long as service is willingly rendered by servants to masters it is unnecessary to interfere in the conditions existing between them." Blacks absorbed in households by sale or marriage were not officially considered as slaves. Wingate, who became governor-general after Kitchener, declared—as Gordon had done thirty years earlier— that domestic slavery was tolerable and only the export of slaves was illegal. His soldiers were allowed to keep retainers, concubines, and servants, ostensibly to protect them from reverting to slave status. The racism of colonial officials became apparent, as when Slatin spoke of the "inherent bad qualities of these negro races whom we seek in vain to raise to our level." As late as 1918, "runaways were being captured and carried off, tied to camels, all with the knowledge of officials." It was believed that migrants from Nigeria and other African countries would provide a solution. It was commonly said, "the government took away our slaves, but God sent us the Fellata," who provided the labor needed for agricultural development in the modern Sudan.

The indentured servant might be given a certificate of freedom, but even then, he would be encouraged to remain "with the tribe." The Imam Abdul Rahman and other sectarian leaders took the position that Sudanese who keep slaves treat them "as if they were members of their families, because of the increasing need for their work…Their labor was critical to agricultural production, and if set free the women would resort to prostitution, and the men would become 'alcoholic and lazy.'" Individual cases of slavery were often disguised as kinship. "We do not have slaves here, we just have Dinka," Baggara would claim. "They work for us in order to escape poverty in their homeland."

So the legacy of slavery continues to haunt the modern Sudan. Nomads still covet pastures more verdant than their own. They need labor to herd their animals and work their fields. Beset by drought and famine and restricted in their seasonal peregrinations, they seize livestock and laborers, as they were wont to do in the past—but now often with the consent of the government—and sometimes at its behest. The government is guilty not only of knowingly arming and transporting slave-raiding militia, but also in not enforcing its own laws against kidnapping and forced labor, debt bondage, employing children without the consent of their parents or guardian, and coercing or persuading girls or women into marriage while keeping them ignorant of their origins and their rights. Ill-informed human rights advocates who engage in the practice of buying back slaves—recently at $50 a head—only ratchet up the problem. Even Gordon cautioned that "by buying slaves you increase the demand, and indirectly encourage raids." Slave redemptions are subject to abuse, and many of those redeemed are not slaves at all.

Besides, jihad had become, once again, a means of legitimizing the enslavement of people deemed to be racially inferior. Abducted children and women absorbed into the household of another family, whether by sale, false adoption, marriage, or as a result of the passage of time, have never been treated as human rights victims, let alone as victims of slavery, even though denied their heritage, religion, and identity, and coerced into adopting Islam. Instead, it is argued, they are being adopted into a superior culture.

Particularly disturbing are the racial overtones. Janjaweed will say, "As you are black, you are like slaves...We don't want any black skin here...You have spoiled the country! We are here to burn you...We will kill your husbands and sons and will sleep with you! You will be our wives!" The Nuba, too, were seen as black people who were racially inferior, and the Arabic names given their tribes reflected this prejudice, such as "Kawalib," which is—mistakenly—said to mean "dogs," (the plural being "kilab,") and "Ghulfan," meaning "uncircumcised." And the distinction in Darfur between "Zurga," meaning "very black," and "Arab." And the Zurga include outsiders. Thus, a politically insignificant epithet of earlier times has taken on an alarming racist meaning, which is often included in rallying calls to militant Arabs.

Can ethnicity be the root source of conflict when centuries of coexistence and intermarriage have so lessened the physical differences between Arabs and Blacks? "The Arab-African dichotomy is historically and anthropologically bogus," writes Alex de Waal, who knows Darfur well. Moreover, "the rebels—who drop their simplistic 'African' versus 'Arab' terminology as soon as they get into details—have no desire to purge Darfur of its indigenous black Arabs," he adds. Over generations Blacks, both Darfurian non-Arabs and West African Fellata, have adopted Arab genealogies and the Arabic language; it is still possible for "Africans" with sizable numbers of cattle to be assimilated into Baggara Arab clans. A prominent Baggara businessman said to me, "If Arab means Muslim and speaking Arabic, then I am an Arab; if African means a black skin, then, as you can see, I am an African." Members of both groups are dark-skinned. Sometimes it is impossible to tell on the basis of skin color to what group an individual belongs.

Sudanese officials use this argument to deny that genocide is occurring—with government complicity—in Darfur despite overwhelming evidence to the contrary. "We know the Arabs don't have planes; they have cows!" an African says after an onslaught by government and Janjaweed on his village. And Brian Steidle, an American on-site investigator, reports: "Brazenly, the GOS (government of Sudan) troops continued to burn and loot the village even as we conducted our investigation."

Also, the conflicting interests of nomadic and sedentary populations aren't a meaningfully significant explanation. Indigenous African groups depend on animal husbandry as well as on subsistence farming, and nomadic Arabs have cultivations. In colonial times, tribes were moved between districts and given permanent land rights for administrative convenience. When their livestock were decimated in times of drought, nomads relied on crops. The same "ethnic" conflicts arise between Arab tribes when a sedentary group lays claim to land within a nomad dar. "No guest can stay when he claims part of the house," Rizaigat said when the sedentary Maaliya claimed a dar of their own.

Sudanese Arabs believe that they are descended from an Arab father and an African mother and identify with the father, whose genealogy they cherish. After a few generations, "non-Arabs" assimilated into Arab tribes will claim an authentic Arab genealogy. It has even been suggested that the stigmatizing of Blacks may be "an outward suppression of the mother inside the northern self." When government has selectively armed tribesmen as proxy militias, ethnic distinctions are drawn more sharply; so it is best to place all such ethnic differences within quotation marks. To label what is happening in Darfur as "ethnic cleansing" glosses over a complex muddle of ethnic relationships.

Nor is religion a key factor in explaining present-day animosities. If it were, how do we explain the conflict in the Nuba Mountains, where people have faced government violence even though seventy percent of them are Muslims? The Nuba supported the Mahdi and many were in the ranks of the Jihadiya. Allied with Baggara, they annihilated Shallali's troops that were sent against the Mahdi. Four thousand Nuba were killed at Kerari, where they remained loyal to Mahdism until the bitter end. And in Darfur the Fur, Masalit, and Zaghawa villagers are Muslims as are the Janjaweed who attack them. Some Dinka are Muslims, and at one time many were followers of the Mahdi. Like the Baggara, they, too, were Ansar and supported the Mahdist jihad against the infidel foreigners. Darfurian "non-Arabs" and Nubawi comprised seventy-five percent of the professional army fighters sent against separatists in the South.

Drawing on Tijaniya traditions of the western Sudan, the Khalifa convinced the Mahdi to modify his broadly defined missionary view of jihad as self-discipline and use it for the more narrow purpose of creating a state. An activist definition of jihad was appropriate in the struggle against outside intervention and government corruption. This militant interpretation remained dominant through the early years of colonial rule. The British were the Antichrist, and wasn't Abdul Rahman the Second Coming that presaged the millennium? Abdul Rahman repudiated this belief, but that didn't deter thousands of pilgrims from joining him on Aba. To rid the land of infidels, Turks and foreign mercenaries, such as Gordon, may have once been necessary in defending against outsiders who threaten the faith, he said, but times have changed; so jihad should denote internal engagement and personal effort to suppress evil in oneself and to promote peaceful means to improve society. According to Abdul Rahman, only self-defense justified jihad.

Only in the Nuba Mountains did ethnic conflict become a jihad, properly speaking. In 1992, during the most violent phase of hostilities, religious dignitaries in Kordofan issued a fatwa calling for jihad against the "rebel infidels" backed by the SPLA, and a new force of Jihadis was recruited and given military training. In the south, the application of Islamic law on non-Muslim consolidated opinion against the north as well as political exclusion and inequitable access to oil resources led to conflict. In the west, it was also a reaction to the dominance of the Nile-based "Jellaba" who neglected the development and security needs of the indigenous Muslims in Darfur.

To characterize these developments as stemming from inherent confrontation between Muslims and Christians—as some U.S. evangelists claim—or between pastoralists and farmers, or between Arabs and Africans is simplistic and unhelpful. Presented in this way, media stereotypes give rise to apocalyptic rhetoric and political posturing, not meaningful solutions. The only common denominator has been the marginalization of peripheral areas that have been successively exploited, stigmatized, and ignored since Mahdist times by Nile-centered authority.

In this context, the ideology of Mahdism appears to have little to offer. National dialogue no longer centers on ideology but on power sharing and regional identities—as Nubians, Beja, Nuba, Dinka, Fur, Zaghawa, and such. Does this suggest a resurgence of tribalism and violation of the umma, which was the Mahdi's greatest achievement? Perhaps. But tribal chiefs no longer have the grassroots authority they had in the past. Authority now rests with Khartoum representing powerful Nile-based families who use for political ends the "ethnic" and regional grievances of their rural constituents—with whom they have little in common. Only through regional connections can someone share in the power; being Umma or Islamist is not enough in itself.

Mahdism may still have value. It is as myth, however, one that is infinitely malleable and subject to different interpretations. It isn't a doctrine to be followed, even by those who say the ratib two times a day. But as myth, it can still capture popular imagination. It is not just a footnote in history. It can mobilize the energies of people who feel exploited and look to the Mahdi's legacy for salvation. Politicians adopt it to suit their particular purposes. It was used to mobilize Ansar against the threat of Communist takeover during Nimeiri's presidency. In Nigeria, the people used to say, "We are Ansar, but don't tell anybody." Student leftists in the 1960s interpreted Mahdism as a national liberation movement, as anti-colonialism. That is not the way conventional historians saw it. How could British rule be justified if that were the case? The Mahdi's revolt was against the corruption of power, not against colonialism. The Turks didn't have a civilizing mission as the British did. At the time of independence, the Mahdist heritage became the first successful nationalist revolution. The Umma party adopted Mahdism as part of its Ansar identity and commitment to the independence and unity of the Sudan. Is it unavoidable that the fractioning that portends a failed state will thwart this overarching and laudable goal?

The End

Endnotes and Illustrations

Preface

p. x "…crushed under the weight of books…," Hill, *Egypt in the Sudan*, p. 144.

"Too late," Theobald, *The Mahdiya,* p. 123, quoting Cromer, *Modern Egypt.*

Chapter 1: Setting

The Best View of the Town is from the Blue Nile

p. 2   Illustration: "The Palace" from *ILN (Illustrated London News)* **Sept. 10, 1898.**

Descriptions are from SNR Vol. 18 (1935); C. E. J. Walkley, *The Story of Khartoum* ; G. Melly, *Khartoum and the Blue and White Nile* (1851); John Petherick, *Egypt, the Sudan and Central Africa* (1861) and *Travels in Central Africa* (1869).

p. 4 "The Sudan is not a residence for a person like me…." Quoted in Kushsha, Sulaiman, *Ta'sis Madinat al-Khartum wa al-Mahdiya.*

p. 5 From *Journal of C. M. Brownell*, an American doctor and explorer, who accompanied Petherick as botonist on a journey up the White Nile in 1862; SAD (Sudan Archives, Durham).

p. 5 From Dr. W. Junker (*Travels in Africa, 1875-1878, 1890*) who described the Austrian Consulate and residence of the Consul Hansel.

Hansel's clothing are from SNR (Sudan Notes and Records), vol. 19, *The story of Khartoum.*

Illustration: "Frank Power" from *Cassell's History of the War in the Soudan,* p. 140.

p. 7 "...Bass's pale ale and Giesaler's extra superior..." Power, Frank, *Letters from Khartotum Written During the Siege,* p.89.

"...temper the sun's ardour with frequent libations..." *Journal of Licurgo Santoni* in Santi & Hill, pp. 208.

"... A more miserable, filthy and unhealthy place..." Moorehead, *White Nile,* p. 90.

"...If any person should wish..." Schuver, *Travels,* p. 270.

"...to their own great profit, endeavour to..." *Ibid.,* p. 280.

White Nile and Fearful Sudd

p. 8 Illustration: "Dhahabiya" from SAD (Sudan Archives, Durham) 744/1/77.

"One of them, a tall, debauched-looking fellow..." Baker, *N'yanza,* p. 22.

p. 10 Illustration: "Khartoum at the Confluence" is from Archer, *The War in Egypt and the Sudan,* on the website of Cornell Library Historical Monographs.

"The steamer whistled, the crew screamed..." Schuver, p. 330.

Illustration: "Shadouf" from SAD 1/6/73.

p. 11 "A huge elephant, trunk up ..." described in Petherick, p. 337.

p. 12 "Take my word..." *Letters of Adolfo Antognoli*, Santi & Hill.

"...depriving eighteen captives of their generative parts..." is from *Brief summary of the efforts of Mr John Petherick, F.R.G.S. to counteract the despotic measures of the Egyptian Government against the extension of British Commerce to and from Central Africa, commencing in the year 1849 and terminating in December 1863.*

"…a commodious boat and some tons of glass…" Petherick, p. 337.

p. 13 The Franz Binder story is told by Stiansen, Endre, "Franz Binder: A European Arab in the Sudan, 1852-1863" in *White Nile, Black Blood*, pp. 3-21.

Baker's Impossible Mission

Illustration: "Baker" from frontispiece of Baker's *Ismailia*, v. i.

"There was not a dog…" quoted by Cromer, *Modern Egypt*, i, p. 349.

"…The Negro does not appreciate…" quoted in Abbas, p. 35.

p. 14 "…the rumor that Baker…" Scroggins, Deborah, *Emma's War*, p. 47.

"…a taste for agriculture…" Abbas, p. 48.

"…being a good rifle shot…" Budge, ii, 317.

p. 15 "How many troops have you here?… Baker, *Ismailia* i, p. 88.

p. 16 "This was the Sudan method of collecting taxes…" *Ibid.*, p. 93.

"From white ivory to black ivory…" Jackson, *Black Ivory*, p. 99.

Americans in the Service of the Khedive

p. 17 Illustration: "Chaillé-Long" *My life in Four Continents*, p. 158.

p. 18 "…a queer character…" Chaillé-Long, i, *Ibid.*, p. 18.

p. 18 "…a bottle of Bordeaux wine with a red seal…" *Ibid.*, p. 26.

p. 19 Illustration: "Ismail Pasha"

p. 19 '…sphinx-like expression…,' Crabites, p. 42.

"Yes…and I think with them both." Hesseltine & Wolf, *The Blue and Gray on the Nile*, p. 30.

"Bear it with patience…" Chaillé -Long, i, p. 32.

With Chinese Gordon to the Sudan

p. 20 Illustration: "Gordon" from Junker, *Travels in Africa*.

"My dear Chaillé-Long, will you come with me…" Chaillé-Long, p. 66.

"How are you, old fellow? Come take a b and s…" *Ibid.*, p. 66.

p. 21 "I do not want a British officer…"*Ibid.*, p. 70.

"He could charm the birds…" Moorehead, *White Nile,* p. 178.

p. 22 Illustration: "Dancers" from Junker, *op. cit.*

Chapter 2: Slaves

Every Household has its Slaves

p. 23 "I never saw one of these beings ill-treated…" Abbas, p. 75 quoting Pallme.

"Except for their infernal tom-tomming…" Power, p. 23.

Illustration: "Master and slave" from Cassell's, *op.cit.*, p. 80.

p. 24 "…father of all dogs…" Power, p. 40.

"…entering the crocodile's stomach…" *Ibid.*, p. 41.

p. 24 "…repaid the kindness…" Baker, *N'yanza,* p. 86.

It's the Slave Trade that Keeps the Place Alive

p. 25 By 1836, between ten and twelve thousand slaves were being imported into Egypt; from Segal, *Islam's Black Slaves*, p. 150.

p. 26"…like pheasants…"; the description is from Baker, *op.cit.*, p. 15.

Illustration: "Slave convoy" from *ILN* 5/10/1884.

p. 27 "…Where does this black man come from?…" Deng, *Africans of Two Worlds,* p. 153.

p. 28 A boy sees his father and mother die of starvation; from the *Journal of J. A. Vayssiers (1853-4)* in Santi & Hill, pp. 122-68.

"A young Galla girl named 'Azamiya…"; from "A journey to Sennar and the Hijaz, 1837-1840" in Hill, *On the Frontiers of Islam,* p. 172.

p. 29 "…for every ten slaves who reached…" Segal, *op.cit.*, p. 151.

"…how people, who, when in Europe…" Quoted in Hill, *A Journey to Sinnar….,* xxvi.

"…unspeakable cruelties are described…" Taylor, "Journey to Central Africa" in Hill, *On the Frontiers of Islam,* p. 37.

p. 29 "…the grass never grows…" Baker, *N'yanza,* p. 10.

"…the nose again recalled the savoury old times…" *Ibid.*

p. 30 The U.S. consular agent in Khartoum; from *Bulletin of Sudanese Studies*, Khartoum, vol. vi, no.1 (Feb. 1981).

"I am not ashamed to say that I feel the greatest…" Power, p. 24.

The Greatest Slave-trader of Them All

p. 31 Illustration: "Zubair" from *ILN*, May 10, 1881.

p. 31 "I was born on the island of W*awissi* …" The account is from Jackson, *Black Ivory,* pp. 49-50.

p. 32 On Daim Zubair; see Schweinfurth, ii, pp. 355-64.

"…hawkers of living human flesh…" *Ibid.,* pp. 355.

p. 34 "…to consider himself a permanent guest …" Mire, Lawrence, "Al-Zubayr Pasha and the Zariba based Slave Trade in the Bahr al-Ghazal 1855-1879," in Willis, J.R., *Slaves and Slavery in Muslim Africa,* p. 120.

"…I never sent a single slave…" Jackson, *Modern Sudan,* p. 105.

Chapter 3: Cultures

Khartoumers and Jellaba

p. 36 "Fawzi was by no means a stickler…" Junker, i, p. 417

p. 37 "…the luckless fowl, plucked…" *Ibid.*, i, p. 425.

p. 37 "Foreign parts ease the hearts…,' Bedri, i.

"The north gives birth, the south gives manhood…" Bjorkelo, p. 139.

p. 39 "…the most rigid observers of…" Pallme, p. 186.

Wild Sons of the Steppe

p. 41 Illustration: "Baggara Family" from SAD (Sudan Archives Durham) 705/4/5.

p. 42 Illustration: "Baggara Hut" photo by author.

p. 44 "The beard orders…" Bedri, i, p. 146.

"This is our land — we know no Effendina here."

Below the Bahr al-Arab

p. 45 Illustration: "Dinka Cattle Camp" from Sudan Archives Durham 835/4/20.

p. 46 "The owl is a wise bird…" Deng, *Cry of the Owl*, pp. 46-7.

p. 47 "All the cattle of the …" Deng, *Africans of Two Worlds*, p. 131.

The Land Between the Niles

p. 48 "Robust, bombastic and noisy…" Schuver. pp. lx-lxi.

"… like a stretched fishing net…" *Ibid.*

p. 48 "…almost like an elephant's spittle…" *Ibid.*

p. 48 "…by the chicanery of soldiers passing through…" *Ibid.*, p. 286.

"Without merisa, no Sudan…" *Ibid.*, p. 293.

p. 49 "…swearing on the Quran, the Prophet…" *Ibid.*, p. 305.

The Western Frontier

Illustration: "Kordofan village" from *Cassell's History,* p. 111.

Illustration: "At the Well" photo by author.

p. 52 "…easier in this country to find a slave…" Pallme, p. 39.

p. 53 "…the most delightful and the cleanest town…" Fr. Stanislao Carcereri (1862), SAD "Catholic Missionaries Reports."

p. 54 Illustration: "Tabeldi" from SAD A67/14.

p. 56 "…all of the semi- or full Negro type…" *Ensor*, pp. 88-9.

p. 57 "By moistening a small gold coin…" Petherick, p. 138.

Illustration: "Feki and Pupils" photo by author.

p. 59 "His father served me faithfully…" Purdy, quoted in Crabites, *Americans,* p. 59.

p. 59 "My left leg showed symptoms of paralysis…,' Colston, quoted in Crabites, *op. cit.*

"Oh, Night of Hell!…" Hesseltine and Wolf, *The Blue and the Gray on the Nile,* p. 142

"His Highness, expressing great sympathy..." Prout, General Report on the province of Kordofan, 1877 in Dye, *Modern Egypt,* p. 100.

Chapter 4: Gordon

Gordon in Equatoria

p. 61 "What I shall have done will..." Strachey, p. 203.

"Events will go as God likes." *Ibid.,* p. 201.

p. 63 "As I do not talk Arabic..." Hill, p. 47.

p. 63 "Inaction is to me..." Phipps, *More about Gordon,* p. 139.

p. 63 "Writing orders to be obeyed by others..." Hill, p. 93.

p. 63 "If you sit in all day and smoke..." *Ibid.,* p. 170.

p. 64 "Lads and women came to do certain work..." Abbas, p. 80.

p. 65 "The slaves I buy are already torn..." *Ibid.,* p. 104.

p. 65 "...never reaches Gondokoro..." Phipps, *op. cit.,* p. 131.

p. 66 "Old fellow, now don't be angry..." Chaillé -Long, p. 66.

"Gessi paid dearly for the privilege..." *Ibid.,* p. 218.

"...foq al-qanun..." Crabites, *Gordon, the Sudan and Slavery,* p. 22.

"...exerted such zeal...a despicable creature..." SNR, v. 10 (1927): "Unpublished letters of Charles George Gordon."

p. 67 "You have but little idea of what work ..." "Unpublished letters...," *op. cit.*

"No one can conceive the utter misery..." Farwell, p. 66.

He Gave Me the Sudan

p. 68 "He gave me the Sudan..." Allen, p. 106.

"...with eyes like blue diamonds..." Moorehead, p. 200.

p. 68 "My dear fellow, whoever you are...He greeted me coldly...You came rather too soon..." Giegler, *Sudan Memoirs.*

p. 69 "I expect to ride 5000 miles this year..." Allen, p. 118.

"I came flying into this station like a madman..." *Ibid.,* p. 118.

p. 69 "The old trod on the young..." Nur, p. 28.

"The camels and I are of the same race..." Hill, *Col. Gordon,* p. 235.

p. 70 "Every fortnight I have a new skin..." *Ibid.,* p. 269.

"...such a road through the forest..." *Ibid.,* p. 365.

"Gordon summoned me to guide him..." *Ibid.,* p. 365.

"I would infinitely rather travel alone..." *Ibid.,* p. 277.

p. 71 "I have no pleasure in eating or drinking..." I*bid.,* p. 365.

"...reportedly despise the Englishman..." Crabitis, *op. cit.,* p. 98.

"To die quickly would be to me nothing..." Allen, p. 153.

p. 72 "In camel riding you ought to..." Hill, *Col. Gordon,* p. 297.

"I own nothing and am nothing..." Allen, p. 112.

"A lover of danger and the audacities..." Strachey, p. 199.

p. 72 "My huge palace is a dreary..." Hill, *Col. Gordon,* p. 275?

"I sent out an expedition..." *Ibid.,* p. 265.

p. 73 "The steamer has just brought four little hippopotamuses..." Crabites, *Gordon, the Sudan,* p. 138.

"This morning, without any apparent reason..." *Ibid.,* p. 139.

p. 74 Illustration: "Junker" from Junker, *Travels.*

"...a most lovable character..." Allen, p. 276.

p. 74 "Marriage spoils human beings..." Blunt, p. 92.

"...he would run half-way up the stairs..." Phipps, p. 34.

p. 75 Illustration: 'Coup de grace of an exhausted slave' from *ILN* (*Illustrated London News*).

p. 76 "Why should I, at every mile..." Hill, *Col. Gordon,* p. 366.

p. 76 "I smell slaves..." *Ibid.,* p. 341.

"One man met on the trail..." *Ibid.,* p. 285.

"There are numbers of children..." *Ibid,* p. 288.

p. 77 "It is the slaves who suffer..." Crabites, *Gordon, the Sudan,* p. 101.

"Poor souls, I cannot feed..." Hill, *Col. Gordon,* p. 253.

p. 78 "I was met by the son of Zubair..." *Ibid.,* p. 271.

p. 78 "…down to the very babes…" Gessi, p. 302?

"…every stitch of clothing, and they were driven…,' Slatin, p. 10.

p. 79 "Free Bahr al-Ghazal from the Egyptian troops;…' Gessi, p. 307 footnote.

Gessi to the Bahr al-Ghazal

Illustration: "Romolo Gessi" from Junker, p. 99.

p. 80 "…He ought to have been born in the 16th century…" Allen.

p. 80 "Do you know Gessi yet?…" Giegler, *Sudan Memoirs.*

"…It was so near I could have grasped its head…" *Ibid.*

"Gordon was sending to certain death…" Gessi, p. 187.

p. 80 "…a safe retreat for the scum…" Junker, i, p. 394.

Illustration: 'Meshra al-Rikk' from Junker, *op. cit.*

p. 81 " What is their use to natives who never eat meat…" Gessi, p. 53.

p. 81 "…riding like a scourge of God…" Allen, p. 150.

p. 82 But are you not afraid…,' Gessi, p. 335.

p. 82 "I have seen master and slave sitting eating…" Gessi, p. 226.

p. 83 "It is all I possess…" *Ibid.,* p. 240.

"Let us destroy their infamous commerce…" *Ibid.,* 270.

"I shall give Gessi £1000…" Abbas, p. 109.

"No one can escape his destiny…" Gessi, p. 255.

p. 84 "…massacred by Jellaba slave dealers…" Hill, *Colonel Gordon in Central Africa*, p.383.

"…a poor little girl with a beautiful face…" *Ibid.,* p. 281.

"…offer up their last prayer…" *Ibid.,* p. 282.

p. 85 "I give you five minutes…" *Ibid.,* p. 321. Details of the execution of Suleiman and his eight relatives are given by Jabari, Muhammad Ahmed, *Fi shan Allah,* p. 52.

"What, Have you no other troops?…" Hill, *Colonel Gordon,* p. 387.

p. 85 Account of Aza bint Idris and her followers comes from al-Jabari, *op.cit.,* pp. 56-66.

p. 86 Illustration: "Daim Sulaiman" from Junker, *op. cit.*

"Gessi has kept his word…" Gessi, p. 345.

p. 87 "…a silent leave-taking…" Junker, ii, p. 92.

"I like the Mussulman…" Hill, *Col. Gordon*, p. 282.

p. 88 "…a fundamental to the Muslim way…" Moorehead, p. 205.

"…as thick as a violin string…" Gessi, p. 379.

p. 88 "I turned the Bahr al-Ghazal into a garden…" Gessi, p. 390.?

"As I cannot give milk to my son, take him…" Gessi, p. 400.?

p. 89 "Scarcely does someone die than he is devoured…" *Ibid.*, p. 400.?

p. 89 "And now must I die ingloriously…" *Ibid.*, p. 407.

"Courage, Gessi. Egypt has need of you…" *Ibid.*, p. 407.

"Gessi! Gessi! Gessi!…" Moorehead, p. 211.

Chapter 5: The Mahdi

Holy men and the Mahdi of Allah

p. 90 Illustration: "Feki preaching" from Archer, *op. cit.*

p. 92 "If it were not for my food…" Al Hassan, *On Ideology,* p. 99.

p. 93 "Miserable Dongolawi, how true…" Farwell, p. 6.

"Get away, you wretched Dongolawi…" Slatin, p. 47.

p. 94 Illustration: "The Mahdi" from *ILN*, May 10, 1881

p. 95 "Put aside everything…" Farwell, p. 8.

"The cursed tax gatherer…" Wingate, Mahdiism, p. 14.

p. 95 "…like a cart without wheels…" Jabari, pp. 14-15.

"Often when we were students…" Bedri, i, p. 19.

The Mahdi's visit to El Obeid is described in Nur, op. cit.

p. 96 "Men who profess…" Jackson, *Black Ivory,* p. 9.

"What do you want? Go back to your country…" Slatin, p. 51.

"From the first moment I saw his face…" *Ibid.*, p. 52.

"He is of the Mahdi…" Shaked, p. 226.

"There is no god but God…" *Ibid.*, p. 115.

p. 97 Abu'l-Su'ud's meeting with the Mahdi are from Shaked, p. 204 and from Hasan, Abdullah Muhammad Ahmed, *Jihad fi sabil Allah*, pp. 9-10.

"…as long as I have it, I was told, no one can defeat me." Nicholl, Fergus, *The Sword of the Prophet*, p. 71.

p. 97 "…with stones and clay…" Shaked, p. 79.

p. 98 "Ansar" since his followers were promised paradise as a reward for their devotion and willingness to die in Jihad, they could not go by their previous sufi title of dervish, which indicates poverty. See Warburg, *Islam, Sectarianism & Politics in the Sudan since the Mahdiyya*, p. 33.

p. 101 Illustration: "With the Mahdi" from *Cassell's History*.

"If you yield, you will be safe…" "Notes of Sudan History," Wingate file, SAD 113/2 Attack on El Obeid is described by Ohrwalder, pp. 43-45.

"Now, what will you do…" Wingate file, *op. cit.*

p. 102 "…master and slave behaved like brothers…" Nur, p. 118

"El Menna Ismail…," SNR, 17 (1934)

p. 104 "We rang the for the last time…" H.C. Jackson file, SAD.

"May Allah lead you into the way of truth…" Farwell, p. 191.

"During the night they gathered in groups…" Ohrwalder, pp. 54-5.

p. 105 "Let all show penitence…" Proclamations are from many sources, including Strachey, op. cit., pp. 212-3, Moorehead, pp. 225-6.

The Ill-fated Expedition

p. 106 Illustration: "Hicks Pasha" from Archer, *op. cit.*

p. 107 "…swaggering bullies…" Hicks, p. 90. ?

"…a high Sheikh or Priest…" *Ibid.*, p. 16.

" My being here is of no use…" Macleod, p. 13.

"…accomplish the reduction of Kordofan…,' *Ibid.*, p. 14.

p. 107 "If my army will only behave well..." Hicks, p. 38. Hicks seemed not to appreciate that firearms captured in previous fights had been brought out to arm the new force of Jihadiya under Hamdan Abu Anga, a client of the Ta'aisha.

Illustration: "Hicks' army on the march" from Archer, *op. cit.*

"...the price of claret...,' *Ibid.*, p. 34.

p. 108 "No other arrangement does ..." *Hicks,* p. 59.

"...the gallant hero, Hicks, his army..." Nur, *op. cit.*, p. 140.

"It was Ramadan when first we hear*d...*" from Ali Julla's account "The defeat of Hicks Pasha," SNR, 8 (1925), pp. 118-23.

p. 109 "I am like Jesus Christ..." Hicks, p. 129.

p. 110 "Is this what they call the skill..." from "The diary of 'Abbas Bey," SNR (1951),Vol 32, p. 192.

p. 111 "Now here I am ready..." *Ibid.* (SNR, 32) p. 188.

"He who surrenders shall be saved..." Wingate, *Mahdiism*, p. 85.

"...full of courage and like an elephant..." Ali Julla's account, "The defeat of Hicks Pasha," SNR v. 8, p. 119.

p. 112 "Oh, our Lady Zainab..." Slatin, p. 133.

"Allahu Akbar; you need not fear..." Wingate, p. 89.

"I have brought Hicks and all the infidels..." Nur, p. 140.

"The thick trees hindered our horses..." Ali Julla's account, *op. cit.*

p. 112 "No other shall ever ride on you as well ..." Wingate, p. 90.

p. 113 "You see, this dysentery that I cursed..." Power, p. 49.

Slatin to Darfur

p. 114 "I could not serve under you..." Moorehead, p. 203, footnote.

p. 114 "This motley of expatriates..." Hill, *Slatin Pasha,* p. 8.

"No man could lift his hand..." Moorehead, p. 204.

Illustration: 'Young Slatin' from Junker, *op. cit.*

"Are you not aware that Yusuf Pasha..." Slatin, p. 6.

p. 115 "Good-bye my dear Slatin…" *Ibid.,* p. 7.

"Is he brave and kind-hearted?…" Slatin., p. 20..

p. 115 "We shall first fill our jars…" *Ibid., p. 36.*

"…whose sombre purpose…" Hill, *Slatin Pasha,* p. 12.

Illustration: "Slatin's Blacks" from *ILN* reproduction in SAD 695/5/12.

p. 116 "I have eaten bread and salt with you …" Farwell, p. 113.

p. 117 "Allah is great! I have killed myself…" *Ibid.* p. 121.

"A helpful soldier took a sword…" Hill, p. 16. ?

p. 118 "Isa, where is Morgan…" Slatin, pp. 90-91.

"If he is really an adherent of the Mahdi…" *Ibid.,* p. 101.

p. 119 "The idea has gotten around…" *Ibid.,* p. 113.

"I have shared your joys and your sorrows…" *Ibid.,* p. 115.

"If you are really a brother to me…" *Ibid.,* p. 147.

p. 120 Illustration: "Lupton Bey" from Junker, p. 214.

p. 121 "It was the Mahdi who destroyed the people…" Deng, *Africans of Two Worlds,* p. 131.

"…the government had given him permission…" Collins, p. 35.

p. 121 "The Mahdi's army is now camped…" "Last letters of Lupton Bey to Emin Pasha," SAD, 155/1.

p. 122 "Hold to your faith, you are now one of us…,' Wingate, *Mahdiism,* p. 137.

p. 122 "The Mahdi does not allow…" "Frank Miller Lupton," SNR, 28 (1947), p. 36.

Mahdi Moves to Rahad

p. 123 "I know that you Christians are…" Ohrwalder, p. 122.

p. 124 "Are you satisfied?…" Slatin, p. 161.

"Unlike those who covered themselves with ashes…" One such fearful penitent was Sheikh Muhammad Sharif, the Mahdi's former master and religious leader, who, years before, had called the Mahdi "a wretched Dongolawi" and put the yoke on him. The Mahdi now forgave him and presented him with several horses and two pretty Abyssinian girls.

"My name is Olivier Pain…" Slatin, p. 177.

Illustration: "Olivier Pain" from Junker, op. cit., p. 113.

p. 125 "If Yusuf dies here he is a happy man…" Farwell, p. 144.

"…ass of a French journalist…" Hill, *Slatin,* p. 22.

Account of Harrington is in a paper by Ahmed al-Bashir, *Bulletin of Sudanese studies,* Khartoum, Dec. 1981

p. 125 "I send you Sheikh 'Uthman…" Wingate, *Mahdiism,* p. 93

p. 126 "…sweepings of Cairo…" Owen, "The Hadendowa," SNR, 20 (1937)

"…broke the British square…" *Ibid.*

"So 'ere's to you, Fuzzy Wuzzy…" quoted in Farwell, pp. 51-56.

Gordon Returns

p. 126 "In three days this town…" Shibeika, *British policy,* p. 132.

"…the wreck of the Sudan…" *Pall Mall Gazette,* noted in Crabites, *Gordon, the Sudan,* p. 178.?

p. 126 "You saw me today?…" Allen, p. 218, quoting Barnes, *Charles George Gordon*

"Yes, they would evacuate the Sudan…" *Ibid.* p. 229.

"I leave for the Sudan to-night…" Theobald, *The Mahdiya,* p. 84, quoting Allen.

p. 127 "I know that if I was chief…," Cromer, i, p. 432

p. 128 "Because, it is the hand of the man…" Jackson, *Modern Sudan,* p. 102.

p. 128 "We are friends again…" *Ibid.,* p. 103.

"…the tender mercies of Greek merchants…" Blunt, 191

"Will Zubair ever forgive me the death…" Cromer, i, p. 455.

"…a comparatively low-born Armenian…" Jackson, *Modern Sudan,* p. 101

p. 129 "What the two decided, I do not know…" S.F. Brocklehurst, "Letters from Gordon" 26 January 1884, SAD 630/5.

"…mystic feelings…" Strachey, p. 227.

Almost a decade later, Zubair approaches Chaillé-Long in his Cairo hotel and asks him to intervene with the Khedive Tawfik to let him return to the Sudan. "You will go with me. I promise you to smash the Mahdi within ten days after we reach Khartoum. I wish to return to my country; I will restore the Sudan to Egypt." Chaillé-Long replies: "Tawfik will do nothing; have patience." Chaillé-Long, ii, p. 349. Many years after that Zubair says, "I only once came across a man whose life was absolutely pure and unselfish, and that man was Gordon." Jackson, *Black Ivory,* p. 91

"I have ignored the existence of any rebellion…" Brocklehurst, *op. cit.*

p. 130 "I got a fresh camel near here…" *Ibid.*

Illustration: "Berber" from *Cassell's History,* p. 48.

p. 131 "I have laid the egg which the Mahdi has hatched…" Gordon, *Gen. Gordon's Khartoum Journal,* p. 77.

p. 132 "Weeping and crying loudly…" Cuzzi, p. 53.

"Gordon—sword and Bible—travels like…" Power, p. 76.

" I come without soldiers…" Crabites, *Gordon, the Sudan,* p. 220, quoting Archer

"The glare and the heat…," Strachey, pp. 288-9.

p. 133 Illustration: "Gordon Releasing the Prisoners" Archer, *op. cit.*

"…may have passed the narrow…" *New York Times,* 20 April 1884.

"Today I desire you to recommence…" Nicoll, Fergus, *The Sword of the Prophet,* p. 192, quoting Chaillé-Long, *Three Prophets,* pp. 64-5.

p. 133 "I have no need of the sultanate…" Farwell, p. 87.

"…two hundred Indian troops be sent to 'smash the Mahdi'…" Moorehead, p. 246.

"Even if we could sneak…" "Col. Stewart's Second Mission (Jan-Mar 1884)" SAD.

"I expect that my asking…" Gordon, *Khartoum Journal,* p. 142.

p. 134 "What a queer fellow Gordon is…" Cromer, i, p. 491.

"A man who habitually consults…" Farwell, p. 82, quoting Cromer.

"A man who would govern others…" Cromer, i, p. 371.

"…500 red-blooded Englishmen…" Crabites, *Gordon, the Sudan*, p. 248.

"I will retire to…" Theobald, *Mahdiya*, p. 102, quoting Allen, p. 331.

p. 135 "They will be plundered to the skin…" Allen, p. 214.

"You ask me to state cause…" Moorehead, p. 255.

p. 136 "…walking up and down his room al night…"Allen, p. 378.

p. 136 "…a dreadful lot…" Gordon, *Khartoum Journal*, p. 61.

"They shut themselves in their houses…" *Ibid.*, 156.

Chapter 6: The Siege

Closing the Noose

p. 138 "…at the last banquet these unlucky men …" Cuzzi, p. 39.

"…so that she would never become the slave…" *Ibid.*, p.26.

"Khartoum is encircled …" Cuzzi, p. 57.

p. 139 "My wife had only just recovered…" *Cuzzi*, p. 63.

"You are Guiseppe Cuzzi, the English Consul…" Cuzzi , p. 65.

"…to play the farce…" *Ibid.*, p. 67.

"You have joined the true religion…" *Ibid.*, p. 79.

"…even if it were to show our enemies…" *Ibid.*, p. 82.

p. 140 "…who had abjured his faith to save his skin…' Maugham, *The Last Encounter*, p. 60.

"As you may be aware…" Cuzzi, p. 84.

"In view of my imminent journey…" *Ibid.*, p. 100.

"I shall capture Khartoum, then conquer Egypt…" Cuzzi, p. 103.

"…two camels, fifty dollars and a slave-girl." *Ibid.*, p. 106. Fawzi (v. i, p. 420) says that the Mahdi gave Cuzzi the name of Muhammed Yusuf, two slave girls, two male slaves, and two she-camels.

"Although I knew of Gordon's often unjustified…" *Ibid.*, p. 109.

p. 141 Illustration: "Umm Dubban" photo by author.

"The fighting pasha...stood on his fur." Wingate, *Mahdiism*, p. 162.

"...the blind carrying the crippled..." Nur, p. 150.

p. 142 Illustration: "Ansari warrior" from *Cassell's History*, p. 21.

"Does your excellency believe..." Wingate, p. 133.

"I will have nothing to do with Slatin's..." Moorehead, p. 266.

p. 143 "When it is a question..." Gordon, *Khartoum Journal*, p. 37.

p. 143 "Does Abdul Qadir think..." Slatin, p. 199.

p. 144 "...a dreadfully itchy..." Gordon, *Khartoum Journal*, p. 74.

"...grinned and smirked at her reflections..." *Ibid.,* p. 75.

"Why, the Arabs give us nothing..." *Ibid.,* p. 119.

"So it is true that the belly governs..." *Ibid.,* p. 119.

p. 145 Thames penny steamers described in Watson, SNR, 12 (1929).

"I never feel anxious..." *Gordon's Last Journal,* Nov. 13, 1884.

'...they cannot run away...,' Gordon, *Khartoum Journal*, p. 79.

"I have put most of you in prison..." *Last Journal,* p. 188.

"...even though the Anti-Slavery Society would ..." *Ibid.,* p. 188.

p. 145 "My beautiful steamer..." *Ibid.,* p. 80.

p. 146 "...that the Arabs could not dare..." *Gordon's Last Journal,* Nov. 5, 1884

"The *Abbas* struck a rock..." Account is from Archer, iii, pp. 246-8.

"Stewart was a brave..." Gordon, *Khartoum Journal*, p. 177.

The Relief Expedition

p. 147 Illustration: "Gordon Relief " from Archer, *op. cit.*

p. 148 "...as if a man on the bank..." Gordon, *Khartoum Journal*, p. 64.

"...beautiful black soldiers..." Farwell, p. 92.

"I declare positively..." *Gordon's Last Journal,* Nov. 9, 1884.

p. 148 "If the expedition comes here…" *Ibid.,* Nov. 22, 1884.

"…they will enter Paradise…" Gordon, *Khartoum Journal,* p. 141.

Illustration: "Whaler Boat on the Second Cataract" from *ILN*.

p. 149 "…floating merrily…" Grant, *Cassell's History…,* iii, p. 118.

"The novice son learns…" Archer, iii, p. 230.

"Before engaging the enemy…" 'Nile Campaign,' Wingate papers, SAD.

p. 150 "You know that you are quite unable…" *Ibid.*

"…quite a walk from the desk …,' Maugham, *op. cit.,* p. 97.

p. 151 "The eye that mocketh at his father…" Allen, p. 378.

"…to comfort her black soul…,' Gordon, *Khartoum journal,* p. 80

p. 151 "…he let his pen rush on…" Strachey, p. 252.

"If the Arabs are not eating…" *Khartoum Journal,* p. 137.

"I would sooner live like a Dervish…" *Ibid.,* p. 139.

p. 152 "The wretched peasant…" *Khartoum Journal,* p. 72.

"…judicially murdered…" *Ibid.,* p. 180.

British officials in Cairo thought otherwise: "I can hear no good of Fawzi. I spoke to the Khedive about him and found he had a very poor opinion of him, and I also interviewed two old officers who were also with Gordon in Khartoum and they had nothing to say in his favour. I am afraid he is something of an imposter." Ibrahim Pasha Fawzi, SAD.

The Siege of Khartoum

"…nigger dances…" Archer, iii, p. 263.

p. 153 Illustration: "Battle of Abu Tulaih" from *Cassell's History*

"I saw a fine old sheikh…" Archer, iv, p. 21.

p. 154 "November 12th: One tumbles…" Gordon, *Khartoum Journal.*

"Khartoum all right, could hold out for years …" *Ibid., p.* 22.?

p. 156 "If only a couple of English soldiers…" Holt, *History of the Sudan,* p. 170 as recounted in *Bordeini Bey's Journal.*

p. 156 Illustration: "Wilson Approaching Khartoum" from Archer, *op. cit.*

"I would that all could look on death…" Cromer, ii, p. 11.

p. 157 "Go and collect all the people…" Moorehead, p. 284.

"If any people want to go over to the Mahdi…" Allen, p. 393.

"The English will be here tomorrow …" Holt, *History,* op. cit., p. 198.

p. 157 "What more can I say…,' *Ibid*. p. 169 as recounted in *Bordeini Bey's Journal.*

p. 158 Story of how Gordon spent his last night: told by Maugham, *op. cit.*

"God is most great. Advance…" Theobald,, *The Mahdiya,* p. 121.

"Slay not the man Gordon…" Zulfo, op. cit., p. 21.

p. 159 "…withal, a spice of madness…" Wingate, *Mahdiism,* p. 239.

"Companions of the Mahdi!…" Bedri, i, p. 24.

"O cursed one, your time is come…" Moorehead, p. 287.

There are other accounts. A more elaborate (and self-serving) account given by Gordon's head *kavass*, Khalil Agha Ahmed, *Eyewitness account of Gordon's death*; SAD A.P.Bolland 439/1-4, follows: "At about sunrise on that day I heard the shouting of the enemy coming from the direction of the White Nile. I at once went down to General Gordon, who was then in his office, and told him that the enemy had entered Khartoum. He at once took his field glasses and went out to the staircases and with his glasses saw the enemy weaving about through the streets from all directions and advancing towards the palace. He then returned to the room, put on his sword, and carried his revolver in his hand. Shortly after, the rebels broke into the garden, and with axes broke open the southern gate of the palace. They climbed the staircases and rushed straight to Gordon Pasha's room. I struggled with them but I was speared in my right hand. In Gordon Pasha's room there was a secret small door overlooking the staircases. The enemy rushed to enter the room from that door. General Gordon fired at them, and they retired to the bottom of the staircases, apparently thinking that there were many men occupying the room. General Gordon then came out to my assistance, and an Arab, whose name and tribe I do not know, threw a spear at him hitting him on the shoulder. The Dervishes rushed on us again, but we stopped their rush by both of us continually firing at the same time. General Gordon, who had his sword drawn, struck the man but missed him and hit another man. A Dervish, who was not far from the staircases, fired at General Gordon hitting him on the chest and forced him to lean against the wall. General Gordon and myself then drove them to the bottom of the staircases, where General Gordon received a spear thrust on his left side and also I was thrown down by spear thrusts. I do not know what happened then to General Gordon. I was wounded on my hand, shoulder and both legs. All the Kavasses who were in the Palace, three farashes and the Bashibuzuk guard were killed with the exception of one name Ibrahim who jumped out of the window and saved himself. A farash name Hasan was wounded but did not die."

p. 160 Illustration: "Bringing Gordon's Head to Slatin" from Slatin, *Fire and in the Sudan*, p. 206.

p. 160 "Is this the head of your uncle…" Slatin, p. 206.

'What is this?' asked the Mahdi…' Zulfo, p. 22.

"…by those for whom he lived he died." "For the grave of Gordon," by Tennyson, quoted in SNR, "The story of Khartoum."

"…and he thanks God for that…" Al-'Atabani, *Memoires* (in Arabic), p. 132ff.

p. 162 "He is of the Mahdi…"

"…whom they wryly styled 'Our lords the Taaisha'…," Holt, *Modern History,* p. 92

Chapter 7: The Khalifa

The Khalifa's rule

p. 163 Illustration: "Khalifa Abdullahi" from postcard provided by the Khalifa's grandson, Muhammad Daud al-Khalifa, in March 2002.

"Miracles were attributed to him…" Yaji, p. 22, recounts when the was no water in the Atbara to quench the thirst of the army of Abu

Anja. Learning of this in a dream, the Khalifa the next morning went down into the Nile with his mulazimin and, three times, ordered them to drink and ask God for to deliver their brothers from hunger and thirst whereupon the clouds formed over the distant army and the rain poured down.

p. 164 "Once I was young and beautiful girl..." Mann, p. 82.

p. 164 "One will never succeed me..." Yaji, *Rijal...,* p. 19.

p. 165 "If you rely on delaying in your land..." *Ibid,* pp. 54-5.

"I have never asked for mercy..." Farwell, 173; described also by Yaji, pp. 62-66.

"You miserable slave..." *Ibid.,* p. 68.

p. 166 "O Ansar, the whole land ..." Wingate, *Mahdiism,* p. 420.

Nujumi into Egypt

"...which had been the Mahdi's firmest resolve..." In fact, the main object of the Mahdi's *jihad* extended even further abroad to include Mecca, Medina, Jerusalem, and Kufa in Iraq. Warburg, *Islam...,* p. 45.

p. 167 "My father said that al-Nujumi was a fool..." Bedri, i, p. 225.

"No, by God, I will retreat only as a cold corpse..." Zulfo, p. 31.

"I took the two water-skins and the two donkeys..." Bedri, i , p. 57.

p. 168 "You intend to reach Binban..." *Ibid.,* p. 57.

Ohrwalder and Slatin Escape

p. 170 "Abdul Qadir, are you well?..." *Ibid.,* p. 220.

"...an ugly black face, two little eyes..." *Ibid.,* p. 227.

p. 171 "See, this is the man who was formerly..." Farwell, p. 164.

"I want to go to Abu Ruf jetty to buy some sorghum..." Nur, p. 212.

Illustration: "Slatin's" from Slatin, *Fire and Sword in the Sudan.*

p. 172 "On the day of my arrival..." *Ibid.,* p. 395.

"There is a man outside..." Farwell, p. 238.

Battle of Omdurman

p. 173 Illustration: "Gunboat Passage through the Rapids" from *ILN*.

"Why did you come here to burn and kill?..." Zulfo, p. 80.

"They fear not God but have destroyed the qubba." Zulfo, p. 148.

"Our men were perfect, but the Dervishes were superb..." Farwell, p. 309, quoting G.W. Steevens, *With Kitchener to Khartoum.*

"Where is Yaqub?..." Zulfo, p. 214.

p. 175 Illustration: "Ya'qub killed with the black flag," *ILN*.

"Ansar, look at us now!..." Zulfo, p. 213.

"...he lost interest in the course of the battle..." *Ibid.*, p. 222.

p. 176 "It was not a battle..." Moorehead, p. 360, quoting Steevens.

"...the harvest of the 300 50-pounder shells..." Zulfo, p. 235.

"Cease fire! What a dreadful..." Huband, *Warriors of the Prophet*. p. 145.

p. 176 The quiet hills each night listened..." Zulfo, op.cit. p. 237.

"The Khalifa has left the city..." *Ibid.*, p. 235.

"I remember, ya Khalifa al-Mahdi..." Yaji, p. 43.

"You have been with me throughout..." Huband, *op. cit.*, p. 244.

Chapter 8: The Legacy

The Mahdist legacy

p. 181 Churchill, *Winston S. Churchill* (London: 1966) v. i, p. 424.

"...even the Queen expressed shock.' See Philip Magnus, *Kitchener: portrait of a imperialist* (London: John Murray 1958), p. 133.

p. 182 "...waving blood-stained swords..." Quoting a British district commissioner in Warburg, *Islam, Sectarianism* p. 63.

Preservation of the Legacy

p. 184 "...that he might better defend..."

Erosion of the Legacy

p. 189 "Where are the cattle..." Deng, *Seed of Redemption*, p. 80.

p. 189 "The Arabs want to occupy our land…" Human Rights Watch, *Famine in Sudan,* pp. 31-34.

For accounts of the Daein massacre see Mahmud Ushari and Sulaiman Baldo, *Al Diein Massacre – slavery in the Sudan,* especially pp. 30-32.

"They amputated their arms …" Deng, *Cry of the Owl,* p. 175.

p. 190 "They used to share our water…" African Rights, *Facing Genocide.* p. 29.

"What is your farm? Let the cows eat…" *Ibid.* p. 47.

"The soldiers burned the whole village…" African Rights, *op.cit.,* p. 209.

"We are not kufar, we are Muslims…" *Ibid.* p. 292.

p. 192 "When we harvest our crops…" Tim Judah, "The stakes in Darfur," *N.Y. Review of Books,* Jan. 13, 2005.

p. 193 "…counter-insurgency on the cheap…" This is from de Waal in *London Review of Books,* Aug. 5, 2004.

"…good Sudanese Arabs…" *Independent,* Aug 6, 2004.

"The Arabs and the government forces arrived…" Amnesty International, "Darfur: Too many people killed for no reason," Jan. 2004, p. 20.

p. 194 "We die here or we get shot outside…" *Ibid.*

"…surpassed the numbers killed by violence." Flint and de Waal, *Darfur: A New History of a Long War,* p. 146.

"I found my son with someone…"

p. 195 "Slavery is not recognized in the Sudan…" Daly, M. W., *Empires on the Nile* (Cambridge University Press, 1986), p. 232.

p. 195 "…inherent bad qualities of these negro races…" *Ibid.,* p.233.

"…runaways were being captured and carried off…" *Ibid.,* p. 234.

"…the government took away our slaves…" *Ibid.* p. 238.

p. 195 "…as if they were members of their families…" Jok. p. 102.

"…We do not have slaves, we just have Dinka…" *Ibid.* p. 49.

"...by buying slaves you increase the demand..." Hill, *Col. Gordon*, p. 253.

p. 196 "As you are black, you are like slaves," Amnesty International: "Darfur: Too many people killed for no reason.," p. 12; UN Integrated Regional Information Networks [Nyala, Darfur], Apr. 8, 2004.

"The Arab-African dichotomy..." A. de Waal, "Tragedy in Darfur," *Sudan Tribune*, Oct. 14, 2004.

"...the rebels—who drop their simplistic 'African' versus 'Arab' terminology..." de Waal, 'Darfur's Deep Grievances,' *Sudan Studies Association Newsletter*, Sept. 2004.

"If Arab means Muslim and speaking Arabic..." Adam Musa Madibo interview, Mar. 10, 2004.

p. 197 "We know [the Arabs] don't have planes....,' Flint and de Waal, op. cit., p. 132

"Brazenly, the GOS troops ..." Brian Steidle, *The Devil Came on Horseback,* Public Affairs, N.Y., p.192.

"The governor in El Fasher replied that genocide was literally impossible..." Tim Judah, "The Stakes in Darfur," *NY Review of Books*, Jan. 13, 2005.

'No guest can stay....,' Madibo interview. March 10, 2004

"...and in a few generations his descendants would have an 'authentic" Arab genealogy." O'Fahey, R.S., "W. Sudan: a complex ethnic reality with a long history," *International Herald Tribune*, May 15, 2004

"...an outward suppression of the mother inside the northern self." Albaqir Alafif Mukhtar, "Darfur: Hell on Earth."

Tradition has the Prophet Muhammad saying after a military victory: "We are coming back from the Lesser *Jihad* [i.e., the battle] and returning to the Greater *Jihad*" - the far more important, difficult and momentous struggle to reform our own society and our own hearts. (Karen Armstrong, *Guardian*, July 11, 1005.

p. 199 "We are Ansar but don't tell anybody." Jaifar Mirghani Ahmad, interview 2002.

On the competition for oil resources, see Scroggins, *op. cit.,* p. 208, who quotes Nuer who say, "Yes we are fighting for the oil…We are fighting for the Arabs will not let us develop…The Jellaba are wanting the oil."

GLOSSARY

amir	commander, prince
ansar	helpers (first applied to supporters of the Prophet)
angareb	bedstead of wood and woven rope or palm leaves
asida	thick sorghum or millet paste
Baggara	cattle-owning tribes
Bahhara	people of Nile river origin
bait al-mal	treasury of Islam
baraka	blessing, special virtue
bashibazuk	irregular cavalry
bashkatib	chief clerk
bazingers	slave troops
baksheesh	present, tip
daim	fortified armed camp
Danagla	Nubian Arab people
da'wa	mission
dhahabiya	large sailing vessel

dhikr	Sufi "remembrance"
Dinka	most numerous of the Nilotic cattle herders
divan	large office, reception area
dukhn	bulrush millet
durra	sorghum
falja	vee-shaped gap between two front teeth
farwa	sheepskin under a saddle
fatwa	legal opinion
fellahin	Egyptian peasants
ghazwa	raid
Hadendowa	Beja Arab
hadra	assembly attended by all prophets and holy men
hakim	doctor
hay'at al-shu'un al-ansar	ansar associations
hejira	pilgrimage
hijlij	*Balamitis egyptica*
imma	turban
Ja'aliyin	Nubian Arab people
jibba	dervish patched cloak
jihad	holy war
jallaba	itinerant trader, lit. "packmen"
jallabiya	loose, shirt-like garment
kafir	infidel
kartush	cartridge
kavass	attendant
khalifa	successor
khalwa	Quranic school
kurbaj	rhinoceros hide whip
kisra	wafer from sorghum paste

mamur	sub-district official
merisa	native beer
miralai	colonel
mulazim	a kind of servant-courtier-bodyguard
Nuer	Nilotic tribe
nuggar	lanteen-rigged barge
ombaya	horn made from elephant's tusk (*umm bay'a*)
qaimmaqam	major
qubba	domed tomb of a saint
rahad	a thong girdle
rakuba	rectangular straw shelter
ridaa	overcoat
Rizaigat	Baggara tribe
sagiya	Persian water wheel
Shaigiya	Nubian Arab people
shadouf	counterbalance for irrigation
sibha	beads
sirwal	drawers
stambouli	Turkish official dress
shi'ba	heavy forked pole or yoke
tebeldi	baobab with huge trunk for storing water
takiya	skull-cap
tariqa	Sufi order
tukl	conical roofed hut
ulama	orthodox clergy
wakil	deputy or agent
wali	saint
zariba	thorn-enclosed encampment
zuhd	self-denial, asceticism
zahid	ascetic

BIBLIOGRAPHY

Abbas, Ibrahim Mohammed Ali, *The British, the slave trade and policy in the Sudan, 1820-1881* (Khartoum: Khartoum University Press, 1972)

Abu Salim, Muhammed Ibrahim, *Ta'rikh al-Khartoum* (Dar al-Arshad)

——— *Shakhsiyya Sudaniyya*

——— "The man who believed in the Mahdi," *Sudanic Africa*, 2 (1991), pp. 29-52

African Rights, *Facing Genocide: the Nuba of Sudan* (London: African Rights, July 1995)

Ahmad, Abd Allah Muhammed (ed.), *Jihad fi sabil allah* (Khartoum: Government Printing Office, 1925)

Ali Julla, "The defeat of Hicks Pasha," *Sudan Notes and Records*, VIII (1925), 119-24.

Allen, Bernard M., *Gordon and the Sudan* (London: Macmillian 1931).

Archer, Thomas, *The war in Egypt and the Sudan* 4 vols. (London: Blackie & Son, 1886)

Asad, T., *The Kababish Arabs* (London, 1970)

Abd al-Hadi al-'Ata, Awad, *Tarikh Kordufan al-siyasi fi'l-Mahdiyya 1881-1899*, (Khartoum: Sudan Government, 1973)

Badri, Babikr, *The memoirs of Babikr Bedri*, vol. i, ed. & tr. Yousef Bedri & George Scott, with intro. by P.M. Holt (London: Oxford Univerisity Press, 1969)

Bahlman, Dudley W., *The diary of Sir Edward Walker Hamilton, 1880-1885* , 2 vols. (Oxford: Clarendon Press, 1972)

Baker, Ann, *Morning star* (London: William Kinder, 1972)

Baker, Sir Samuel W., *Albert N'yanza, great basin of the Nile*, 2 vols. (London: Macmillan, 1866)

——— *Ismailia, a narrative of the expedition to central Africa for the suppression of the slave trade*, 2 vols. (London: Macmillan, 1874)

Beshir Mohammed Said, *The Sudan, crossroads of Africa* (London: The Bodley Head, 1965)

Bennett, Ernest N., *The Downfall of the Dervishes* (London: Methuen, 1898)

Berman, Richard A., *The Mahdi of Allah* (New York: Macmillan, 1932)

Bjorkelo, Anders, *Prelude to the Mahdiyya: peasants and traders in the Shendi region, 1821-1885* (Cambridge: Cambridge Univ. Press, 1989)

Blunt, Wilfrid Seawan, *Gordon at Khartoum* (New York: Stephen Swift, 1911)

——— *Secret History of the English Occupation of Egypt* (New York: Knoph, 1922).

Budge, E. A. Wallis, *The Egyptian Sudan* (London: Kegan Paul, 1907)

Burnham, G.H., "Chaillé-Long, C." *Dictionary of American Biography*, 1929

Burr, Millard and Collins, *Requiem for the Sudan: War, drought and disaster relief on the Nile* (Boulder, CO: Westview Press, 1995)

Casati, Gaetano, *Ten years in Equatoria* (London: Frederick Warne, 1891

Chaillé-Long, Colonel, *My Life in Four Continents*, 2 vols. (London: Hutchinson & Co, 1912)

Colston, R.E., "Report on northern and central Kordofan...1875," *Publications of the General Staff* (Cairo, 1878)

Churchill, Winston S., *The River War* (N.Y.: Carroll & Graf Publishers, Inc., 2000)

Churi, Joseph H., *Sea Nile, the desert, and Nigritia: Travels in the Company with Captain Peal, 1851-52* (London: published by the author, 1853)

Colborne, J., *With Hicks Pasha in the Sudan* (London: Smith and Co. 1885)

Collins, Robert O., *Shadows in the grass: Britian in the southern Sudan, 1918-1956* (New Haven, CT: Yale University Press, 1962)

——— *The Southern Sudan 1883-1898* (Yale, 1962)

——— "The Nilotic Slave Trade: Past and present" in *The Human Commodity: Perspectives of the Trans-Saharan Slave Trade*, ed. by Savage, E. (London: F. Cass, 1992)

Colville, H.E., *History of the Sudan Campaign*, 2 vols. (London: Harrison & Sons, 1889)

Crabites, Pierre, *Gordon, the Sudan and slavery* (London: George Routledge, 1933)

——— *Americans in the Egyptian army* (London: Routledge, 1938)

Cromer, Earl of, *Modern Egypt*, 2 vols. (New York, Macmillan, 1908)

Cunnison, Ian, *Baggara Arabs*, Oxford, 1966

Cuzzi, Guiseppi, *Fifteen years prisoner of the false prophet*, trans. Hildegund Sharma (Sudan Heritage Series No. 8, Univ. of Khartoum Research Unit, 1968)

Daly, M. W., *Empires on the Nile* (Cambridge University Press, 1986),

Daly, Martin and Ahmad Sikainga, eds., *Civil War in Sudan* (London: British Academic Press, 1993)

Deng, Francis Mading., *Africans of two worlds: The Dinka in Afro-Arab Sudan* (Inst. Of Asian and African Studies, Univ. of Khartoum, 1978)

――― *The Dinka of the Sudan* (NY: Holt, Reinhart & Winston, 1972)

――― *The recollections of Babo Nimr* (London: Ithaca Press, 1982

――― *War of visions: conflicts of identities in the Sudan* (Washington: Brookings Institution, 1992)

――― *Seed of Redemption: a political novel* (N.Y.: Lilian Barber Press, 1986)

――― *Cry of the Owl* (N.Y.: Lilian Barber Press, 1989)

De Waal (ed.), *Facing Genocide: The Nuba of Sudan* (London: African Rights, 1995)

"Diary of Abbas Bey" (secretary to General Gordon) *Sudan Notes and Records*, vol. 32 (1951)

Dye, William McC., *Modern Egypt and Christian Abyssinia* (NY: Atkin & Prout 1880)

Ensor, F. Sidney, *Incidents on a journey through Nubia to Darfoor* (London: W.H. Allen & Co., 1881)

Ewald, Janet J., *Soldiers, traders, and slaves: state formation and econimic transformation in the Greater Nile valley, 1779-1885* (Madison: Univ. of Wisconsin Press, 1990

Fawzi, Ibrahim Pasha, *The History of the Sudan between the times of Gordon and Kitchener,* vol. I (1974-85), tr. by Khalid Deemer and Zohaa El Gamal, (Mafraq, Jordon: Al-Bayt Univ., 1997)

Farwell, Byron, *Prisoners of the Mahdi* (New York: Harper & Row, 1967).

Finnegan, William, "The Invisible War," *New Yorker*, Jan. 25, 1999

Flint, J. and de Waal, A, Darfur: *A New History of a Long War* (London: Zed Books, 2008)

Fluehr-Lobban, C., Lobban, R.A., Voll, J.O., *Historical Dictionary of the Sudan*, 2nd ed. 1992

Freese, Mrs. *More about Gordon by one who knew him well* (London: Richard Bentley & Son, 1894)

Gessi, Romolo, *Seven years in the Sudan* (London: Sampson Low, 1892)

Giegler Pasha, Carl Christian, *The Sudan Memoirs of Carl Christian Giegler Pasha, 1873-1883* ed. by Richard Hill (London: Oxford University Press, 1984)

Gleichen, A.E.W., ed., *The Anglo-Egyptian Sudan*, 2 vols. (London: Wyman & Sons, 1905)

Gordon, Charles G., *General Gordon's Khartoum Journal*, ed. Lord Elton (New York: Vanguard Press, 1956).

——— *General Gordon's last journal: facsimile of the last six volumes dispatched before the fall of Khartoum* (London: Kegan Paul, Trench, 1885)

——— *Equatoria under Egyptian rule: the unpublished correspondence of Col. C.G Gordon* (Cairo: Cairo Univ. Press, 1953)

——— *Colonel Gordon in Central Africa, 1874-1879*, ed. George Birbeck Hill, London 1885.

Gordon, Murray, *Slavery in the Arab world* (New York: New Amsterdam, 1992)

Grant, James, *Cassell's history of the war in the Soudan*, 5 vols (London: Cassell & Co.)

Hake, A. Egmont, ed., *The Journals of Major-General C.G. Gordon, C.B. at Khartoum* (Kegan Paul, 1885)

Hasan, 'Abdallah Muhammed Ahmed, *Jihad fi sabil Allah* (Khartoum: Government Printing Office, n.d.)

Hasan, Ahmad Ibrahim, "Mahdist Risings against the Condominium government in the Sudan, 1900-1927," *International Journal of African Historical Studies*, 12/3 (1979), pp 440-82

——— "Imperialism and neo-Mahdism in the Sudan," *International J of African Historical Studies* 13(1980), #2, pp. 14-39

Hasan, Idris Salim, *On ideology: the case of religion in Northern Sudan*, (University of Connecticut Ph.D. dissertation, 1980)

Hasan, Yusuf Fadl, *Tabaqat wa Dayf Allah* (Khartoum Univ. Press, 1974)

——— *Sudan in Africa* (Khartoum University Press, 1971)

——— *Some aspects of the writing of history* (Univ. of Khartoum: Inst. of African and Asian Studies, occasional paper #12)

Henderson, K.D.D., *The making of the modern Sudan* (London: Faber, 1953)

——— "Migration of the Missiriya into South West Kordofan," *Sudan Notes and Records*, vol. 22 (1939)

Hesseltine, William & Hazel C. Wolf, *The blue and the gray on the Nile* (Chicago, 1961)

Hicks, William, *The road to Shaykan* (Durham Center for Middle East and Islamic Studies, Occasional Papers #20, 1983)

Hill, George Birbeck, ed., *Colonel Gordon in Central Africa, 1874-1879* (London: Thos. De La Rue & Co., 1881)

Hill, Richard S., *Egypt in the Sudan 1820-1881* (Oxford Univ. Press, 1959)

——— *A bibliography of the Anglo-Egyptian Sudan from earliest times to 1937* (London: Oxford University Press, 1939)

——— *Slatin Pasha* (London, NY: Oxford University Press 1965)

——— *Biographical dictionary of the Anglo-Egyptian Sudan* (London: Frank Cass & Co, 1967)

——— *On the frontiers of Islam*, two manuscripts 1822-1845 (Oxford, 1970)

——— *A bibliography of the Anglo-Egyptian Sudan from the earliest time to 1937* (London, 1939)

——— *The Sudan memoirs of Carl Christian Giegler Pasha, 1873-83* (London: Oxford Univ. Press, 1959)

——— "An unpublished chronicle of the Sudan, 1822-41" (*Sudan Notes and Records*, vol. 37, 1956)

Holt, P.M., *Modern History of the Sudan* (New York: Grove Press, 1961).

——— *The Mahdist State in the Sudan, 1881-1898* (London: Oxford University Press, 1958).

——— "The Archives of the Mahdia" *Sudan Notes and Records*, vol. 36 (1955)

Huband, Mark, *Warriors of the Prophet* (Boulder, Colorado: Westview Press, 1998)

Human Rights Watch, *Sudan, Oil and Human Rights Abuses* (N.Y., April, 2000)

——— *Famine in Sudan, 1998* (N.Y., Feb. 1999)

——— *Denying the honor of living: Sudan, a human rights disaster* (N.Y., March 1990

——— *Facing Genocide: the Nuba of Sudan* (N.Y., July 1995)

Hurreiz, Sayyid H., *Ja'aliyyin folktales*, ed. T. Hodge (Indiana Univ. Africa Series, vol 8, 1977)

Ibrahim, Abd Allah Ali, *Al-Sira' bein al-Mahdi wa al-'Ulama* (Struggle between the Mahdi and the Ulama) (Khartoum, 1966)

Jackson, Henry C., *Behind the modern Sudan* (London: Macmillan, 1955)

——— *Black ivory* (Khartoum, 1913; NY: Negro Universities Press, 1970)

——— *Osman Digna* (London, 1926)

Jackson, H.W., "Description of Gordon's steamers *Bordein* and *Telahawieh*, 1884-5," *Sudan Notes and Records* 15, 1933

James, Wendy, Gerd Baumann and Douglas Johnson (eds.), *Juan Maria Schuver's Travels in North East Africa 1880-1883* (London: The Hakluyt Society, 1996)

Johnson, Douglas H., *The Root Causes of Sudan's Civil Wars* (Int. African Inst. & James Curry, Oxford, 2004)

Jok, Jok Madut, *War and slavery in Sudan* (Philadelphia: Univ. of Pennsylvania Press, 2001)

Junker, Wilhelm J., *Travels in Africa during the years 1875-1886*, 3 vols. (London, 1890-2)

Karrar, Ali Salih, *The Sufi Brotherhoods in the Sudan* (London: C. Hurst & Co., 1992)

Al-Karsani, Awad Al-Sid, "Beyond Sufism: The Case of Millennial Islam in the Sudan," in Louis Brenner (ed.) *Muslim Identity and Social Change in Sub-Saharan Africa* (Indiana University Press, 1993)

Keen, David, *The benefits of famine: a political economy of famine and relief in southwestern Sudan, 1983-1989* (Princeton: Princeton University Press, 1994)

Keown-Boyd, Henry, *A good dusting: a centenary review of the Sudan campaign 1883-1899* (London: Leo Cooper 1986)

Khalid, Mansour, *The government they deserve: the role of the elite in Sudan's political evolution* (London & NY: Kegan Paul International, 1990)

Khartoum University, *Studies of history of Mahdiya* (in arabic) (Conference on history of Mahdiya, Khartoum, 1981)

Kramer, Robert S. *Omdurman, 1885-1898: a holy city on the Nile* (Ph.D. thesis, Northwestern University, 1991)

Lea, C.A.E., *On Trek in Kordofan: the diaries of a British District Officer in the Sudan 1931-1933*, ed. by M.W. Daly, (Oxford Univ. Press, 1994)

Macleod, W.E., *Hicks Pasha and the Government*, (London: Edward Stanford, 1884)

MacMichael, Sir Harold, *A history of the Arabs in the Sudan*, 2 vols. (Cambridge, 1922)

——— *The tribes of central and northern Kordofan* (Cambridge, 1912)

Mahjoub, Mohamed Ahmed, *Democracy on trial* (London: Andre Deutsch Ltd., 1974)

Manger, Leif O. (ed.), *Trade and traders in the Sudan* (Bergen: Dept of Social Anthropology, 1984)

——— *The sand swallows our land* (Bergen: Dept of Social Anthropology, 1981)

Magnus, Sir Philip, *Kitchener, the portrait of an imperialist* (London: John Murray, 1958)

Mahmud, Ushari Ahmad and Suleyman Ali Baldo, *The Al Dhiein Masssacre: Human Rights Violations in the Sudan* (Khartoum: University of Khartoum, 1987)

Manger, Leif O., *The sand swallows our land* (Univ. of Bergen: Dept. of Social Anthropology, 1 1981)

Maugham, Robin, *The last encounter* (New York: McGraw Hill, 1972)

McHugh, Neil, *Holymen of the Blue Nile* (Evanston, Illinois: Northwestern University Press, 1994)

Melly, G., *Khartoum and the Blue and White Nile*, 2 vols. (London, 1851)

Middleton, Dorothy, *Baker on the Nile* (London, 1949)

Miller, Judith, *God has Ninety-nine Names* (New York: Simon and Schuster, 1996).

Milayka, Yusuf Mikha'il, *Memoirs* (Archives of Republic of Sudan 101489; ed. by Salih Muhammad Nur. Ph.D. thesis Nr. 101490, Univ. of London, 1962)

Mire, Lawrence: "Al-Zubayr Pasha and the zariba-based slave trade in Bahr al-Ghazal," *Slaves and slavery in Muslim Africa*, vol. 2 (London: Frank Cass, 1985)

Moore-Harell and Gabriel Warburg, *Gordon and the Sudan: Prologue to the Mahdiyya, 1877-1880* (London: Frank Cass, 2001)

Moorehead, Alan, *The White Nile* (New York: Dell Publishing, 1960)

Newbold, Douglas, *The making of the modern Sudan: the life and letters of Sir Douglas Newbold*, ed. K.D.D. Henderson (Westport, 1974)

Newfeld, Charles, *A Prisoner of the Khaleefa* (N.Y.: Putnam, 1899)

Nuqd, Muhammed Ibrahim, *'Alaqat al-riqq fi sudan* (Cairo: Dar al-thaqafa al-jaddida, 1995)

O'Fahey, R.S., "Slavery and the slave trade in Dar Fur," *J. of African History*, vol. 14-1, 29-43 (1973)

———— "Kordofan in the eighteenth century," *Sudan Notes and Records*, liv, 32-42

———— & Jay L. Spalding, *Kingdoms of the Sudan* (Studies in African History, 9, 1974)

———— "Slavery and Society in Dar Fur," *Slaves and slavery in Muslim Africa,*_ed. by Willis, J.R. (London: Frank Cass and Co. Ltd, 1985)

Ohrwalder, Father Joseph, *Ten Years Captivity in the Mahdi's Camp, 1882-1892*, trans. by F.R. Wingate (London: Sampson Low, 1892)

Pall Mall Gazette extra, 14 (1885): "Too late"

Pallme, Ignatius, *Travels in Kordofan* (London: J. Madden, 1844)

Petherick, John, *Egypt, the Sudan and central Africa* (Edinburgh and London: Wm. Blackwood & Sons, 1861)

———— & Katherine Petherick, *Travels in central Africa and explorations on the White Nile*, 2 vols. (London, 1869)

———— *Brief summary of the efforts...*(London: Public Records Office)

Power, Frank, *Letters from Khartoum written during the siege* (London: Sampson Low, 1885)

Prout, Henry Gosslee (Major), *General report on the province of Kordofan*, (Cairo: Publication of the Egyptian General Staff, 1877); also *New York Times* 9 June (or July) 1878

Rafiq, Mustafa Abd al-Hamid Kab, *Social history of the Mahdiyya* (in Arabic), MA thesis (Khartoum University: National Records Office)

Rehfisch, F. translation from Rosignoli, "Omdurman during the Mahdiya" (*Sudan Notes and Records*, vol. 48, 1967)

Reid, J.A., "The story of a Mahdist Amir," *Sudan Notes and Records*, vol. 9 (1926)

"Reminiscences of a Berber Merchant," *Sudan Notes and Records*, vol. 23 (1940)

Santi, Paul. and R. Hill, eds. *The Europeans in the Sudan, 1834-1878* (Oxford: Clarendom Press, 1980)

Schuster, G., *Private work and public causes, a personal record 1881-1978* (Cambridge, 1979)

Schuver, Juan Maria: *Schuver's travels between two Niles* (Hakluyt Society, 1996)

Schweinfurth, Georg, *The Heart of Africa*, vols. 1-2 (NY: Harper & Brothers, 1874)

Scroggins, Deborah, *Emma's war* (N.Y.: Pantheon Books, 2002)

Segal, Ronald, *Islam's black slaves* (N.Y.: Ferrar, Straus & Giiroux, 2001)

Al-Shahi, A., *Themes from the Northern Sudan* (Ithaca Press, 1986)

Shaked, Haim, *The life of the Sudanese Mahdi* (New Brunswick, NJ, 1978)

Shibikah, Makki al-Tayyib [Mekki Shibeika] *British policy in the Sudan, 1882-1902* (London: Oxford Univ. Press 1952)

——— *Sudan wa al-thawrah al-Mahdiyah* (Khartoum: Univ. Press, 1978)

Shukry, M.F., *The Khedive Ismail and slavery in the* <u>Sudan</u> (Cairo, 1938)

——— *Equatoria under Egyptian rule* (Cairo: Cairo University Press, 1953)

Shuqayr, Naum [Na'um], *Tarikh al-Sudan* (Beirut: Dar al-Thaqafa, 1967)

Sikainga, Ahmad A., *Slaves into workers* (Austin: Univ. of Texas Press, 1996)

Slatin, Sir Rudolf Carl, *Fire and Sword in the Sudan, 1879—1895,* trans. by Major F.R. Wingate (London: Edward Arnold, 1896).

Spalding, Jay, "Slavery, land tenure and social class in the northern Turkish Sudan," *International journal of African historical studies* 15, 1 (1982) pp. 1-20

———— "The business of slave trading," (*African Economic History*, 1988)

———— & Stephanie Beswick, editors, *White Nile and Black Blood* (Lawrenceville, N.J.: Red Sea Press, 2000)

Steevens, G.W., *With Kitchener to Khartoum* (New York: Dodd, Mead & Co., 1899)

Steidle, Brian, *The Devil Came on Horseback* (N.Y: Public Affairs, 2007)

Stiansen, Endre & Michael Kevane, *Kordofan Invaded: peripheral incorporation and social transformation in Islamic Africa* (Leiden, Boston: Brill, 1998)

Sterling-Decker, David F., *Politics and profits*, (Michigan State Univ. Ph.D., 1990)

Stewart, H., "Account of the battle of Abu Klea," *London Gazette*, 20 Feb 1885

Stewart, J.D.H., *Report on the Sudan* (London: HMSO 1883)

Strachey, Lytton, *Eminent Victorians* (New York: Capricorn Books, 1963)

Sudan Intelligence Report, Nos. 1-40, 41-59, 60-111.

Theobald, A.B., *The Mahdiya* (London, 1951)

———— *'Ali Dinar: Last Sultan of Darfur, 1896-1916* (London, 1965)

Toniolo, Elias & Richard Hill, *The opening of the Nile basin* (London: C. Hurst & Co, 1974; NY: Harper & Row, 1975)

Trimingham, J. Spencer, *Islam in the Sudan*, (London, 1949)

Voll, J. U., "The Sudanese_Mahdi: frontier fundamentalist," *Int. J. of Middle Eastern Studies*, 10, 1979, 145-66.

———— *Historical dictionary of the Sudan*, 3rd edition (London: Scarecrow Press, Inc. 2002)

Warburg, Gabriel, *Historical discord in the Nile valley* (Evanston. Ill.: Northwestern University Press, 1992)

——— *Islam, sectarianism & politics in the Sudan since the Mahdiyya* (London: C. Hurst & Co., 2002)

——— "Ideological and practical considerations regarding slavery in the Mahdist state and the Anglo-Egyptian Sudan, 1881-1918" in Paul Lovejoy, ed., *The ideology of slavery in Africa* (Beverly Hills and London, 1981)

Watson, C.M., "The campaign of Gordon's steamers" (*Sudan Notes and Records*, vol. 12, 1929)

Wilson, C,T, (Rev.) and R.W. Felkin, *Uganda and the Egyptian Sudan* (London: Sampson Low, Marston, Searle and Rivington, 1882)

Wilson, Sir Charles W., *From Korti to Khartoum* (London: Blackwood, 1886)

Wingate, F.R., *Mahdiism and the Egyptian Sudan* (London: Macmillan, 1891)

——— *Ten years' captivity in the Mahdi's camp, 1882-1892, from the original manuscripts of Father Joseph Ohrwalder* (London, 1892)

——— "The siege and fall of Khartoum," *Sudan Notes and Records* vol. 13 (1930)

Wylde, Augustus Blandy, *'83 to '87 in the Soudan*, 2 vols. (London: Remington, 1888; Negro Universities Press, 1969)

Yaji, Vivian Amina, *Rijal howl al-Mahdi* (Khartoum, Manshurat Bait al-Khartum, 2001)

Zulfo, Ismat Hasan, *Karari, the Sudanese account of the battle of Omdurman*, tr. from the Arabic by Peter Clark (London: Frederick Warne, 1980)